Also by Neville Sarony

The Max Devlin Series:
The Dharma Expedient

Memoir
Counsel in the Clouds

To Naomi – with best wishes

DEVLIN'S *Chakra*

NEVILLE SARONY

[signature: Neville Sarony]

Published and Distributed 2016 by
Vajra Books
Jyatha, Thamel, P.O. Box 21779, Kathmandu, Nepal
Tel.: 977-1-4220562, Fax: 977-1-4246536
e-mail: bidur_la@mos.com.np
www.vajrabooks.com.np

© Neville Sarony, 2016. All rights reserved.
*No part of this book may be reproduced in any form or
by any means electronic or mechanical,
including photography, recording, or by any information storage
or retrieval system or technologies now known or
later developed, without permission in writing from the publisher.*

ISBN 978-9937-623-68-1

Printed in Nepal

For my darling Tara
यी तारा मात्र होइन आमाम पनि बसाई दिउँला

Sculpted by Psyche Chong

Dharma chakra

Literally, the 'wheel of law', a Buddhist emblem resembling a wagon wheel, with eight spokes, each representing one of the eight tenets of Buddhist belief. The circle symbolises the completeness of the Dharma. The spokes represent the eightfold path leading to right endeavour, right mindfulness, and right enlightenment; right faith, right intention, and right speech; right action, and right livelihood.

Dramatis Personae

Max Devlin. Irishman, ex-Royal Gurkha Rifles, took early retirement as Major but often referred to as Colonel; linguist, Orientalist and Special Operations veteran; all assets in Nepal seized in Communist coup; smuggled the infant 15th Dalai Lama out of Tibet – an adventure told in ***The Dharma Expedient*** (2012).

Deepraj Rai. Nepalese, ex-Royal Gurkha Rifles Sergeant, Devlin's long-time Man Friday.

Geljen Ladenla. Personal assistant to the prime minister of the Tibetan government-in-exile.

Lieutenant General Sidartha Chopra (retired). Indian Army General, one-time 5th Gurkha.

Francis 'Freddie' Fernandes. Chief of Indian Intelligence Bureau; highly influential in the Indian bureaucracy; educated at an English public school and Jesus College, Oxford.

General Ranjit Singh. Commander of the Indian National Security Guard, the 'Black Cats'.

Havildar (Sergeant) Dewan. Member of the Indian COBRA team, a 'Black Cat'; highly trained.

Bo Ziling. Commissioner of the Department of Ethnic Integration in the People's Republic of China with principal role to eradicate dissident ethnic groups of Tibetans and Uyghurs.

General Wang Gui. Commander of the 8341 Unit Central Security Regiment of DGS2 (Chinese intelligence); close associate of Bo Ziling.

Colonel Ji Guan. Commandant of the PLA's 128 Mountain Rapid Reaction Regiment.

Captain Wu Zihan. Team commander of PLA's 128 Mountain Rapid Reaction Regiment, Chinese Special Forces.

Kim Namgyal. Sikkimese, educated at Loreto Convent in Darjeeling and the London School of Economics, UK.

Norbu. Tibetan from good family; codename 'Notebook'.

Tenzing. Chinese agent passing himself off as Sikkimese; codename 'Chopsticks'.

Ashok Dariwallah. Indian foreign exchange dealer.

Peter Rougier QC. English, criminal law specialist in Hong Kong.

Annie Xu. Hong Kong Chinese, barrister-at-law.

Anita Seto. Hong Kong Chinese, solicitor.

Jonathan Tang Ching-yee. Hong Kong Chinese, District Court judge.

Eastern Magistracy

Hong Kong

The courtroom was a tribute to the tacky excesses of institutional architecture. Through the bars of the dock which was located against the left-hand wall he observed a large open space, mainly occupied by the smell of the synthetic carpet, the magnetism of its nylon strands drawing a faintly visible coating of dirt over everything and everyone within its range. The walls were lined with a mid-brown thin plasticky wood veneer to lend it mock dignity and the cheap seats in the public gallery were reminiscent of a barracks lecture room. If he had been hoping for a civilised break from the windowless interview room at the ICAC HQ or its mildewed smelling cell, the court proved a serious disappointment.

'Maxwell Quentin Devlin?' 'Yes.'

'Sit down.'

'May it please, sir, I represent the accused.' An attractive young Chinese woman stood up in the front row of benches and addressed the magistrate who glanced up momentarily, gave a curt nod and resumed writing. A Chinese man sitting next to the defence counsel stood up and started to speak in Cantonese. The magistrate's head came up sharply.

'Better do it in English, Mr Poon. I doubt the defendant understands *Punti*.' His mouth twitched in a condescending leer as he shared the joke with the prosecutor who rewarded him with an obsequious smile.

'If you please, sir, the accused is charged under the money laundering provisions, knowing or believing that he was dealing with the proceeds of an indictable offence under Cap.455.' The magistrate studied the man in the dock for a moment, his expression giving nothing away.

'The prosecution are seeking advice from the Department of Justice and ask for a remand for one month. Bail is opposed.' Defence counsel got to her feet.

'May it please, sir, I ask that my client be granted bail. My client has a complete defence to the charge and the allegation is vigorously denied...'

'I'm not taking a plea now.' The magistrate interrupted impatiently.

'Mr Devlin is a man of impeccable character...'

'You mean he's never actually been convicted.' Again a private joke with prosecuting counsel. Two spots of red flushed the young woman's cheeks, she appeared to be about to retort but held herself in check.

'My client is an ex-British Army officer. He has surrendered his passport and is willing to comply with whatever restrictions the court imposes.'

'Is he a Hong Kong resident?'

'No, sir, he is visiting.'

'So, no fixed abode?'

'Like any other visitor, sir, he was staying in a hotel at the time of his arrest by the ICAC.'

'Employment?'

'Mr Devlin is an independent adventure travel consultant, specialising in expeditions and tours in the Himalayan regions.'

'You mean he's unemployed.' It was not a question. Another quick grin shared with Poon. Max spoke softly, trying to catch the young woman's attention. She looked at the magistrate.

'If I may have a moment, sir?' She walked from her seat towards the dock without waiting for a response from the bench.

'Tell him about me being on a commission for His Holiness the Dalai Lama.' He whispered. She frowned and bit her lip then turned back to face the magistrate.

'No, sir. He has a commission on behalf of a most respected Buddhist organisation.'

Poon was quickly on his feet.

'The Commission does not accept this story, sir. The accused is, as you observed, of no fixed abode and currently unemployed.' Defence counsel threw him an angry look.

'Can he offer any financial surety?' The magistrate asked her.

'My client has substantial funds but the ICAC have frozen his bank account.'

'Huh.' The magistrate's patience hit the buffers. He looked down at a piece of paper on his desk. 'Miss Xu, surely the Duty Lawyer court officer told you that this court won't grant bail to an unemployed visitor with no means of support who is charged with laundering more than 50 million US dollars?' He threw his pen down. 'Why do you waste my time?'

'But...'

'Remanded in custody to...' He leaned forward and spoke to the court clerk, then continued, '...9.30 on October 15th, court one, and I reserve this case to myself.' He busied himself writing, affording Max an unrestricted view of the thin strands of hair arranged with judicious economy across his bald head, which completed his assessment of the man as an indefensibly rude narcissist. The young woman looked apologetically at Max who managed a half-smile and shake of his head to indicate that it was not her fault.

He was marshalled out of the dock and walked through the door into a bleak cement corridor. Correctional services officers pointed to a wooden bench, indicating that he sit down. His barrister had warned him that this was virtually certain to be the outcome but Max was astounded by the pantomime in which he had been the central but monumentally irrelevant player. What had happened to the celebrated justice that Hong Kong proudly trumpeted?

He found himself almost more aggrieved at the disdain shown towards his counsel than at the futility of his own position but realised that she was just a necessary cosmetic feature, to enable the system to go through the motions presenting a façade of judicial integrity.

He'd been through the training programme to resist hostile interrogation and though he knew that everyone had their breaking point, all that belonged to the theatre of war which endowed the prisoner with self-respect, but this was different. Arrested and imprisoned for a crime he hadn't committed, his bank account frozen so that he was destitute in a city with a reputation for some of the most expensive lawyers in the world, he was a man in no hurry to anywhere good.

Waiting for the prison bus that would transport him to Lai Chi Kok Reception Centre, the first stop for most people in custody, Max stared at the cracks in the discoloured cement wall as the smell of stale urine and mild disinfectant filled his nostrils; he balanced his anger at himself with his loathing of his surroundings. He replayed in his mind the events of the previous months, mentally punching himself for his own credulous stupidity. How could he have been taken in so easily and so soon?

First it had been the expedition that he had been deceived into believing was to catalogue Buddhist iconography in Nepal but had turned out to be the operation to extract the new infant Dalai Lama secretly out of Tibet, an enterprise that had caused the death of several good friends and nearly his own, and now this. 'Christ Almighty!'

His left eyelid suddenly twitched and he lifted his hand to stay it only to be reminded that his hands were manacled. It was pointless to berate himself for his predicament but if he believed the old Nepalese superstition, the eyelid's uncontrollable convulsions boded ill. He sat up straight and controlled his breathing to regain control over his mind. Without funds he would be unable to set about contesting the charge against him; stuck in gaol he could not even begin to work on his defence and anyway he could not think of anyone in Hong Kong to whom he could turn for help. His gut felt as though he had been hollowed out.

This time he'd been well and truly screwed.

Once inside his chambers, the magistrate sank back into his chair and reached for his mobile phone. He accessed 'Recent' and tapped the number. It rang four times before it was picked up.

'Done?'

'Done.'

'Your co-operation will be duly noted.'

'*Xie xie*.' He was glad that his command of Putonghua, rudimentary as it might be, had proved beneficial. The prospect of appointment to the provincial Communist party committee was another step on his career path in the Judiciary, even though it would not be publicised. There were still too many senior judges who would question his commitment to judicial independence if it got out. True, he was only a small potato now but by the time Hong Kong had been properly integrated into the mainland, he would be poised for high office. Beijing's characterisation of judges as administrators was a practical approach that channelled them into a bureaucratic system with which he was more comfortable than all the colonial nonsense. The patriot in him could not wait for 'one country, one system.'

North of Taplejung, Eastern Nepal

15 months earlier

Nyima felt less uneasy now that they were out of the Arun Valley. All the Sherpas had left *mane* stone altars at auspicious places on the mountains to propitiate the spirits that inhabited them but he could not rid himself of the sense of foreboding. The Arun was the deepest valley in the world. The dark forces dwelt in its bowels but the *seto bhairabs*, the white gods, lived on the mountain peaks and protected their people. Yet he admitted to himself that it was not the spirits that troubled him so much as the logistical burden that Max Saheb had committed him to. He had been so proud of being made Sherpa *Sardar* that the enormity of the task had not hit him until they were almost a day's trek away and the logistics of transporting such a load, weighed politically as much as physically, had led to several of the Sherpas grumbling.

'*Chiyah*.' Dendi thrust the mug of steaming tea towards him and hunkered down beside him, nursing his own battered aluminium mug between his gloved palms. Both men lifted their snow goggles up to prevent the steam from clouding the glass. Nyima looked up at the threatening black walls of ice and stone that encased them in their dark shadow, their peaks consumed by the mist. A brief tremor ran down his spine, not from the cold. The mountains were beautiful in a starkly chilling sense but he knew they could be terrible in their fury. He mumbled a short prayer.

'Where shall we deliver the goods?'

Nyima registered Dendi's neutral choice of words to describe their load. Max Saheb had told him that it was the Dalai Lama's treasure that had been smuggled out of Tibet. If the Chinese soldiers killed all those *khambas* they had left behind with Max Saheb, it would have been far too high a price to pay. His instructions were to get the treasure safely into India. Max had left it to his discretion whether to take all the other Sherpas into his confidence. Given the risks, he had decided that he owed it to them. Once they knew, they had been unable to contain their curiosity and had taken the first opportunity to examine the contents of the baskets of woven bamboo lined with cloth. That was when they discovered the bars of 24-carat gold and packets of different currencies, US dollars, Swiss francs and Chinese yuan. He estimated that there must be tens of millions of US dollars, quite apart from the value of the gold. One or two of the younger men had suggested that they help themselves and make a run for it and though spoken in jest he detected a serious undertone. He had had to remind them that their reputations as Sherpas were at stake; once lost it could never be regained and no mountaineer would ever trust them for any future ascent of the major peaks.

'We'd never need to work again.' One of them observed dryly. So he changed tack, emphasising that as Buddhists, their *karma* would consign them to countless reincarnations of a nature that would make achievement of enlightenment impossible. Despite his best endeavours he sensed that he was losing them. Dendi had intervened. They all knew he was a *jākri* and a very few words from him had settled the issue. Some of them had witnessed his 'healing' powers but they were all fully aware that those same powers could be deployed to cause people serious harm. Nonetheless, Nyima wanted their voluntary co-operation rather than the risk of retribution. Too many things could go wrong. They had all been paid half their wages before they had set out on the expedition but once the true nature of it had been disclosed and they had agreed to carry on in what had become illegal, Max had promised them a generous bonus. If they were caught in possession of the treasure they would all be fugitives. What really troubled Nyima now was whether Max would survive to make good on his promise. Without the co-operation of the entire group of Sherpas he would never be able to carry out his instructions. They were all solid mountaineers with whom he had worked on many expeditions but their willingness to continue to put themselves at risk entitled them to an appropriate reward. He had made his decision and would have to answer for it.

'When we make delivery, out of the money we are carrying I will pay each of you the balance of your wages and the bonus Max Saheb promised. It will be my responsibility to account for it.' The smiles that greeted this announcement were all the response he had needed.

Pulling his face mask down a little, carefully, he sipped his tea.

'Max Saheb told me to find somewhere safe and then contact Ong Chu, explain the situation to him and he would take over.'

'But he'll be getting his jaw fixed and we don't even know where he is.' Nyima did not need to be reminded of this. Ong Chu's jaw had been fractured and needed a level of skilled surgery that would only have been available in a hospital setting, probably down in Dharan or the border town of Biratnagar. Nor was he unaware that with both the Nepal Army and the PLA closing in on Max Saheb the chances of him getting out alive had looked pretty slim.

'We have to get all this stuff to Dharmasala, that's where His Holiness has his headquarters.'

'Yes.' They both sat nursing their thoughts. It sounded simple but they knew that there was no realistic prospect of them achieving it. Even if they could carry it down to the border with India without getting caught by the police, customs or the Nepal Army, moving a fortune in gold and currency through India posed a far more dangerous and difficult task than traversing the Himalayas in which they were in their natural habitat. Dendi sucked at the hot tea then said abruptly:

'Sikkim…the Karmapa, isn't he the leader of the Karma Kagyu order? He's the most important spiritual leader after the Dalai Lama.'

'Leave it with him?'

'Why not?' Nyima pondered the suggestion. He'd felt immense pride when Max Saheb had given him the responsibility but now that the full significance of what it was about had come home to him, he felt distinctly uncomfortable being put in charge of so much money. He was committed to seeing it delivered safely and had every intention of doing so. Did it make much difference if it was handed over to a different sect in the Buddhist hierarchy?

'It would be in India and it's their responsibility once we hand it over.' Dendi sounded as though he had convinced himself.

'True.'

'I know two smugglers routes we could use which would avoid the authorities.'

Nyima glanced at Dendi, a smile hovering around his mouth.

'I remember you working with those *Manangis* a while back.'

'Just showed them the route.' The tone was defensive.

'Naturally.' Nyima nodded then let his mind slip back to the suggestion. He frowned.

'Isn't there a dispute about who's the genuine Karmapa?'

'What do we care? Deliver the goods and leave them to sort it out amongst themselves.' He drained his tea and cleaned out the mug with a handful of snow. 'Max Saheb would approve. He always says the best way is the way that works. This'll work.'

'If we can shift this stuff into Sikkim and if we can contact the Karmapa's people.'

'If we don't get our arses shot or imprisoned.' Dendi added ruefully.

Nyima stood up and looked down at him.

'Easier than taking a bunch of arrogant foreign climbers up Everest.' Both men grinned.

Maidens Hotel

Old Delhi

9 months later – February 28

He folded the letter carefully and put it back inside its envelope as he tried to sort out his reaction. In the three months since he'd stormed out of the bungalow in Dharmasala he had focused on putting Tashi out of his mind. The fact that she filled his thoughts every night before he fell asleep had become a dull ache that he had attempted to replace with anger. It had not been a success. Now this. He poured himself two fingers of Glenfiddich and let it slide down his throat. The minute he had recognised her handwriting, hope gave him a fillip. Hope hit the buffers as he read on. Her tone was courteous, distant as though she knew damn well what effect her letter would have. So, she was handling it in a far more mature way than he was. Would he please meet His Holiness's representative Geljen Ladenla as there was an urgent matter upon which they needed his help. Not Dondhup, he registered, but 'His Holiness'. Max still thought of him as an enigmatic, brave little boy rather than the Dalai Lama. She had signed off: 'I wish you well'. He could not explain why, but those words hurt him, better if she had just written her name and kept it formal.

He stood looking out of the window. This was his favourite room with its view over the white stucco pillars and swimming pool. Sam Khan still treated him as though he was a valued professional client, charging him a fraction of the room rate and sharing his private store of booze with him. Old Delhi's ghosts were everywhere, its dusty niches, crumbling stone edifices, wearing its history like a garment eaten away by white ants. But now he felt uncomfortable in what was intended to be one of his comfort zones. His involvement in the flight of the Dalai Lama meant that there was no way he would be permitted back into Nepal under the current regime, maybe under any regime. That effectively deprived him of the opportunity to deploy his knowledge and expertise across the majority of the Eastern Himalaya. Privately, he acknowledged that his skill sets in the remainder of the mountain range were not of the same order. What he still had to offer, for what it was worth, was the confidence that foreign visitors to a strange, marginally threatening part of the world felt when their tour guide was an expatriate himself. He permitted himself a wry smile as he recalled his ex-partner Chuck's typically politically incorrect description.

'Hell man, you're the genuine white face. These dumbfuck rich dames from Idaho find themselves surrounded by natives, get the General Custer syndrome and you're Dr friggin' Livingstone!' There was no denying that clients visibly relaxed when they saw him so obviously at ease with the inhabitants of locales as diverse as Delhi, Darjeeling and Dhankuta.

He had always resisted the temptation to adopt a PT Barnum persona and play up to the visitors, conscious that he enjoyed the mutual trust of the people of the host countries, something far too valuable to sacrifice to a careless moment's showing off. But his genuine empathy was part of his stock in trade and two of the leading Indian tour companies had already engaged him to chaperone VIP clients.

He tapped the envelope on the old-fashioned air conditioning unit. They must have known that he would not refuse a request from Tashi. Had it been anyone else he would have binned it. They had tricked him into compromising himself with the Nepal government which effectively severed his source of income. But he acknowledged that he could have abandoned the expedition before his little party became desperate fugitives from the PLA on one side and the Nepal Army on the other. He had only himself to blame, so why put himself at risk again?

He felt his mobile vibrate momentarily before he heard the ring tone.

The display showed a number that meant nothing to him. 'Devlin.' He was non-committal.

'Good afternoon sir.' The accent was American.

'Who is this?'

'I'm the one that a certain Tibetan lady told you would contact you.' Max was about to say the name then hesitated as he realised that the man was avoiding identifying himself.

'And?'

'Please join me at your favourite Kashmiri restaurant this evening. Shall we say 7.30?' Max silently admonished himself. 'Go on sucker, don't say I didn't warn you.'

'7.30.' He ended the call.

Directorate of Income Tax (Intelligence and Criminal Investigation)

Same Day

'Potala has made contact with the target, sir.' Shahnaz called out to her supervisor.

'They've set up a meeting for 7.30 at the target's favourite Kashmiri restaurant but they didn't say which it was.' Neerav nodded. His instructions were simply to relay the information to the intelligence bureau, presumably they would know. He sighed, if the left hand did not know what the right hand was doing, how could intelligence gathering be interpreted properly? He had not even been told the target's name, just provided with his mobile phone number and told to monitor all calls, listening for any initiated by senior members of the Tibetan government-in-exile. 'Potala' he had deduced from earlier traffic was their prime minister's closest aide. Secretly he sympathised with them, poor devils, forced to live as refugees and watch their homeland's population being diluted and their religion suppressed. He had been given a senior post in the directorate with the most modern surveillance equipment supplied by a small secret R&D unit of Reliance Industries. All the other surveillance units had to make do with second-rate Russian equipment that often failed to function properly but the tax authorities were the spoiled children of Indian bureaucracy.

'OK.' He looked over her shoulder, noting the precise time of the call then opened an encrypted email and forwarded the information to his anonymous contact at the intelligence bureau. He had no intention of prejudicing his promotion prospects: earning his PhD in IT had cost his family a small fortune.

Karim's Restaurant, Jama Masjid

Old Delhi
March 1, 1900 hours

'*Salaam awalehkum Shaukat.*'

'*Awalelkhum salaam mere dost.*' Max sensed that Shaukat's welcome was guarded, almost nervous as he hurried to meet him. The elderly maître d's Urdu was usually a joy on the ear but it had an edge to it this evening.

'You alright?' Max asked softly.

'*Mashallah.*' But this was delivered with a slight flick of his eyes towards the only solitary diner in the restaurant that was already almost fully occupied.

'Intelligence?'

'*Afsos hei.*'

'Not your fault, it's a free country.' Max patted him on the shoulder. 'I'll wait for my guest before ordering. Just bring me a spiced *lassi.*' The solitary diner looked as though he was absorbed in a book but Max recognised this as a typical way of disguising surveillance. He had deliberately arrived early to give him an edge but it appeared that someone had beaten him to it. He decided to have a little fun.

'Shaukat?' The maître d' walked over quickly. 'May I have that table over there?' He pointed to the empty table on the same side as the intelligence official but in the opposite corner which would take him out of the man's line of sight.

'Assuredly.' Laid for four, a waiter swiftly removed two places and Max sat facing outward. Just as his *lassi* was served, the door opened and an unmistakably Tibetan man stood in the entrance and surveyed the room, quickly making eye contact with Max. Tall and patrician in appearance he was smartly dressed in a well-cut European suit and what looked like an open-neck silk shirt. Pausing fractionally he gave a small nod of recognition and extended his hand.

'Colonel Devlin, thank you for joining me.' Max shook hands and indicated the chair opposite him.

'Drink?' The Tibetan's eyes registered Max's *lassi*. 'Good?'

'Excellent.'

'Then I shall have one too.' The maître d' gave them their menus and they busied themselves with polite exchanges whilst ordering.

'Mr Ladenla.'

'Geljen please.'

'If you'll call me Max.' He spoke in Tibetan. 'If what you have to tell me is confidential, I don't think this is an ideal venue, even if we continue speaking Tibetan. As I'm sure you are aware, there is a large Tibetan community here in Delhi, added to which the presence of someone from the intelligence bureau,' he indicated the far corner with his head, 'suggests that this place is as secure as a rice paper nappy.'

'They keep close tabs on us I'm afraid.' He gave a wry twist of his mouth. 'Let us enjoy the excellent food here and then perhaps we could find ourselves a little privacy.' Max nodded. 'But I would like to add my own most sincere appreciation for everything that you did to secure His Holiness's safety.' He glanced at Max's left shoulder. 'Your arm, has it healed completely?' He felt like saying 'Yes, until you reminded me' but thought better of it.

'Fully functional.' Which it was, technically. But it still ached from time to time. They did scant justice to the superb food whilst engaging in pleasantries. Max caught Shaukat's eye, indicating that he wanted the bill. The maître d' was uncomfortable.

'Was the food not to your liking Colonel?' Max gave him a reassuring smile and spoke loud enough for his voice to carry.

'Delicious, as usual. Thank you but my friend and I would like a nightcap at the Intercontinental.'

They walked out into the dusky night air and a figure detached itself from the shadows as a car engine started up.

'Rinchen, my personal protection.' Max noted the man's professionalism. 'Not the Intercontinental, I think?'

'I thought we'd find a corner of the bar at the Imperial. They have a very good pianist playing there at the moment.' Ladenla waited until they were inside the Mercedes and had moved off before instructing the driver.

Twenty minutes later they were ensconced in an alcove in the tastefully designed cocktail bar, the piano playing softly, Ladenla with a Johnnie Walker on the rocks and Max a Bacardi and coke. If they had been followed it was not noticeable, no-one had entered the bar after them.

'So, what's on your mind, Geljen?' The Tibetan sipped his drink and set it down carefully.

'After your past experience with us I can well imagine that you would have little appetite for anything more to do with us.' He smiled apologetically. It was a question framed as a statement but Max was not minded to respond. He studied his drink, drawing the man out. His curiosity was intrigued but a sixth sense was raising red flags.

'We're already indebted to you.' His hand rested on the table and he raised it from the wrist, signalling that he had no option but to press on. 'But we're in a quandary and…'

'You need my help.' He shook his head. 'I'm not available.' Anything that exposed him to the risk of seeing Tashi again would only rekindle that fire and the kindling was still far too flammable. The Tibetan's hand came up again.

'There's more.' He leaned forward, lowering his voice. 'The bullion, the money…'

'Was delivered to your people in Sikkim.' He said it curtly. The Tibetan nodded.

'Yes, yes but there is a…' He hesitated, looking for the right word, '… difficulty.'

'My men delivered it. That little excursion caused the death of three of my friends, smashed two of us up and led to me being banned from Nepal. So where's *your difficulty*?' Now he was angry. The Tibetan's mouth compressed and it was obvious he was undecided how to respond. His expression changed and he nodded. 'We owe you, I know. But just hear me out first.' He waited for a response but Max just stared at him, his face set hard.

'You must know about the controversy over the 17th Karmapa *tulku*?'

'I know that there are two claimants, Urgen Trinley and Thaye Dorje and though the previous Dalai Lama endorsed Urgen Trinley both claimants have a devoted following and no-one is backing down. You people are manufacturing your own problems.'

'The Karmapa is the head of the Karma Kagyu school of Buddhism. After the Dalai Lama, the Karmapa is the most revered tulku in the Buddhist community. Like the Dalai Lama, the 16th Karmapa fled from the Tsurphu monastery near Lhasa. Prior to the Chinese invasion, Tsurphu had been the seat of the Karma Kagyu for eight centuries. The 16th Karmapa was a highly influential tulku, responsible for spreading Buddhism throughout the western world, indeed, he died in America. It was he who constructed a new monastery for the order at Rumtek in Sikkim and oversaw the accumulation of considerable wealth, wealth to be used to spread Sakyamuni Buddha's enlightenment throughout the world. But now the Karma Kagyu lineage is at risk.' He leaned back in his chair and his eyes measured the room before he continued.

'Remarkably, in the 14th century the 5th Karmapa actually foretold that between the 16th and 17th Karmapas a demon would arise and through his powers he would bring the Karma Kagyu school near to destruction. There have already been several violent clashes between the adherents of each claimant.'

'So, which one's the demon, Urgen or Thaye?' The Tibetan managed an uncomfortable smile as he shook his head.

'Neither. The prediction suggests that the demon is more likely someone close to them.' He frowned. 'It's not the first time there have been multiple claimants to a reincarnation. No.' He gave a short dismissive shake of his head. 'It's not the dissension over the claimants, it's the political dimension that troubles us.'

'By "us" I take it you mean the Tibetan government-in-exile?'

'Precisely. You see, Urgen Trinley was found in Tibet by two of the Rumtek Monastery regents. In 1992 he was officially installed in the Tsurphu monastery and the Chinese Communist authorities seized the opportunity to declare him to be the living reincarnation, the 17th Karmapa. Later, the same regents who found him smuggled him into India. However, the other two Karma Kagyu regents declared that the true 17th Karmapa is Thaye Dorje. There is a large body of Karma Kagyu adherents who are afraid that the Chinese are behind Urgen, manipulating him in order to gain spiritual control over our people.' Max flicked the side of his glass with his fingernail.

'I'm sorry, but I don't see what this has to do with me.'

'Outside Tibet, the seat of the Karma Kagyu sect is the Rumtek Monastery in Sikkim. Presently, neither of the Karmapas has been able to take up the position of head of the monastery; Urgen is in Dharmasala because the Indian government won't allow him to go to Sikkim and Thaye lives in Kalimpong in the Gorkha Hill District of West Bengal. The monastery is presently occupied by Urgen's followers which is why Thaye Dorje cannot take up his post there either.'

'I still don't see what this has to do with me.' Max allowed his impatience to colour his words.

'The money and the bullion, your Sherpas handed it over to Urgen's people in occupation of the monastery and we cannot get hold of it. They have become a law unto themselves.' His face was grim. 'That is what it has to do with you Max.'

'Well, I'm sorry but I still don't see how the internal politics of the Tibetan community makes it my responsibility. My people would never have made it to Dharmasala. They made the best, frankly the only choice open to them. If you think your funds are unlawfully held, why don't you just inform the police in Sikkim and get the place searched and your funds handed over.'

'The Sikkim government has its own agenda. We can't get co-operation from them and anyway the occupants of the monastery have defied a Sikkim court order.' Max was losing patience rapidly.

'Look, good men died getting that load delivered. We did our job and now it's up to you to sort it out.' It was frustrating to think that the cost in men and effort had become entangled in infighting amongst the Tibetans, added to which he could not help empathising with little Dondhup who seemed to have inherited a multitude of problems. Try though he might, he realised that Tashi would be shouldering a large portion of all these troubles and now he had the distinct feeling that this man was deploying emotional blackmail.

'If you people can't sort it out amongst yourselves what possesses you to think I can?' It was on the tip of his tongue to challenge him to deny that it was emotional leverage, but he held himself in check.

'Colonel.' Ah, he thought, the deference play. 'We cannot make a move that is not immediately public, the people in the monastery would know well in advance if any of His Holiness's entourage set off for Sikkim. You have to understand that neither of the Karmapas are involved personally. Regrettable though it is, those in the monastery have their own agenda, frankly speaking they are nothing more than thieves.' The quiet reserve had been abandoned and the anger was in his tone and his eyes.

'What makes you think I can do anything more than your own people?' Max silently kicked himself, the question carried an implicit recognition that he had not rejected it completely out of hand.

'Sikkim, Kalimpong, Darjeeling, these are your stamping grounds, you know the geography, the politics and most important, you know the people and they know you. Even more to the point, it's a hotbed of dissension, all this clamour for a separate state for the hill people, there is a high degree of sensitivity amongst the ethnic Nepalese there and the fact that Sikkimese have their own state has created an added tension.' Why? Max questioned himself, why was he continuing this conversation? Even as he did so he acknowledged that there was nothing that gave him the adrenalin rush so much as a challenge laced with risk.

'What is it exactly that you have in mind?' The momentary flash of triumph in the Tibetan's body language almost prompted him to add 'whatever it is I don't want to be involved.' But he didn't.

'We would like you to retrieve the funds and deliver them to a trusted intermediary who would ensure that they are banked safely.'

'This trusted intermediary, where does he operate?'

'In Bhutan.'

'Don't tell me you're going to bank them in Bhutan.' The disbelief bordered on sarcasm.

'No.' Ladenla smiled. 'The intermediary will remit them to an account to be opened on behalf of His Holiness outside India.' Dropping his voice and suddenly looking a little embarrassed, he added, 'We are prepared to pay your usual fees and add in a success fee.'

'If you want me to put my head in a noose, especially risk getting banned from India, what you refer to as my usual fee would be rather unusual.'

'As you wish.' The acceptance was too quick.

'Without even knowing what it would be?' Max queried sharply. Ladenla leaned forward.

'Beijing is tightening the net around our people everywhere. If it is true that they want to put their candidate into Rumtek, the next step would be for him to be returned to Tsurphu and the Karma Kagyu sect would fall under Chinese dominion. For them it would be a major victory but it would be a potentially fatal wound to Buddhism and the Tibetan people. Surely you can see that?'

'But you told me that the last Dalai Lama endorsed him.' Ladenla opened his arms in a gesture that signalled that he was in a quandary.

'In strict confidence Colonel, we have more confidence in the Rinpoche who found Thaye Dorje and we cannot afford to allow this division to be exploited by the Chinese.' Max pushed the ice cubes in his glass with the swizzle stick as he digested the situation.

'Geljen, I sympathise with your predicament and I would like to help Dond…His Holiness.' The Tibetan nodded appreciatively ignoring the overfamiliarity. 'I'm also constitutionally opposed to what that collection of hair-dyed megalomaniacs in Beijing are doing to Tibet.' He looked the man in the eye. 'But I'm not your man, not for this. I'm sorry.' He signalled the barman for the bill.

'No, please, this is mine.' His courtesy could not disguise the resignation. Max took the bill folder off the tray first and inserted enough currency notes to include a decent tip, then got to his feet. Geljen took out his wallet and extracted a card.

'Please.' He proffered it and Max accepted it. They shook hands.

'May I at least offer you a lift back to your hotel?' Max shook his head.

'No thank you. I fancy a little walk. This part of Delhi has a certain charm at this time of night.'

They strode in silence to the entrance to the hotel and he waved the Tibetan off.

The sound of laughter snagged his attention and he heard his name being called.

'Max Devlin, what're you doing here?' Tempted to say that it was none of his business, Max saw that Steve Manthos was accompanied by his lovely but long-suffering wife Jessica and another young woman.

'How lovely to see you, Jessica.' His smile was genuine. For the life of him he could not understand what she saw in the brash Australian banker with his moustache of insecurity. She was charming, intelligent and highly literate having read Medieval English at Oxford whereas her husband was a barely articulate neo-con with an MBA from some dubious Middle American university that no-one had heard of and a 'little man' complex of giant proportions. Apparently they had met when Manthos was investigating a possible investment in a Sikkim hydro-power project that Jessica's father was promoting. He nodded in the Australian's direction.

'Steve.'

'Max, I don't think you've met my younger sister Kim?' Jessica gestured towards the elegantly slim figure standing behind them. 'Honey, this is Max Devlin, an old friend.'

'With the accent on old.' Manthos leered. 'I soon put a stop to the friend bit.'

Max barely registered the usual animus so taken was he by the smile on the girl's face which, typical of the *Chamling* women, was strikingly fine-featured. Her eyes held his so directly that he almost forgot his manners.

'*Malai khub kushi lagyo, bhainilai bhetnu.*' Excluding Manthos was easy for he regarded all foreign languages with suspicion.

'Oh, you don't have to go native with Kim, speaks English, got a degree from the London School of Economics and nice tits too.'

'How would you know?' The younger woman's tone was as icy as her eyes as she bit back at him.

'Do you think you could behave civilly in public, Steve? Not everyone appreciates your Aussie sense of humour.' Jessica frowned and Max had the urge to knock his teeth down his throat.

'Let's have a drink.' Manthos managed what for him was a sheepish grin which did little to ease the uncomfortable tension.

'*A la banc.*' Max's smile embraced both women. He would make the banker pay, literally and metaphorically.

'*Bien sur.*' Jessica put her hand on Max's arm to lead him to the bar and he held back to allow Kim to walk beside them.

'Why all the bullshit foreign gab? English is the international lingo.'

'Such a pity you don't speak it.' Kim's barb, thrown over her shoulder, made both women laugh. Max's appreciation for the younger woman went up several notches.

By the time they had settled at the bar with their drinks the atmosphere had lightened; for whatever reason Manthos was on his best behaviour, leaving his wife and sister-in-law to engage with Max.

'Need to shake hands with my best friend.' Manthos stood up and walked towards the rest rooms. Jessica gave Max an apologetic look.

'He's incorrigible.' Max was tempted to say openly what he had long asked himself what on earth possessed her to stay with him but Kim's presence constrained him. Suddenly he felt as though he was an awkward teenager, afraid that the girl would brush him off.

'Would you be free for dinner tomorrow?'

'If that's an invitation, I'd be happy to accept.' Her smile lit her face and quieted his anxiety.

'Kim's staying with us temporarily.' Jessica said. 'You remember our address?'

'Of course.' He turned back to connect to those compelling eyes. 'I'll call for you at eight if that's OK?' A little flick of her head signalled that it was.

'You girls don't need any beauty sleep but I should be on an intravenous drip.' They both rose as he stood up and gave Jessica a light farewell embrace. He paused fractionally before placing his hands on Kim's shoulders, caught in the twin magnets of her eyes before his face brushed against her hair and he caught the scent of her skin.

'Until tomorrow.' What could he read into those words? He hid behind formal 'goodnights' and headed for the main door.

Standing on the drive leading to Janpath he made a heroic effort to restore a semblance of order to his mind in which Kim was lighting up corners that had been in deep shadow. A natural process of prioritising relegated Tashi to the role of valued client, in parallel with Dondhup. Though his ever present sense of responsibility made him uncomfortable with the decision he had reached with Geljen, yet his instinct counselled him that it was correct.

'*Lat Saheb*.' An old woman, little more than a bag of bones on which an unrecognisable garment hung from her skeletal shoulders sat cross-legged and motionless, her back to the leprous looking brick wall and a little wooden begging bowl in front of her. It was a long time since anyone had addressed him as 'Lord Saheb'. Breaking a lifetime habit, he rooted around in his trouser pocket for change and dropped all the loose coins into her bowl. The old woman could well have been dead for all the acknowledgment she gave. As he walked away he muttered to himself.

'Max Devlin, you're a shit and giving that beggar a few coins does nothing to change the situation. You're still a shit.'

It was gone midnight by the time he got back to Maidens. The night duty receptionist caught his attention.

'Colonel, sir.' Reaching behind him, he extracted an envelope from the pigeon holes and handed it to Max who stuffed it into his trouser pocket. It was not until he had showered and was sorting out his clothes for the *dhobi* that he came across it and tore it open. The note was short, in army telegraph style 'Drinks, my place, 20.00 hours. Undress Order. Sid.'

'Damn.' Lieutenant-General (Retired) Sidartha Chopra, 'Sid' to his friends, was as regimental as shiny boots and puttees. If Max turned up without wearing a tie he'd be castigated for allowing standards to slip. They had met at a Commonwealth Services introduction to counter-insurgency techniques when both of them were comparatively junior officers. Sid was Indian Army 5th Gurkhas and Max British Army's Royal Gurkha Rifles, there was an almost symbiotic bond. Whereas Max had taken early retirement, Sid had soldiered on, highly successfully. But there was no way that he was going to postpone seeing Kim again. He would call Sid in the morning and trust that he could re-arrange the invitation. The general was his most important contact in India as well as a man to whom he was greatly indebted for arranging the successful surgery for both Deepraj and himself. But Kim was a promise of a future, something he had not had the luxury of for a long time. He noted the time as he put his wristwatch on the bedside table. Quite out of the blue, the day ahead held out hope.

General Chopra's House

Defence Colony, New Delhi
March 2, 1810 hours

'Devlin, you idle bugger, you're not properly dressed!' The general's smile belied both the content and tone of his voice.

'And a good evening to you, Sid.' Max held out a bottle of Dimple Haig. The general turned to the two men he had been talking to.

'Gentlemen, beware of the Irish bearing gifts. They rot your standards of good order and military discipline.' He took the bottle in one hand and gripped Max's hand with the other. 'Apart from this apology for making me change the timing of my invitation, it's damn good to see you.' He glanced at Max's left arm. 'If you can carry a bottle of whisky you can carry a rifle. Good.' The Indian Army had cocooned Max's little party in a security shutdown which had protected both him and Deepraj from being identified as having smuggled the infant Dalai Lama and his mother out of Tibet and into India. Despite being technically retired, Sid had a wide circle of contacts and very considerable influence and once he learned of Max's involvement he channelled the pair of them into the military medical circuit. It had been Sid who had ensured that Max's arm, damaged in the train crash, had been attended to by one of India's top hand and arm surgeons. Despite every reasonable effort to protect his anonymity, as the surgeon removed slivers of coal from Max's arm he had observed, 'I may only be a hand and arm wallah but it doesn't take a brain surgeon to fathom out how you came by these coal inserts!' Inevitably, rumours were rife but Max tried his best to dismiss them out of hand.

The general steered Max towards his other guests. 'Max I'd like you to meet Professor Harish Mitra, a member of our Rajya Sabha, nominated by the president for his contribution to literature, which means he is incorruptible.'

They shook hands and Max had a quick impression of an ascetic looking academic.

'And this is Freddie Fernandes, he's a bureaucrat.' He gave Max a theatrical wink.

'It's a pleasure, Colonel.' Fernandes appeared to be in his mid-forties, medium height, a full head of neatly groomed, grey streaked hair. His smile was professional but his eyes gave the impression that he was amused. 'Pay no attention to Sid, Colonel, he forgets that a soldier is only a bureaucrat in uniform.' He smiled broadly.

'Let's not start that crap again Freddie.' The general moaned. 'Your envy is so tangible I could strangle it.' He gave Fernandes a slow stare. 'As you're among friends here, don't be hiding your light under a bush.' The bureaucrat chided him.

'Are you not offering your guest a drink?' He beckoned to a smartly dressed bearer standing next to the drinks cabinet. The general snorted dismissively.

'Raju, pour the Colonel Saheb a straight rum on ice.' He gestured towards the bearer. 'Raju was my orderly and driver when I retired, so he came with me. He's my Man Friday.' The bearer smiled his acknowledgment.

'Sid, forgive me.' The professor put his empty glass on a side table. 'I promised Nisha I'd join her for dinner tonight.' He turned to Max, 'I'm sure you will understand. My poor wife is a legislative widow. These family occasions are something of a rarity.' Whilst the general saw him out, Fernandes pointed to an L-shaped sofa. 'Shall we?' Max sat on the short horizontal stroke and accepted the charged glass. Fernandes's face was distinctly familiar, thinner and without the moustache. He was struggling to place it.

'*Chakrata*...you're trying to recall where we met.' Max gave no sign that he had recognised the man. Simply mentioning Chakrata brought the whole disaster back. It had been during his secondment to SIS. He had been sent to India to help train a unit of Tibetan members of their special services force, known as 'the 22s' who were to be infiltrated into Tibet on a clandestine operation. Only after he had reached the training camp had he learned that the Indian government, fearing that the slightest border incident could provoke a further invasion by the PLA, had not only banned such cross-border incursions by their own forces but had prohibited the 22s from being posted any closer to the border than ten kilometres. Consequently, he had become unwittingly complicit in activities which were not only capable of bringing the PLA pouring over the border but were also categorised as unlawful by the Indian government. The training camp's senior officer was a *Dapon*, an Indian Army Tibetan whose rank was equivalent to a brigadier general and the second-in-command of the unit was an American Rangers Major. Max had enjoyed the work. The men he was training were a mix of Tibetans, Gurkhas, Sikkimese and Bhutanese and not only were they outstanding in their martial qualities but as it had originally been planned that they would be deployed in the eastern Himalayas, they were motivated because they would be protecting their homelands. But added to Max's discomfort was the fact that the men had not been informed that any such cross-border operation had been expressly prohibited by their own government. He was surprised that he had forgotten that the government official to whom he had voiced his concerns was this same Fernandes. The general came back into the room and spoke to the bearer who then left. He recovered his glass and joined them on the sofa.

'Max, Freddie is Director-General of Security at the Research and Development wing of the Intelligence Bureau.'

'We've met before.' Max's voice was cold. The fact that Sid had not warned him was an abuse of friendship. The invitation was plainly a setup.

'I owe you the apology, Colonel.' Fernandes leaned forward, an earnest expression on his face. 'I told the General not to forewarn you.' Max shot a glance of reproval at Sid and received an apologetic flick of his eyebrows.

'I suspected that you would decline the invitation if you knew that I'd be here.' He was bloody well right about that Max thought. It had been on Fernandes's adamant assurance that the then prime minister of India had authorised Max's team of 22s to make a clandestine incursion into Tibet to plant a nuclear test monitoring device supplied by the CIA. When it all went horribly wrong, three of the 22s had been killed, they'd had to abandon the monitoring device and he and the rest of his team had escaped by the skin of their teeth only to learn that no such authorisation had been given. The whole operation had been a renegade CIA-Indian Intelligence Bureau project premised on presenting the Indian government with a successful *fait accompli*. When it had not succeeded, both the Tibetan Dapon and the Rangers Major were made the scapegoats. Max had been whisked out of India still in his filthy camouflage gear but there had been no sign of

Fernandes when the shit hit the fan. The man wore the same earnest expression that Max recalled from Chakrata, his brown eyes shone with earnest credulity.

'I don't give a monkey's for running an unauthorised covert operation and the Americans are big enough and ugly enough to look after themselves. But what you allowed to happen to the Dapon was disgraceful. You sacrificed him to the politicians, claiming that he'd gone AWOL and run a private show for his own purposes.' Fernandes held both hands up in surrender.

'I'm not going to hide behind my orders, but as Sophocles rendered it "No-one loves the messenger who brings bad news."'

Max shook his head in self-wonder. The man's English was accentless and now he remembered that he was a product of an English public school education and Jesus College, Oxford.

'I'm not apologising for my service's record but we had to mollify the Chinese, we simply were not in a position to go to war with them. So, we were between the Scylla of China and the Charybdis of America, and we Indians are a very pragmatic race.' The half-smile invited assent. Max chose to remain silent, it was history and he needed some pragmatism for himself. With Nepal barred to him, India was the one country in which he could exploit his talents and experience: he could not afford to fall out with the intelligence bureau's chief. He gave the merest nod and Fernandes visibly relaxed, observing:

'I'm uncomfortably aware that we can rely upon you're absolute discretion.'

'*Ji ha!*' The general nodded.

'We have a sensitive situation.' He paused and locked eyes with Max. 'We regard you as a staunch friend of India.' Max wondered who the 'we' was but assumed that he was being softened up.

'Yesterday, you met Geljen Ladenla, the PA to the prime minister of the Tibetan government-in-exile. Of course...' he smiled, '...we are fully aware of your role in bringing the infant Dalai Lama to India, your commitment to their cause is entirely admirable, isn't it?' Max stifled a grin, Haileybury and Jesus couldn't quite cure the man of his vernacular speech.

'Our government's hospitality sprang from a genuine veneration for the late Dalai Lama and, remarkably, it rarely figured in our relations with the Chinese which, again as you know, blow hot and cold. But this business over the 17th Karmapa is a source of genuine concern. Whether Urgen Trinley is a conscious tool of Chinese policy towards India, perhaps only that young man himself knows for sure. But if he were to ascend to the Karma Kagyu throne in Rumtek, it is far from inconceivable that Beijing would use this as a pretext to move into Sikkim, adding physical occupation to their long-standing claim. That is something we cannot permit to happen, under any circumstances.' He struck the palm of his left hand with two rigid fingers of his right.

'It is imperative that he never take up his position at Rumtek.'

'I understand that he's prohibited from leaving Dharmasala, so the prospect of that happening is illusory.' Max countered.

'In theory, you are correct.' He leaned back on the sofa and ran his hand through his hair. 'But India is a democracy and in a democracy we cannot always control people as one would wish.' It was the expression of distaste on Fernandes's face more than the words that carried the message to Max's mind that the man was a control freak.

'The Karma Kagyu followers are split amongst themselves but they have a worldwide constituency. If Urgen Trinley's adherents were to mount an international campaign for his enthronement in Rumtek, our government could be gravely embarrassed, it could be taken up in the United Nations and the Chinese would only have to sit and wait.' Max thought he could see where all this was leading.

'That sort of campaign would require generous funding and the Rumtek rebels are sitting on a small fortune?'

'Precisely.' Fernandes's eyes seemed to bulge out of their sockets. 'Which you want to prevent them from using.'

'What was it that the character in *House of Cards* said? "You may very well think so. I couldn't possibly comment."'

'What's to stop you from seizing it on any number of pretexts?'

'We cannot be seen to be taking sides in what is essentially a spiritual conflict amongst the Buddhist community. My political masters are particularly nervous at the moment. They think it would be dynamite. We have an election coming up and the government is walking on the proverbial eggs.' Max allowed the mixed metaphors to run freely through his imagination. With a picture of exploding eggs still in his mental window, he inquired gently.

'So?'

Fernandes sat back sharply as though surprised at the query.

'So, if the Tibetan government-in-exile asks for your help to recover the funds, you have no connection with the Indian government and any repercussions would not involve us.' He opened his arms wide with a smile that would have graced any magician at the successful outcome of a trick.

'And when it goes wrong, you can drop me in the shit, just like you did to the Dapon.' Max stood up and stepped away from the sofa. In a soft tone that belied his words he addressed the general. 'I will assume that you were unaware of what Mr Fernandes had in mind when he set up this encounter, Sid, and even if you had an inkling, I owe you so I shan't hold it against you.' Then, facing Fernandes, in the same softly modulated voice he said, 'You make Machiavelli look like Mother Teresa. I hope that our paths won't have to cross again.' Turning on his heel he began to walk out of the room.

'Max!' The general called after him but he ignored him.

'Let him go, Sid. He's a slave to his principles.' Fernandes's smile came from hooded eyes. The general nodded emphatically. They heard the front door close. Still with a residue of a smile Fernandes wagged his head gently from side to side. 'Of course, principles come at a price. Not to worry, he'll come around. Every principle has a price, isn't it?'

By the time Max reached the Manthos' apartment building his anger had dissipated, displaced by an almost nervous anticipation at the prospect of having Kim to himself for an evening. He deliberately asked the taxi driver to stop a good distance from their address to allow him time to collect himself. Though he berated himself for being an idiot, he could not suppress the nervous energy that made beads of perspiration stand out on his forehead. The elderly *chowkidar* at the main gate phoned his name through to the apartment and gave what he obviously thought was a smart salute on being instructed to admit Max. Taking the lift to the second floor, he stepped out into a marbled lobby, one door of which was held open by a uniformed bearer.

'Good evening Saheb.' Max acknowledged the greeting and steeled himself to have to deal with Manthos in as minimally courteous a way as possible, but it proved unnecessary.

'Hello Max.' He was held momentarily speechless by her smile.

'Jessica and Steve are attending some financial cocktail. Would you like to come in for a drink?' He shook his head, conscious that he was smiling like a loon and still had said nothing.

'No, thanks.' Other than that she was wearing something that clung gently to her figure, he was unaware of anything but her face.

'I've booked a table at Bokhara. Is that OK?'

'Wonderful, I love their food.' Suddenly serious she asked, 'Do you have a car?'

'No.' She turned to the bearer.

'Sammy, *local cab bolau*.' She touched his elbow. 'There's a cab rank at the corner of the road. By the time we get to the main gate, one will be there.' She put her head back inside the door and called out. 'Goodnight Jason.' Once seated on the slippery plastic covered seat of the cab they found themselves sliding together as the driver diced with death in the night-time traffic. Max held the back of the driver's seat with one hand and held her firmly across the shoulders with the other.

'I didn't bribe him.' He joked.

'Are you sure?' She responded. 'Steve says that you're some sort of spook and you plan your every move.' He gave a derisive laugh.

'Steve has a vivid imagination, especially for a banker.'

'You don't like him, do you?'

'He's the sort of little creep that gives Australians a bad name.' Then, aware that this could be a reflection on Jessica he added, 'I've never understood what Jessica sees in him.' He turned to face her. 'Sorry, that was thoughtless of me.'

'Don't apologise. He's always coming on to me, thinks he's God's gift. Jessica is well aware but she's protective of Jason.' Max had guessed that their autistic son could well be an explanation for why Jessica put up with her husband.

'She's scared that if they broke up, the emotional stress could damage the tenuous channel of communication they have with him.'

'Poor girl, poor child. It's a lose-lose situation if ever there was one.' Not for the first time, Max was struck by what he believed to be the disproportionately high incidence of very intelligent mothers with autistic children. Their conversation revolved around autism and the catastrophic effect on the lives of both parent and child until the cab drew up at the main entrance to the Maurya.

Max had taken the trouble to talk to the restaurant captain earlier and they were shown to their shiny wooden table for two, slightly set apart from the other diners.

'I'd like the baby lamb.' She volunteered.

'If I order the paneer and their dhall, with roti Chennai, would that suit you?'

She smiled enthusiastically. They both chose to drink lassi, she sweet and he salty. Studying the menu forced him to take his eyes away from her. She wore her hair loose, down to her shoulders and he was entranced by her habit of sweeping it away from the left side of her face, only for it to fall back moments later, almost veiling the classic lozenge-shaped eye peculiar to the Mongol races. The dark pupils had an intensity that drew him back. They both started to speak at the same time.

'What are you doing in…' Both stopped and then laughed. Max held out his open palm. 'You first.' Her expression grew serious, a tiny crease puckering the space between her eyebrows.

'I heard about the communists in Nepal seizing your business. That was outrageous.' She leaned forward a little. 'Could you not start again in Sikkim? We have the Kanchenjunga national park and several wildlife sanctuaries.' He gave a little shake of his head.

'I'm afraid all my capital was invested in Nepal.'

'But with your reputation you could easily get backers.' He loved her enthusiasm and was loath to dampen it.

'Nepal was a wake-up call. It brought home to me just how precarious it is for a foreigner in lands where he has no real security of tenure.'

'But the Indian government is relaxing the restrictions on foreign investment.'

'If you are Starbucks or Walmart, but not the SMEs.' He caught the hint of iron in his voice. 'Let's not dwell on the past, tell me about your plans. What did you read at LSE?' He watched the little worry lines ebb out of her face as she began to talk animatedly about herself.

Kim acknowledged that both her parents were much more liberal in their attitudes than the majority of the Gangtok community. They had welcomed Hope Cook's marriage to the Chogyal, seeing it as providing tacit

American support for the little kingdom's continuing independence. But when everything went wrong and India engineered the annexation of Sikkim they had retreated into their traditional thinking and Jessica had been compelled to fight a lonely battle against conventions that would have crushed the spirit of anyone less determined. Her insistence on marrying Steve Manthos had put an almost intolerable strain on her relationship with her parents, her mother in particular. Kim believed that it had been Jessica's way of demonstrating her independence rather than a romantic union. Whichever it was, Jessica had pioneered the way for her younger sister who had enjoyed a far greater measure of freedom in consequence. Conscious of the debt she owed, Kim had been careful not to squander the licence thus bestowed. Both at Loreto Convent in Darjeeling and later at LSE, young men quickly learned that her academic studies took precedence over everything else and after being politely rebuffed a few times they gave up. On her return to Sikkim she had soon become involved in the underground campaign for the resumption of sovereign status. The Congress Party's vote to create a new state out of Uttar Pradesh had triggered similar claims from various groupings around India and lent renewed impetus to those in Sikkim who wanted to see the Chogyal reinstated and its independent status reclaimed. However that put them on a collision course with the central government in Delhi and those Sikkimese politicians who were milking the system under the current administration. At Jessica's insistence but with marked reluctance, she had agreed to accompany them to Delhi because feelings were increasingly febrile and there had been several instances of violence. It suddenly dawned on Kim that she was telling Max everything, her hopes and fears, her relationship with Jessica, things she would never have dreamt of revealing to a stranger in the past. Her hand flew to her mouth and she stopped mid-sentence.

'I…I'm so sorry. I've run on and on about myself.' He gave her a reassuring smile.

'Apart from letting your food go cold I'm happy for you to keep going on.' They both laughed and the momentary awkwardness she had experienced was replaced by a warm sense of sharing. She ate a little of the *Raan* and nodded appreciatively.

'Delicious.' She noticed that he ate with his hand and he, following her glance, responded.

'Food like this can't be enjoyed with a knife and fork. I often get critical stares when I eat *dhall bhat* this way. I can tell what they're thinking

"Disgusting, the man's gone totally native, eating curry and rice with his fingers.'" He laughed. 'I always think poor ignorant bastards. They don't know any better!'

It struck her that whatever he did made her feel totally comfortable. It was not until they had finished eating that her curiosity got the better of her.

'So, what are your plans now?' She saw his expression darken for a moment and hurried to repair any damage she had caused. 'I'm sorry. I didn't mean to pry, but…' He waved his hand to dismiss her concerns.

'It's kind of you to take an interest.' Why, he couldn't really say, but it seemed perfectly natural to share his thoughts with her.

'Call it a coincidence if you will, but some people would like me to go to Sikkim and help sort out a problem they have.' As he spoke he chided himself for the veiled way he was expressing himself but there was no way he could burden her with the story, not at this stage anyway, much though he felt inclined to be open with her.

'Well, that's great!' Her face lit up in a smile that made him think of butter, he wanted to taste it. 'We could go together and then Jessica won't need to worry about me.'

'Whoah!' He held his palms up. 'For starters, I haven't decided whether to go.' His mind scrabbled around for an excuse that would not make her think that her company was unwelcome or that gave a hint as to what he might be involved in. 'And from what you've told me, you might need 24-hour protection.'

'That's nonsense.' She made an impatient gesture with her hand. 'Jessica pays too much attention to Manthos *bhena*. He's a banker spelled with a "w".' She grinned and it broke the moment of tension. 'Anyway, I can't waste my time in Delhi when there's important work to be done at home.' He hesitated a moment before saying something that might give offence.

'Do you not think that trying to put the clock back, what is it, 50 years is a bit over optimistic?' He studied her face for signs of the shutters going up but her eyes were alive.

'Of course it's a big jump but if the Gorkhaland movement can succeed in the Darjeeling District, why shouldn't Sikkim nationalism triumph? They have to start from scratch but we want reinstatement.'

'True.' He nodded. Her hair had fallen across her face again and she brushed it back, giving him another moment's delight. He was already revising his plans but had no intention of telling her anything yet. He looked at his watch.

'I'd better get you home, it's gone midnight.' She looked around suddenly aware that they were the only diners left in the restaurant and smiled apologetically at the captain who was hovering nearby with the bill. Max paid in cash and bade the staff goodnight as he escorted her out into the hotel proper.

'I'd like to show you around Old Delhi tomorrow if you'd be interested.' Her head turned towards him, her smile of acceptance putting to rest his fear that she might refuse. He placed his hand lightly in the small of her back as they mounted the staircase, enjoying a contrived moment of contact. At the entrance she touched his arm.

'There's no need to see me back. I'll take a taxi from here.'

'Would you deprive me of your company so readily?' She laughed.

'Thank you.'

In the taxi back to Maidens he took stock of his feelings. What he had felt for Tashi had grown out of the traumatic experiences which they had gone through together. Even now he acknowledged that theirs was a bond that would survive, yet, as he was compelled to accept, it had not been strong enough to overcome her sense of duty to her son. Though he had resented it at the time, he also recognised that what he had asked of her was selfish. So, where did that put his feelings for Kim? Anyone looking into the taxi would have seen a mature male with his face fixed in a smile for no apparent reason. Happiness, he concluded: just being with her made him happy. Perhaps he was being foolish but there had been so little to be happy about over the recent past that he had grown accustomed to the grim expression reflected in his shaving mirror. He had no need to pursue happiness, she carried it with her.

Maidens Hotel

Old Delhi
March 3, 0700 hours

As he walked back into his room after his morning swim, his mobile phone signalled that he had a message.

'Café Coffee Day, Gymkhana 0800. Sid.' Despite the cryptic message, he was glad that Sid wanted to see him. On reflection, he felt that he'd been less than courteous to his friend.

At five to eight he alighted from his taxi in front of the colonial façade of the Gymkhana Club and was saluted by the uniformed chowkidar. He walked inside and Sid waved to him from a corner table.

'I suppose you'll want a cappuccino?'

'Please.' The general ordered for him and a cup of English breakfast tea for himself.

'I apologise for my rudeness to you the other night.' The general gave a dismissive wave of his arm.

'You gave him what he deserved.' His expression darkened. 'Max, you don't have to tell me but have you got what the licentious British soldiers call "Fuck off money"?' Max shook his head.

'I've enough to see me over the next two or three years, if I spend cautiously, that's about it, then I'll be indigent again.'

'Thought so.' The general glanced around quickly, other than a solitary member in the far corner of the room and the staff hanging around the entrance, the café was deserted.

'Fernandes wields a great deal of influence…' Max started to interrupt.

'Hear me out.' The general raised his hand and Max subsided into his chair.

'I subscribe to your principles but civilians don't, which makes us akin to the Dodo. For what it's worth, I think you ought to have remained in the army, you had excellent prospects and it was an environment in which the ideals that you adhere to were appreciated. But you didn't, so now you have to play politics instead of soldiers. God knows, you must have been a Premier League player to have survived for as long as you did in Nepal!' Max managed a wry grin.

'Whether or not you play along with him on this Tibetan business, I want you to mend fences with the man.' He paused to allow Max to digest this for a moment. 'He could facilitate things for you but he can also get you frozen out.' He dropped his voice. 'And I believe that's what he intends to do.' Max felt anger rising but kept it under control.

'What are you suggesting, Sid?' The older man sat back as their tea and coffee was served and waited for the bearer to withdraw.

'Clausewitz. Attack before he does.'

'How?'

'Use me as a channel to set up a meeting between the two of you, then give him some of that Irish blarney about India's interests being more important than personal impressions. Oh, I don't know, I'm sure you can think of something.'

'What makes you think he'll freeze me out?'

'Not in so many words but he left me with the clear impression that he intended to bring you around to his way of thinking. I'd rather you volunteer than be conscripted against your will. He could do a lot of damage to your reputation.'

Max's mind was preoccupied with Kim and the prospect of going to Sikkim with her. Fernandes could find himself the unwitting facilitator or at the very least not erecting hurdles in his path. He gave a friendly nod.

'You're right, Sid.' The older man's face beamed.

'My God, that's a relief, I thought your stubborn streak would defeat me.' He brushed his moustache with his forefinger. 'I'll call him this morning.'

'Don't set anything up for today. I have a full programme and I don't want to give the impression that I'm worried.'

'Agreed. I'll be in touch. Can I drop you anywhere? My car and driver are in the car park.' Max had arranged to meet Kim at the Red Fort at 10 o'clock. It would mean arriving a bit early but being chauffeur-driven was always better than a taxi in Delhi.

They spent the morning walking through the Red Fort and he explained its symbolic status as the residence of the last of the great Mughal emperors. That led in turn to the Indian Mutiny.

'Don't you mean the first war of independence?' She teased him.

'No, that's far too facile a description for the culmination of a process of breaking down the unique synergy that had evolved between the indigenous population and the early British officers.' He looked and sounded so serious that her hand flew to her mouth and she giggled.

'I was only joking.' Taken aback by his own response, a chastened smile lit his face. 'Sorry.'

'Don't be.' She shook her head and her hair fell across her face again. 'What you were saying reminds me of what my dad used to tell us, that there had been a time when marriage between Englishmen and Indian women was perfectly normal, even more so amongst the Mongol hill girls where the genes matched so well.' Suddenly embarrassed, she looked away. It took him a couple of moments to catch on.

'I've met a couple of blue-eyed beauties but both of them were elderly Raini ladies, so perhaps the genes are running out.' He took her hand. 'Come on, I'll take you to Subba Rao's house where the 2nd Goorkhas made their name during the siege of Delhi. Before the British Army disbanded all the old Gurkha regiments, we used to joke at the expense of the 2nd, nicknamed them "God's Own" but their defence of the Ridge during the mutiny was a sort of Rorke's Drift but much much longer or as if the Americans had succeeded in holding the Alamo.' The momentary awkwardness dissolved and they went in search of a taxi.

'I'm not surprised that people want you to act as their guide, you make history come alive.'

'Half the world's mistakes are because politicians lack a sense of history.'

Martial Arts Club

Janakpuri, New Delhi
2030 hours

Deepraj was not in the best of humours. He had been enjoying a mildly alcoholic evening with several friends when his mobile rang and Max's angry voice told him to get himself over to the Martial Arts Club in Janakpuri. His ringtone of 'Colonel Bogey' had set off uncontrollable laughter amongst the other *Lahoreys* who were all ex-Indian Army Gurkhas which only served to irritate him further. An hour later both he and Max were drenched in sweat as they went at each other hammer and tongs, kick-boxing. Despite Max having a height advantage, Deepraj was quick and built like an armoured car so that he absorbed Max's kicks and punches. Whereas he took out his irritation at having his evening ruined, he had no idea why his employer was trying to knock several shades of shit out of him. His injured leg was giving him hell but he was damned if he was going to admit it. Max was not wearing a headband and the sweat was rolling into his eyes, making him blink. Deepraj focused on the Saheb's eyes and in the second that they closed he shot out a right to the head which landed with a satisfying thud jolting his opponent backwards.

'Whoah!' Max held up his hands. '*Pugyio!*' Deepraj was in total agreement, it was enough. They showered and changed and sat at the empty health bar nursing large fruit smoothies. The Gurkha gave Max a sideways glance.

'What's up *huzoor?*' They were an odd couple: an ex-Major who everyone addressed as 'Colonel' because he had held the temporary rank of Lt-Colonel immediately before he took early retirement and the ex-Corporal. Despite the fact that Deepraj always used the respectful form of address, his often disrespectful idiosyncrasies would never have been permitted whilst they were serving soldiers but they were comfortable in each other's company and in the course of their shared experiences they had acquired an unspoken respect for each other's qualities. Men who have fought together develop a seventh dimension, no matter differences in rank.

In a dry, emotionless voice, Max recounted his meetings with Geljen Ladenla and Freddie Fernandes without saying how he had reacted. The kick-boxing session had drawn out the venom, leaving him emotionally balanced. Whereas he understood and even sympathised with the Tibetan's request, despite his promise to Sid, his feelings towards Fernandes were of profound dislike and, even more, distrust. Regardless of the ease with which Max could blend into a variety of Indian communities, the fact remained that he was a foreigner. A Sikh might quarrel with a Bengali or a Tamil with a Scindi but they were all Indian nationals and could not be forced to leave their country. The intelligence chief would not need to have him thrown out. He could just make his work impossible. He was genuinely saddened that Sid had lent himself to the intelligence chief's design, he had thought better of him. It was a rock and a hard place syndrome.

'And?' The Gurkha prompted him.

'*Kunni?*' He really did not know.

'The *Bhotia* will pay us and I need a proper pension.' There it was, the practical old soldier's approach, unencumbered by Max's emotional baggage or his history of Fernandes's deceit. To give Deepraj the full flavour of the intelligence chief, Max recounted succinctly and without comment the cross-border incident and the scapegoating of the Dapon.

'Hmph, all soldiers are expendable in the eyes of politicians and bureaucrats.' Suddenly changing into English he added: 'We eat and they cheat.'

Whilst acknowledging all this basic wisdom, until he met Kim, Max had wanted nothing more to do with the Tibetans in exile, especially if, as now seemed unavoidable, it meant an involvement with the Indian intelligence world, in any of its many manifestations. Now that he was actively considering getting involved he needed to get a handle on all the various individuals and organisations that had made it their business to interfere. It was also second nature to have as good a grasp as possible of the background facts of a situation. Deepraj clearly read his thoughts.

'I could go and muck in with the *Bhotia* here in Delhi, drink with them, gamble, provided I'm funded.' He said with a completely straight face. 'They all talk once they get pissed.' Max did not have the intelligence bureau's IT infrastructure or hydra-like surveillance capabilities, but he could put Deepraj's boots on the ground and he was convinced that nothing compares with human intelligence.

'Go and use your hillman's charm on the Tibetan community in Delhi, see what you can pick up about the folk behind the Karmapa Urgen Trinley.'

The more he considered the situation the more bizarre it appeared. 'Curiouser and curiouser' as Alice would have remarked, save that this was not the Wonderland. Though he believed that he had no moral obligation to restore the gold and money to the Dalai Lama in Dharmasala, he had started to justify it to himself. Having accepted payment for completing the task, even though the job itself had changed beyond recognition and it had always been open to him to simply walk away in the mountains, leaving the money, the child and Tashi to their own devices, it would never have occurred to him that he would ever have done so. Yes, he'd been deceived and yes, good friends had lost their lives but one either saw an assignment through to the end or abandoned every principle that gave any meaning to a sense of self-worth. All that had stood in the way of helping Geljen Ladenla and, by necessary extension, Tashi and Dondhup, had been his own wounded psyche. Yet in all too many ways they were also victims, no not victims but pawns in a game being played at a level way out of their league. Some of the players had upped the stakes and made him feel that he was dispensible; whilst recognising the truth inherent in that, he was damned if he would give them the satisfaction of proving it. If the bloody Indian intelligence people wanted to rattle his chain perhaps it was time to teach them a lesson too.

Try as he might, he could not take Kim out of the equation.

At the back of his conscience was the knowledge that the fees that the Tibetans had paid him had relieved him of financial worries, at least for a year or two. Deepraj was correct, it was not sufficient to give them a pension but neither of them was knocking on destitution's door any more. Quite the reverse, the premier travel agents were sniffing around, trying to see how expensive it would be to engage his services. Despite the serious efforts to preserve their anonymity, word had percolated through to the market and he could have charged a premium if he had been prepared to acknowledge his part in the Dalai Lama's flight. By way of contrast, Deepraj entertained no such inhibitions and had only agreed to keep quiet under duress.

'So, do we take the job?'

'I'm thinking about it.'

'What's to think about?' What went unspoken was the notoriety in which he could have basked, enjoying the enhanced fees.

'I said I'm thinking about it.' Max snapped. 'When you get the solid data on Urgen Trinley's hard men in Rumtek we can decide.' Deepraj gave him one of his blank expressions behind which Max believed that he concealed mutinous thoughts. Taking five 1,000-rupee notes out of his wallet he held them out.

'Go and buy some loose tongues.'

'Saheb.' The Gurkha took the proffered notes, a smile ghosting across his mouth. As he watched him leave, Max was reminded of the Guards' Sergeant-Majors at Sandhurst who also imbued the word 'Sir' with a derisive quality when addressing the officer cadets.

Office of Commissioner for Ethnic Integration

Beijing
March 3, 1700 hours

―――⁂―――

Nursing an evil temper, Bo Ziling watched the cavalcade of 7-series BMWs exiting the drab courtyard in front of his building and smarted within himself. Even his wife was complaining about their BYD F6 and its asthmatic 2.0-litre engine. Yet in many respects his was the most politically challenging appointment in the entire PRC. Witness the conference that had just finished, attended by nearly all the provincial governors. They, smug in their knowledge that all the religious dissidents were Bo's responsibility, had shaken his hand warmly and gone back to their 5-star hotels to change for the obligatory banquet at which, regardless of the president's war on profligacy, lakes of the very best *maotai* would be imbibed until they were decorously bundled back into their limousines. But he would be the one nursing the irremediable hangover.

He turned away from the window only to face a wall of photographs of himself with foreign religious leaders and the heads of all the official Chinese religious organisations: the former were a pain in the arse and the latter were of monumental irrelevance or worse. His eyes passed quickly over the Taoists and the characterless Protestants, pausing momentarily on the two-faced Catholic Cardinal Tzu before moving on to the photograph of a placard protesting against the prosecution of the *Falun Gong*. This was his sole joke, no people, just a placard in badly scrawled simplified characters. It was the best that that bunch of lunatics could achieve since he had driven them underground. The next photograph made him wince: both he and the Imam stared icily at the camera. The Uyghur Islamic fanatics were barely under control: no matter how many were arrested and re-educated more of the swine kept popping up and causing mayhem with their vicious knife attacks on the Han residents in Xinjiang, Gansu and Shaanxi provinces. He would have liked to close all the mosques and stop all that caterwauling from the loudspeakers mounted on them but the central committee had ruled against such repressive measures, instructing him to 'get alongside them'. How, in the name of Sun Tzu can you get alongside people who won't even permit you to touch them physically? His grunt of contempt made his personal assistant jump.

'Sir?'

'Nothing, fuck nothing.' He forced himself to contemplate the next photograph in which he was bent forward, the palms of his hands pressed together opposite a boy in the magenta robes of a Buddhist monk who was facing him in the picture in a similar pose. Urgen Trinley, the 17th Karmapa Lama and head of the Karma Kagyu sect, Bo's masterstroke. Ensconced in Tsurphu, he had been a magnet to a significant proportion of the Buddhist bastards in Tibet and represented the most effective method of combating the Dalai Lama's influence. That is, until he had suddenly fled to India. In order to save himself, Bo had allowed the rumour to spread that he had engineered Trinley's flight to give him greater credibility in the eyes of Buddhists all over the world. Fortunately, some of Trinley's closest advisors were in Bo's employment and he had quickly seen how best to exploit the situation: get Trinley set up in Rumtek and slowly spread his influence over the Karma Kagyu sect and by extension over Sikkim. He had presented it to the central committee as his masterstroke and they had bought it. Just when he could see his career path opening before him, two of the stinking Rumtek regents, the Rinpoches, had declared Thaye Dorje the true 17th Karmapa. Now neither of the claimants were seated in Rumtek and Bo's plans were on hold.

He sat down behind his kidney-shaped desk which he had paid a small fortune to a *feng shui* master to design for him, yet another total waste of money, and opened the central drawer. There, positioned over his diary was the newspaper cutting of the infant Dalai Lama: where his face would have been was just a mass of tiny pinholes where Bo had vented his fury. He slammed the drawer shut.

'So, where's all the gold and money those shit-faced Khambas stole?'

'It's with Trinley's people in Sikkim.'

'Sure?'

'The Nepalese Sherpas delivered it to Rumtek thinking that it would be transferred to Dharmasala, fortunately it was handed over to Trinley's supporters. It's under lock and key in the monastery, there's no way they'll let Dorje or his people access it.' The PA was nervous: his chief had been criticised by some senior cadres over the escape of the Dalai Lama and the theft of the bullion and cash. If they could recover it, there would be less loss of face.

'Do you want to send a snatch team in to bring it back?' The PA pointed to a map on the wall. 'We could get a special forces unit in and out in 48 hours.' Bo smiled as he shook his head slowly.

'No. Those funds are off our balance sheet. We can use them to influence Indian officials to permit Urgen to take up the Karma Kagyu throne in Rumtek. Once he is there, we can begin the process that will marginalise the Dalai Lama. With the Tibetans split amongst themselves our task will be so much simpler.' He smiled at the desiccated head of the infant Dalai Lama.

'No, the funds stay in Sikkim for now, but we need an audit, no-one close to that amount of money is trustworthy. We must engineer a way to put them under our direct control. Is this man *Chopsticks* reliable?'

'Our agent in residence says that his loyalty is as deep as our pocket and he's very influential in Trinley's group of the Karma Kagyu sect.'

'I'd rather have someone governed by greed than some crazed Maoist adherent. I hate the Marxist fanatics as much as the Islamic fundamentalists. They're all deep down crazies we can't control.'

He had a good feeling about this operation; it would be his springboard into a position of real power and everything that he had learned about moving funds secretly to destroy all the religious groups meant that his rewards would be untraceable. Nor would he make the mistakes made by his namesake Bo Li in Chongqing. He would only take into his confidence those who became equally compromised. The PA broke into his chain of thought.

'*Notebook* says that the Dalai Lama clique in Dharmasala are trying to get hold of the funds for themselves.' He paused nervous of the reaction to his next item of news. 'He says that the same *laowai* who brought the Dalai Lama to India will help them.'

'Devlin?' Bo's face twisted in disbelief. 'Wasn't he crippled in the train crash?'

'Apparently not.' For the next thirty seconds the PA learned the extent of his chief's repertoire of abuse focused on parts of the body. When the tirade seemed to have run out, he started to explain that they had no confirmation of the information but Bo cut him off.

'This must be prevented. Notebook is the one we caught with the honeytrap, isn't he?' The PA nodded. 'Keep him terrified of exposure. Tell him he has to do whatever is necessary to stop them.' His eyes retreated behind their lids. 'Get rid of the laowai!' A creamy globule of spittle crept out of the corner of his mouth. 'Remind Notebook of what will happen if he fails. Get him put in funds immediately. He'll have to buy help.' He pointed his finger at his PA. 'Use some of the Rumtek money, it's ours, this is what it's for.' He had been on the point of saying 'mine' but saved himself in time.

'Sir.' The PA was cowed by the vehemence, the finger pointing.

'When I say whatever is necessary, I mean *whatever*, is that clear? I want him dead.'

'Sir, absolutely.'

'Make sure that little fuck your mother Notebook gets the message."

'Sir.' The word almost choked in the PA's throat as Bo pulled open his drawer and stabbed his ivory paper knife into it. He had seen the newspaper cutting.

Moti Mahal Restaurant

Old Delhi
March 4, 1315 hours

'Something wrong with your lamb?' Fernandes barely paused as he chewed on his chicken leg.

'I've little appetite.'

'My dear Colonel, one doesn't waste the best tandoori in the world.' He waved a drumstick in the air. '*You're* reputed to be quite an authority on the Indian kitchen. Or is it that your loss of appetite is less to do with the food and more the company?' He smiled.

'You may say so.'

'I see.' He signalled to a waiter. '*Do to Cobra beer.*' He turned to face Max. 'You will join me in a beer?' Max nodded.

'I understood from our good friend General Sid that you have reconsidered your position.'

'I'm willing to listen.'

'Good.' Fernandes's eyes swivelled left and right as he reassured himself that no-one was in listening distance. He stared at Max, his fingers drumming inconsequentially on the table top as he appeared to be making up his mind. 'I'm going to be extraordinarily frank with you.' Max interpreted this as an intention to tell only a half-truth instead of a stonking lie. He was tempted to ask why but held himself in check.

'I think you can help me and by "me" I refer to my bureau.' He tore off a piece of *naan* and punctuated his words with it in his hand.

'Almost all my resources are occupied with the Islamic fundamentalist threat.' He frowned as he leaned forward. 'A major terrorist attack on my watch and I'm history.' Again his eyes rolled quickly around. 'I can't afford to drop my guard against those bastards.' He jerked his head in a way which conveyed that he was referring to Pakistan. 'But they're in the dark ages in comparison to the sophistication of the Chinese.' The piece of naan was twisted in an upward flick of the wrist.

'You doubt me?'

'No, not at all.' Max shook his head. 'I'm just a little surprised that you have so many eggs in the fundamentalist basket.'

'*Eh bhaguwan* my friend.' He grimaced. 'The politicians tie my hands and then expect me to do conjuring tricks! Most of our citizens think that the bureau is omniscient and all powerful but my biggest battles are over my budget allocation with the finance ministry. They demand a Rolls-Royce service for the price of a Hindusthan Standard.' They both laughed, then Fernandes's face grew serious.

'I have developed what I call the "applied China" technique. I can't hope to break into their networks but I can cultivate people within organisations that have known Chinese connections. Which brings me to the Tibetan government-in-exile.' He used the piece of naan to break off some of the tandoori chicken and stuffed it into his mouth.

'The old Dalai Lama was shrewd, he knew how to play the game.' Bits of food flew out of his mouth across the table and Max made a mental note of what not to eat.

'But then he handed over the political reins to laymen who lacked his intuitive skills and now this dispute between the two Karmapas is also causing divisions between the two great Buddhist schools, the red hats and the black hats.' He waved a chicken drumstick in the air for emphasis. 'It's ripe for exploitation by Beijing. It's ironic, we offer the Tibetans sanctuary and now all that money the Dalai Lama brought out with him could be used to give Beijing a base in Sikkim, isn't it?' He tossed the drumstick aside in disgust.

'So why not find an excuse to seize the money, that'd cramp their style?'

'That's just what the Revenue want to do and they've got a good case, claim that it's all contraband under the Foreign Exchange Maintenance Act.' He spread his hands wide. 'Simple, eh?'

'I would have thought so.'

'I wish the greedy bastards would stay out of my hair, all they think about is getting their fingers on everyone's cash, no sense of money as a vital weapon in the wider world of political influence.' He stared out across the heads of diners, lost in his own thoughts. Max saw his facial muscles suddenly assume purpose.

'But the cabinet is terrified of the international opprobrium, can't you see the headlines? "Indian government steals poor Tibetan refugees' money".' He shook his head and pursed his lips in what he obviously intended to be a smile. 'No, it requires a great deal more subtlety than that.' Max felt that it would not have been out of place on a tiger. He could not shake the sense of the bizarre, sharing a meal with India's top security officer and discussing what the country's bureau with its fearsome reputation could not do, the absurd corollary being that it was something he, Max, could.

'There are complications.'

'Why am I not surprised?'

'The Sikkim Supreme Court has ruled in favour of Thaye Dorje but the state government favours Urgen Trinley. Consequently, Urgen's supporters' retention of the funds is, strictly speaking, unlawful. However, the state police are controlled from Gangtok and so they are guarding the monastery at Rumtek, much to the frustration of Thaye Dorje's followers. There have already been several violent clashes.'

'And you want me to go and knock on the monastery door and ask them to please hand over the treasure?' He weighed his words sarcastically.

Fernandes stared at him for a moment, his lips quivered a little as though he was savouring his next pronouncement.

'What I want you to do, Colonel, is to divorce the money from the Urgen Trinley faction.' He sat back in his chair, placed his hands together and steepled his fingers, resting his chin on his fingertips. 'Why me? You may ask. Well, let's just say that you are responsible for dropping this problem in my lap, so to speak.' One eyebrow rose quizzically but he did not wait for a response.

'I don't care how you do it, in fact I don't want to know anything about it and if it all goes terribly wrong.' He paused to give effect to his words. 'I shall deny any knowledge of you.' He glanced at his watch. 'As at this very moment I am delivering a lunchtime lecture to a fresh intake of intelligence officers, where I have been for the last hour or so, as they will all readily confirm.' Reluctant to be seen as an easy pushover, Max made the obvious inquiry.

'And if I refuse?'

'Ah.' He cleaned his fingers in a finger bowl with a wedge of lemon. 'The days of the Raj are no more, dear Colonel, your presence in India would be regarded as an embarrassment, after all, we wish to cultivate excellent relations with our neighbours in Nepal whose government would welcome your extradition.' He smiled. 'All purely hypothetical, you understand?' Max nodded as the intelligence chief wiped his fingers on a napkin, then got up out of his chair and gave a slight bow.

'I relish a good hypothesis and, as our good friend the General told me, you are a good listener.' He began to walk away, stopped and turned back.

'Oh, one more thing, I'm afraid I cannot offer you any assistance, but I'm sure we can count on your initiative, isn't it?' Then he walked off and in seconds was lost to sight. Max surveyed the detritus of their lunch. He had hardly touched his food. Whatever appetite he may have had was long gone.

Outside the restaurant, Fernandes lit a cigarette and drew deeply on it. His driver had spotted him and was hurrying back to his car. The intelligence chief dialled a pre-set number on his mobile phone.

'Ranjit, I have a job for one of your Black Cats.' He laughed appreciatively at the response and rang off. Together with the commander of the National Security Guard they had been developing India's crack special forces along the lines of the British SAS with a view to using them in a clandestine role. It was time to put it to the test.

Maidens Hotel

Old Delhi

1915 hours

Max was stretched out on a sun-lounger beside the pool. The sun had shifted so that he sat in the shade. The vodka-tonic he had ordered thinking it would be refreshing stood on the table beside him, untouched. Everyone else had abandoned the open air for fear of the mosquitoes but as he was fully dressed he did not care. He found himself staring at the polished toes of his ankle length boots which, as his feet were touching at the heels but splayed out reminded him of a gun sight. Soldiering was kindergarten stuff compared to this. Find the enemy, put him in your sights and bang. Well, who was his enemy? It was like asking 'What is truth?' The Maoist revolutionaries in Nepal made no bones about hating him. The Nepal Army generals who had carried out the coup would have killed him if they could and the Chinese authorities would never forgive him for effecting the escape of the infant Dalai Lama. As if that was insufficient forces to be ranged against him, Indian intelligence had presented him with Hobson's choice.

Who, then, were his friends? He supposed the Tibetans in exile, though they were doubtless upset that he had refused to assist them to recover the Dalai Lama's treasure: count them as uncommitted. The assortment of ex-soldiers and Sherpas that he had served with or employed, yes they were on the credit side. So, everyone with influence was ranged against him and all he commanded was a Fred Karno's army of people whose loyalty humbled him. Looking at the options was a sobering business: returning to Nepal was out, operating from India required government approval which, it had been made clear, would not be forthcoming if he did not dance to their tune. Making a fresh start in Ireland or England was laughable given the state of their economies and the lamentably evanescent market for ex-soldiers with travel acumen related to Nepal, Tibet and Northern India. Yet no matter how he tried to focus on the practicalities, it was Kim's face that kept interrupting each chain of thought. Each time her smile or the scent of her hair intruded he embarked on a course of self-justification for restoring the damn treasure to the Dalai Lama. Despite all the inherent problems and his increasing distaste for Fernandes, he knew that accepting the commission meant he could spend time with Kim and lay to rest his unrequited feelings for Tashi.

'*Kuch laiye*?' A bearer interrupted his thought process.

'*Nay, nay shukria*.' He shook his head. There was nothing he wanted, at least nothing that the man could bring him. He swung his legs onto the ground, took his mobile out of his pocket and scrolled down the recent numbers until he found the one he wanted, then hit it.

'Ladenla.'

'Geljen, Max Devlin.' There was a momentary pause before a response that carried a note of optimism.

'Colonel…Max, it's good to hear you.' Max allowed himself a further second or two before responding.

'I'd like to help you.'

'You've changed your mind?'

'Yes.' This time Max responded promptly.

'Er…thank you, we are immensely grateful.'

'Save the gratitude, this is a commercial arrangement.' There was a noticeable pause before the Tibetan replied.

'Of course.'

'I'll SMS you my terms.'

'Of course.' There was no hiding the relief in the man's voice.

'That's all for now. Goodbye.' Max ended the call. Given all the unhealthy interest in the activities of the Tibetans, their conversations were unquestionably monitored. Everyone's security demanded it was essential that he take every precaution against their future contacts being hacked into.

Office of PA to the Prime Minister

Tibetan government-in-exile
Dharmasala

Geljen Ladenla was smiling happily as he turned to face the four other men in his office.

'Devlin-la has agreed to help us.'

'Rumtek?' The deputy prime minister queried.

'Yes.' Geljen nodded.

'See that he has all the information that we have available to us…all those involved up there, ours and theirs, latest indication of location, floor plans of the Rumtek *gumba* and contact details for our…banker.' He allowed himself a small smile on the last word before his features resumed their normal inscrutability. He looked around the room.

'Not a word of this to anyone who is not directly involved.' He caught sight of Geljen about to speak and raised his palm towards him, anticipating the question.

'No, not even him.' He nodded his head in the direction of the prime minister's office. 'What he doesn't know can't compromise him.' He turned to face the young man standing in the corner of the room.

'Since you have overheard this, you'd better make yourself useful. You will assist Geljen-la. I will tell your superior that I am borrowing you for a little while.' Norbu gave a short bow of acknowledgment, quietly excited that he had been taken into the confidence of such a senior figure.

Tibetan Government-in-exile

Dharmasala
March 4

Norbu felt sick. His breath came in short spurts as his lungs refused to fill and the fear of dying served to aggravate the panic that seized him. His mobile phone fell out of his hand and involuntarily he jumped back from it as though it were an insect poised for a fatal strike. He felt disoriented, as though he was half-blind, his arms outstretched reaching for the door, he stumbled out into the open air and wrapped his arms around a wooden pillar on the verandah. Slowly, oh so very slowly, his breathing improved and his vision began to take in his surroundings. But the fear lodged in his stomach like a herald of diarrhoea and a bead of sweat ran down into his left eye, stinging him to a realisation that this was a living nightmare.

'Why?' He muttered at the sky. But he knew only too well why. Three years ago he had been about to graduate from UCLA. Never an outstanding scholar, he had scraped through with the lowest possible grades, studies paled into insignificance as against cocaine parties, drinking competitions and the unlimited supply of girls attracted to his Ferrari and spacious beachfront condo. His parents had indulged their only son, believing he would mature once he had graduated and taken up the promising position in the Tibetan government-in-exile which his influential father had secured for him to return to. Though he would far rather have stayed in California, he was shrewd enough to know that his lifestyle depended upon his father's continued support. Despite the restrictions that Dharmasala would necessarily impose to cramp his style, so long as money was in plentiful supply he did not anticipate that it would prove too inhibiting. The added bonus was that the job would require him to travel to the USA fairly regularly, so all in all he had a sweet life to look forward to.

Mei Mei changed all that.

She was pretty and had the sort of body that made him want to undress her as soon as possible. Even now he could not recall exactly how they had met but they had left the party at Lee Logan's house together, both of them on a high from the top quality coke that Lee's supplier always managed to provide. He recalled little of the drive back to his condo, only that her tongue in his ear had made him drive even more recklessly in his haste to get home. Afterwards, the two empty bottles of champagne on his bedroom floor and traces of two lines of coke on the bedside table told their own story. He had ascended sluggishly from the deepest sleep he could remember, vaguely conscious of a repetitive banging noise which eventually registered as someone hammering on the apartment door. Though it was still dark, there was a low light in the hallway and he slid off the bed, wrapping his discarded shirt around his waist in a semblance of decency. His fuddled mind and clumsy fingers had no sooner released the latch whereupon the door was thrust back, sending him tumbling to the floor. He felt himself being pulled savagely to his feet like a doll and an angry voice shouted at him.

'Where is she? You piece of shit.' Without waiting for a response he was dragged back into the bedroom. The same voice gave a terrifying roar and he was hurled to the floor. Now there were two voices, both men, both talking in furious Putonghua. He felt his head jerked back by the hair.

'You've killed her! Look!' Fear brought him to the surface of his consciousness with a sudden rush. Her body was sprawled across half the super-king size bed, tangled in a bed sheet. Someone had turned the bedside lamps on and he stared at the shadow that ran from her head down to her small breasts, unable to understand why it should be in shadow. The realisation that it was blood soaked into the sheet drove the breath out of his body and he vomited. A massive blow struck the side of his head and he lost consciousness.

When he came to, he was sitting in a rattan armchair in the bedroom, naked apart from his shirt bundled in his lap. Mei Mei's body still lay on the bed and, as far as he could see, nothing had changed. Sitting opposite him, smoking, was a Chinese man of indeterminate age holding a camera in his free hand.

'You rich young Tibetans are worse than your ignorant filthy peasants.'

The tone was devoid of any feeling, aseptically cold. He turned the camera screen towards Norbu. It showed him lying next to the dead girl. Flicking the images with his finger, there was a succession of such pictures.

'I believe Buddhism is not inconsistent with realism?' A tiny flick of one side of his thin lips suggested that this was intended to be humorous. 'We, and by "we" I refer of course to the People's Republic of China of which the Autonomous Region of Tibet is a part, are prepared to spare you the indignity of arrest and imprisonment by the Americans and being subjected to what they laughingly call the greatest system of justice in the world.' He loaded the words with contempt.

'How would your parents like to see you in your orange prisoner's jumpsuit, chained and manacled, their beloved son upon whom they have lavished everything that money can buy?' He drew on his cigarette and tapped the ash into a small tin that had not been on the occasional table before.

'All this,' he said, pointing towards the bed, then tapped the camera with a fingernail, 'can be made to disappear.' Norbu felt his world falling away beneath his feet. His throat was dry, his mouth sticky and his tongue swollen. He wanted to ask what he had to do but got no further than 'Wha…'

'The motherland needs patriotic young men, particularly those who live amongst the enemies of China and the splittists like the Dalai Lama. All I need is your agreement to help us from time to time with information.' What appeared to be a genuine smile made a brief appearance across his otherwise bland features.

'Not really a difficult task but one which will contribute to the integrity of our country and help to combat the ridiculous notions of independence that your stupid monks and the west are so anxious to impose on us.' Though his words were contemptuous, his tone was marginally warmer as though sharing a confidence. Despite the escape avenue being mapped out for him Norbu was sufficiently in possession of his faculties to realise that they would own him. If he could persuade them that he was of no value, perhaps… He could not think it through but some residual defensive instinct prompted him to try.

'But, I'm just a student.' The words came out as thickly as porridge.

'Please, Mr Norbu. Don't insult our intelligence, yours or mine.' The refrigeration had returned to his voice.

'You will be the assistant to the Tibetan government-in-exile's representative for foreign relations with North America.' He managed to give the words 'Tibetan government-in-exile' an acidic quality. 'Which, of course, will require frequent travel to the USA.' He left the significance for Norbu to work out for himself.

'I suggest that you leave now and go to the Brookfields Hotel which you registered into yesterday.' He took a key and room tag out of his pocket and put them on the occasional table. 'A young colleague of mine will accompany you there and provide an alibi for your presence after you left Mr Logan's house. He will also explain when the unfortunate young woman left you.' Norbu felt as though he had been eviscerated. Never a strong character, he felt as helpless as a child: he knew instinctively that this was a setup but his instinct for self-preservation drove him to fall back into the protective web that had been woven for him.

'You and I will never meet again. All future contacts with you will identify themselves as your "calligrapher".'

And so it had begun. Initially the requests were simple, identifying particular people and their responsibilities but gradually 'the calligrapher' or his controller, as he thought of him, wanted more and more: itineraries of various officials, copies of confidential documents, then access to documents classified as 'Secret' which involved him in risky deceptions to obtain codes. It took little time for him to realise that he was utterly compromised once he had started to pass copies of secret communications, so he summoned up the courage to tell his controller that he could not risk getting caught any more. The connection was broken immediately. Four days later he received an envelope through the post. All it contained was a blurred copy of one of the photographs of Mei Mei, but she was alone on the bed. On the next occasion he called the controller said: 'The copies of both of you on the bed are at a high pixel rating.' Norbu almost begged him to give him another task, but the connection was broken and he spent the next few days in an agony of anxiety, not knowing what would happen. In the event, he had not been contacted for several months. His initial desperate worry that they would do something to drive home the message gradually subsided and after the weeks turned to months without a call he began to kindle the embers of hope that they had forgotten him.

Until today.

The number on the LCD screen had shown up 'Unknown' but he knew instinctively that it was his controller. He winced audibly, dreading what was to follow and even thought of not answering. The phone rang and vibrated with a life of its own, compelling and threatening.

'Yes?' It was a querulous response.

'You must prevent the foreign mercenary soldier from leaving Delhi. Cripple him, have him disposed of if necessary.'

'Who…?' Norbu was momentarily at a loss.

'The one who is to steal our money from the monastery in Sikkim.' The words were uttered as though to a backward child. Without waiting for a response the voice continued.

'You will receive enough cash to get the job done.' As the enormity of it struck home, Norbu instinctively sought to duck the responsibility.

'But I can't do this…I don't know how…' His words spluttered out like verbal enuresis.

'You have no choice…' The voice was mechanical, inexorable. '…apart from extradition…probably, what is it the Americans call it…rendition?' The line was cut.

Indian National Museum

Janpath, New Delhi

Max hovered around the entrance, glancing at his watch from time to time and hoping not to arouse too much attention from the security guards. He rebuked himself for his impatience: he had arrived nearly a quarter of an hour before they were due to meet and there was still five minutes to go. Absent-mindedly he massaged his arm and then took his hand away as though he had been caught doing something forbidden.

'Hello. Am I late?' She materialised in front of him, a slight look of concern on her face.

'No, not a bit of it, I was early.'

'Good.' She relaxed and he turned his mind to enjoying their time together. He led the way in.

'Have you been here before?'

'No, I'd no idea it even existed.' He smiled and took her hand.

'Come on, there are some beautiful things I want to show you.' For the next hour they walked through the galleries as he conducted her from exhibit to exhibit, talking her through the ones that most excited his interest. Kim let him talk, occasionally asking questions which he noted were insightful. It was when they stood in front of a beautiful Buddhist stupa said to contain relics of Siddhartha Buddha that she found herself enraptured by his commitment and the depth of his knowledge.

'This stupa was built in the 3rd century on the orders of Ashoka, for me, the greatest emperor of India. Did you know that in his time, virtually all of India was Buddhist? Extraordinary, isn't it? When you consider that Hinduism is not an evangelical religion that you cannot be converted to it, yet the Brahmins systematically destroyed almost every structure that

Ashoka ordained to influence his subjects to follow the path of the Dharma.' She felt herself caught up in the intensity of his words and for reasons that she could not fathom, she felt tears well in her eyes.

'Oh God, I'm so sorry…you must forgive me.' He made a helpless gesture with his arm but she put her hand out and rested it on his arm.

'No, please…I think…I don't know…it's just that it's a side of you that I'd not seen before.' She swept her hair back off her face, allowing her fingers to brush softly under her eyes. 'You really love this, don't you?' He nodded, suddenly aware of an emotional chord that harmonised with her. He took her hands in his, leaning forward so that his head touched hers for a moment.

'Let's get out of here.' She nodded mutely.

In the taxi they sat holding hands, leaning against each other and enjoying confidential little smiles when they caught sight of the driver observing them in his rear view mirror.

He had no recollection of how they got from the hotel entrance to his suite of rooms, nothing registered until they closed and locked the door behind them and their mouths met and did not part until most of their clothes lay on the floor around them. He unclipped her bra and she slipped out of her panties. He wanted to savour every second, every movement, every touch but she was impatient, insistent, wrapping herself around him so that he stopped trying to control himself and gave in with matching abandon.

The Akasi chiya dhokan

New Delhi

'Best *dhall bhat* in Delhi' was all Deepraj said before leading him into the simple but scrupulously clean café hidden in a side alley. Max noted that the place was full of Nepalese, both serving and seated at the scrubbed wooden tables. Several faces were turned towards them and they nodded and smiled a greeting, two or three made *namascar* to Max too. A waitress smiled and pointed to a table in one of the corners of the room. They sat down and Max picked up the menu, printed on handmade Nepali card. The list of drinks was short and to the point: beer, Kukri Rum or tongba.

'What are you drinking?'

'Tongba.' Max ordered one each.

'Try their *dudh choorpi ko achar* Saheb, it's really good.' Following the advice, he ordered plain rice, black *dhall* and the chutney made from the soft white yak's milk cubes crumbled with lemon juice, salt and ground chillies. He looked around at the Mongol faces of their fellow customers.

'What's the story?'

'It belongs to an ex-5th Gurkhas Sergeant, though his wife...' Deepraj inclined his head towards the stout little lady sitting next to the till, '...is the boss.' He grinned. 'It's the favourite *chiya dhokan* for ex-Indian Army Gurkhas and some serving ones too. I warned them that you were coming and asked Anjali...' He indicated the waitress, '...to give us a table where we wouldn't be easily overheard.' Max nodded his appreciation.

'Get a message to Nyima and Dendi in Kathmandu, tell them to go to Kalimpong and wait for us there.'

'Huzoor.'

'What have you learned about the Urgen Trinley people in Sikkim?'

'They're a mixed bunch; like lots of the monks, they have Cartier watches, and do a lot of praying.' He gave a dismissive grunt.

'The *Bhotia* here in Delhi don't like talking about the two Karmapas, some of them are fiercely hostile to one or the other and there have been some fights, so they avoid the subject.' He took a quick look around the room and dropped his voice a little. 'Some of Urgen's followers are furious that they are being called Chinese puppets…' He looked up from under his eyelids, '…but there are some bad buggers in Sikkim, going round beating up those who support Thaye Dorje. Even one or two here have had their shops burned down, nasty bastards.' Max nodded slowly. He had introduced the subject into his talks with Kim from whom he had learned a great deal about the politics involved. A few years previous, there had been an assassination attempt on the most influential of the Rinpoches supporting Thaye Dorje. He could well understand how anxious the Chinese would be to have their man acknowledged and leading the Karma Kagyu school of Buddhists.

'So it doesn't look as though we can just knock on the monastery door and say "Give us the money".' He did not expect an answer and was not disappointed. 'If they're really into assassinating a Rinpoche, it's going to be much more risky than just moving the stuff from point A to point B.' Deepraj shrugged his eyebrows.

'It's a job, Saheb and it pays well.' To Max's eyes, the Gurkha's attitude had changed quite significantly since they had both been injured when the train in which they were escorting the infant Dalai Lama and his mother had crashed across the Nepal border into India. His sense of humour was darker and there was a venal streak that he had never noticed before.

'Don't go back amongst the *Bhotia* here any more.' He was regretting sending him off to gather intelligence. They needed to avoid drawing attention to themselves. 'Get yourself on a train to Darjeeling. We need half a dozen of your Gorkhaland guerrilla friends who could do with some extra *talab* for a few days' work. Ex-British or Indian Army, it doesn't matter so long as they're experienced GD wallahs.' Deepraj looked up and gave him his insubordinate smile.

'No clerks or mess waiters?'

'Drink your tongba.'

'Saheb.'

'Then take your gang of *badmas* to Kalimpong and wait for me there.'

'*Hatiyar?*'

'Each man carries his own weapon of choice. Nothing heavy, but don't get caught for God's sake, and get Nyima and Dendi kitted up too.' This time he was going with his eyes wide open and anticipating the worst, he had no intention of losing any of his men this time round.

Tibetan government-in-exile
Dharmasala

'Rafiq?'

'Who is this?' Norbu hated the way Rafiq always wanted him to identify himself over the phone.

'It's me.' He persisted, knowing that the man's screen would show him the familiar number even if he had not logged it into his contact list, which was highly improbable.

'Who is me?' Back came the same unctuously polite tone of voice. It was bad enough being beholden to him for his cocaine supply, now he wanted a big favour there would be no escaping doing his bidding.

'Me, you know, Norbu.' He tried to keep the irritation out of his voice.

'Ah, my dear young friend. What can I be doing for you, surely not another delivery so soon?' The patronising air by a drug supplier was unbearable. But he had tried to change suppliers and his new contact had suddenly disappeared: he guessed without knowing for sure that Rafiq had disposed of him or frightened him off. It was this that had emboldened him to make the approach to Rafiq: the man was a professional criminal and anyway he knew of no-one else who could do it for him.

'No, no.' He hesitated, not sure how to put it. 'There is a man who has like…to be taken care of.' There, he'd done it. He waited, feeling like one of those frogs that could blow up their chests and block their airway.

'You mean you want this man disposed of, isn't it? Not too difficult, a life is worth no more than four to five thousand rupees at market rates.'

'No, well…not exactly.' He knew that this would happen. There was no way he could have put it in the words of his controller and he clung to the idea that provided he could engineer some serious accident to Devlin, he would not have to answer for his failure; even a botched job would suffice.

'What *exactly* do you want?' The voice purred but the intent was a hard dose of reality.

'Well…could you arrange to disable him, for quite a long time?'

'We're talking about hospitalisation for major injuries?'

'Yes, yes…something like that.'

'Ah, my young friend, hospitalisation is rather more complex.'

'You mean it costs more?' Norbu thought he could see where this was going.

'The executives…' He lingered over the word, giving it a legitimacy that Norbu found ridiculous for what were plainly murdering scumbags. '…often exceed their remit in their zeal to earn their commission.'

'So, what will it cost me?' Scenting that Rafiq would take it off his hands, Norbu was anxious to close the deal.

'I cannot say what it will cost you.' There was more than a hue of dark humour at Norbu's expense. 'But my price will be fifty thousand rupees.' Norbu felt relief both at the tacet acceptance of the job and at a price within what he had expected to pay. The drug dealer continued, 'I will have to confirm with the operatives, but I expect that they will want one hundred thousand rupees.'

Norbu's momentary satisfaction dissolved.

'I thought you said that a life was only worth four to five thousand?'

'My dear young friend, that is what an amorous Punjabi farmer would pay to have a troublesome *ryot* with a pretty wife disposed of, but you are not a Punjabi farmer and I suspect that the object of your disfavour is more important than a troublesome peasant. So, tell me, who is this man you wish to incommode?' Still trying to come to terms with the inflated cost of the enterprise, Norbu needed to be reassured that Rafiq would agree to it.

'So, you can arrange it?'

'You still have not told me the identity or location of your target.' Norbu was loath to disclose the details until Rafiq had agreed the terms.

'I want to be sure, the total cost will be one lakh fifty thousand, yes?'

'*Beta, beta* please don't hurry me, this is important business, isn't it?'

Norbu was infuriated to be addressed as though he was a child and knew that Rafiq was playing with him. He was sick with worry, the Chinese on one side, his job compromised beyond recall and now he was being squeezed by this son of a bitch drug dealer. He was sweating profusely. The screen of his mobile was slippery against his ear.

'Important, yes.' He managed to grind out. 'Have we got a deal, yes or no?' There was no answer from the other side. He gripped the mobile so tightly that he felt it slipping out of his hand. When he spoke he could hear the near panic in his own voice.

'Rafiq? Are you there, Rafiq?' He was sure that the line was still open but there was no response.

He started again. 'Rafiq.'

'*Beta, beta* you must learn patience if you are to engage in this kind of thing.' He paused, dragging out the agony. 'We cannot agree if you are wanting to cripple the prime minister of India or the chief justice, isn't it?' Norbu wanted to tell him not to take him for a complete idiot but even as the thought occurred he realised that indeed, he was a complete idiot to have got himself into such dire circumstances. His response was weary.

'It's an Englishman, called Devlin, staying at Maidens in Old Delhi. He's some sort of independent travel agent, seems to be very supportive of the free Tibetan movement.'

'Is he likely to want to leave Delhi soon?'

'My guess is within the next ten days or so.'

'Then we must move swiftly. I shall need the money by tomorrow.'

'Agreed.' He had only a vague idea of where he would get hold of this amount at such short notice but that seemed far less problematic than getting Rafiq to shoulder the burden.

'My man will contact you in the usual way. If you can get a photograph of Devlin, that would be helpful.'

'I'll see what I can do.' He pressed the button to end the call, the first and only time that he had exercised any control over the communication.

Maidens Hotel

Old Delhi

'You're very quiet about your plans.' Kim turned to face him, resting her head on her hand. Each time she had touched on the topic he had deliberately diverted the conversation away from what he was planning. He had worked on the need-to-know principle, assuming that the less she knew the better. But it was becoming progressively more awkward, especially as she was spending most nights with him at Maidens.

'Jessica has guessed what's going on between us and she keeps pressing me to tell her whether you are really serious.' He put his hand behind her head and kissed her, long and hard.

'I am deeply serious about you.'

'I know that but she keeps fussing.' She ran her fingers through his hair. 'Jessica's concerns are not mine. I love being with you, I'm fascinated by your knowledge and your commitment to we mountain people and I'm not looking for more than that.'

'Not even our time in bed?' Max asked seriously.

'Oh you!' She pulled the bedsheet up to cover her breasts. He laughed and she let the sheet fall as they sought each other again.

Later, he woke with his left arm still across her and he absorbed the way her body flowed from her hairline down through the line of her back to her buttocks. She was beautiful, with an intelligence flavoured with a sense of humour and committed in a way that he both admired yet which troubled him. They were sharing every intimacy except that he was concealing his undertaking to recover the treasure. For the umpteenth time he queried whether he was right to do so. His primary purpose, or so he told himself, was to protect her from being involved, even at a remove, from something that was looking increasingly risky. His latest briefing by Geljen indicated that security at the Rumtek Monastery had been tightened and they suspected that the Urgen Trinley faction was showing an unhealthy interest in the treasure, all of which they believed was being driven by Chinese agents. He was saddened that the black hats and red hats were being driven apart at a time when the whole Buddhist movement needed to be united against one common foe and the willingness to use force, contrary to their whole philosophy, lent weight to the theory of Beijing's hand being involved.

'Max.' She turned and started to trace the scars on his arm with her fingertips. 'Why won't you tell me how you got these?' He had known for some time now that he could not fob her off with delaying tactics. Either he lied or told her the truth.

'Kiss and tell?'

'Don't prevaricate.' She slapped him lightly on his back. Then he told her. His account was a stripped down version, recounted in as dry a manner as he could achieve, glossing over the detail and avoiding all mention of his emotional relationship with Tashi. When he finished she stared at him for a moment before hugging him close to her.

'I could have lost you.' He felt the wetness of her tears on his shoulder.

'Nonsense, I've been in far worse situations.' She pulled away from him.

'This job in Sikkim, it has something to do with His Holiness, doesn't it?' Her tone was both accusing and worried. In for a penny, in for a pound: he told her. She listened in silence, then sat up, something in the way she held her body told him that he'd made a mistake.

'You need my help.'

'No. I don't want you to be involved.'

'Too late, I am.' He started to speak but she put her palm across his mouth.

'Sikkim is a hotbed of political factions and cross-currents. I know who belongs to which and who can be trusted and who most certainly can't.' He removed her hand gently.

'I don't doubt it, but this isn't just politics, it could get very nasty, especially if the Chinese take a hand.' He stopped short of telling her that it could be dangerous, anxious to tell her enough to put her off but not enough to scare her.

'All the more reason for you to have someone with inside knowledge.'

'But you're not privy to what's going on in Rumtek.' He sounded more stern than he had intended. She rolled away from him, wrapped the sheet around her and walked towards the bathroom, throwing her words over her shoulder.

'You don't know half of what I know. I'm coming and that's final.' She tried to shut the bathroom door with a flourish but the trailing sheet stopped it closing.

'Damn!' Tugging it in behind her she closed the door firmly. He smiled and applauded.

He accompanied her back to the Manthos' apartment. She had promised Jessica that she would spend the day with Jason and she wanted to be there early in the morning. The boy responded well to her and she seemed to be able to communicate with him far more easily than with most other people. In the taxi they spoke little but he was relieved when halfway through the journey she felt for his hand.

On the return to the hotel he let his mind roam across the complication that Kim introduced into the equation. He had known for a little while that she had become a fixture in the firmament of his life but he had deliberately avoided tracking their path. Alighting from the taxi under Maidens portico his mind was too busy to contemplate sleep. The chowkidar saluted and bid him goodnight but he turned away from the entrance and wandered into the garden to give himself an opportunity to think things through.

They came out of the darkness.

The thought that they might be hotel workers evaporated the second he saw that the one in the middle was carrying a knife and the other two had weaponry of some sort. His threat mechanism engaged and a bolus of adrenalin hit his system. Every time he faced such a situation the words of Joe, his old ex-marine commando instructor at the Fort, ran through his brain like surtitles at the opera. 'Keep your hands moving, identify the most dangerous one, use any weapon to hand, disable him permanently if you can.'

'Good evening.' He smiled as he continued to walk towards them and saw the momentary hesitation in the knifeman's eyes. He kept up the one-sided conversation, gesticulating with his hands to make his conversational points. The one on the left was short and squat with an ugly looking knuckle duster on his hand, the right-hand thug taller but slimmer looked as though he was carrying a wrench. They were close together: good. There was nothing in the vicinity to cover his back but they had not thought this one out, assuming that sheer numbers and brute force would carry the day. Good again. The knifeman was clearly the leader, bigger than the other two and he was holding the knife so that the blade protruded above his thumb, the classic street fighter's grip, not so good. Max had been carrying his jacket and now he casually flipped it around his left arm.

'Warm night, eh?' He smiled again, stopped at no more than two paces in front of them and gestured with his right hand at the sky. It was only a fraction of a second but the knifeman's eyes followed the direction of Max's hand. This was the riskiest moment. Max had an unconscionably heightened fear of knives which transmuted into a violent hatred for those who fought with them. One of his closest friends had died in his arms in Afghanistan of a terrible knife wound which had ripped through his intestines. It was, he believed, the coward's choice of weapon. He had to take the chance that the minimal padding around his arm would absorb the point of the knife. The coat hindered the use of his left arm but he continued to talk with hand gestures so that when he attacked it did not telegraph the move.

He reached back with his right arm, his hand across the side of his neck in what must have looked like a defensive move, then with the force of his shoulder behind it he delivered a forearm smash into the man's neck. There was a comforting grunt followed by a scream of pain as he grated his boot sideways down the front of the man's shin. Being this close made it difficult for the other two to intervene without risking hitting their leader. Max now had his back to the knifeman with the other two flanking him. Two-handed, he grabbed the tall one's clothing and swung him viciously at the man on his right, then smashed his boot into the back of his knees so that he fell against the short thug. Swinging himself round he was just in time to catch the knifeman's head as he was rising up from having doubled over with the pain in his shin. He joined his fists together and brought them down on the exposed neck with furious force. He heard the satisfying crack that told him that the knifeman would play no further part in this attack. The tall man was on all fours on the ground but the squat one threw himself at him in a mad rush. Max let him come and fell backwards onto the ground, his legs coiled like twin springs, then they shot out and his boots struck the man in the midriff so that his own momentum catapulted him over Max's head in a somersault that landed him on his back, knocking the breath out of him. As Max rolled to his feet he saw the tall one scrabbling to his feet. The man's head was perfectly positioned for a drop shot at goal and it took the full satisfying force of Max's boot, the head flopping like a broken doll. Without waiting to see the result, he turned back to find the squat one who, though still catching his breath on the ground had somehow managed to get hold of the knife. Ignoring the hand with the knife, Max stamped on the man's face but this failed to make him release his grip on the knife and he swung it up towards Max's groin causing him to jump back. For a squat man he was remarkably nimble on his feet and sprung up making a growling animal noise, the blood running down his face where Max's boot had split his nose. Max registered that he clutched the knife in his raised right hand, ready to strike down. Not a knife fighter at all. But he might just as well have signed his own death warrant.

'Ana kutta...ana.' Max goaded him, beckoning him forward: if he was going to growl like a dog, then he could be summoned like one. It had the desired effect: with a feral howl he launched himself at Max, the knife stabbing down towards his chest. Turning his body in towards his attacker, Max seized the knife arm with his left hand and got his shoulder under the man's elbow, then heaved. The sharp crack and the scream were almost simultaneous. The contained fury that Max had been channelling into fighting was instinctive and dictated his thinking. A cursory glance towards the other two men satisfied him that they were both out of it. He was gravely tempted to leave no survivors. They had wanted him dead. The squat thug was kneeling on the ground whimpering and holding his broken arm. Max put in a kick to the side of his head and the whimpering stopped.

'Even a mad dog should not have to suffer.' He observed to himself. Letting the body slump to the ground he did a quick search of the men's pockets each of which yielded some 1,000-rupee notes which he threw into the bushes and various keys which he kept. The tall man had an imitation leather wallet with a photograph of a small boy: he removed the photograph and threw the wallet away. The knifeman lay face down on the ground, his back pocket bulging with a wallet. Max checked it, ignored the thicker bundle of rupee notes but put a folded piece of paper together with the keys and the photograph. In a trouser pocket there was a cheap mobile phone which he also collected. Then he picked up his jacket and discovered that the knife had slashed through the fabric. Only then did he realise that his left arm was bleeding. Though the musculature had repaired after the train crash, he still had a loss of sensation between the elbow and the wrist which accounted for the absence of pain. It was a penetrating wound rather than a linear slash. He wrapped his jacket around it and looked around him. It seemed that they had been sufficiently distant from the hotel building that whatever noise had been made had not aroused anyone. Doubtless that had been their original plan. Now it worked in his favour. But if he returned to the hotel the chowkidar would note the time and doubtless notice that the Saheb was looking distinctly unkempt, a fact that would draw his attention to the blood spreading on his jacket. Distancing himself from the three bodies was an imperative.

There was no way he could go to Jessica's in his present state. That left only one option.

'I think you should tell Fernandes.' The general was still in his dressing gown and pyjamas, a silk scarf round his neck in a Noel Coward throwback.

'I was pondering that.' Max nursed a glass of brandy whilst Raju, the general's Man Friday, cleaned and dressed the knife wound. He had discovered some bruises on his chest and arm thanks to the knuckle duster and wrench, blows that he had not noticed whilst they were fighting but which had now got his attention.

'Fernandes can clean it up, sort out the Delhi police, keep your name out of it and then see if he can trace back to where these *badmash* got their orders.'

'Not much chance of that.' There was a pause and then the general, his head cocked interrogatively to one side, said with a slightly pained smile: 'Did you kill any of 'em?' The look Max gave him decided him not to push this one any further.

Max took the mobile phone, keys, photograph and pieces of paper out of his jacket pocket and put them on a side table.

'Fernandes can have these, for starters, but it wasn't intended to be just a good kicking and being blagged, the knife says it all, plus the thousand rupee notes they all had on them. This was a contract and the only folk who want rid of me currently are that bunch of hair-dyed goons in Beijing. The Tibetans may well be exercised amongst themselves over the rightful claimant to be *Karmapa* but it's not their style to send the local *goondas* out to knock off a foreigner.'

'Freddie'll most likely agree with you.' The general swirled the ice round his glass and took a sip. 'Your little Sikkim trip's beginnin' to look as though you need to review the staff work.'

'Mm.' Max had been thinking of nothing else since he'd left the grounds of Maidens. The general looked at his watch.

'It's nearly oh four hundred, get your head down for a couple of hours, you can use the spare bedroom. I'll contact Fernandes at sparrow fart and he can get himself over here.' He looked up at the bearer. 'Raju, show the Colonel upstairs and get him some Ibuprofen.'

'Thanks, Sid.' Max welcomed the idea of a nap but he doubted whether his mind would allow him that respite.

He lay staring at the ceiling trying to piece it all together. The most likely source of the leak was Geljen's office. Not surprising that the Chinese would be monitoring what was going on there. It did not bode well for the success of the venture now that they knew he was involved. But what really troubled him was Kim's determination to accompany him. He could not allow her to be exposed to the same risks. He made up his mind. She would not understand and would undoubtedly be hurt but it was a cheaper price to pay than the alternatives.

General Chopra's House

Defence Colony, New Delhi

Later that morning he had a letter hand-delivered to Kim. The general arranged for his bill at Maidens to be paid and his clothes and scant belongings collected and brought to the house. Fernandes had been like a dog with a new bone and Max thought he detected more than a touch of *schadenfreude* in the man's commiseration at the knife wound and discolouring bruises. It was agreed that Max would lie low at Sid's for a couple of days whilst the intelligence chief made his inquiries and generally mopped up. On the evening of the third day Fernandes dropped in with his news.

'Your victims were heavies who worked for a drug dealer of our acquaintance, Rafiq Hussein. I was going to have him picked up but my contact in the drug squad informed me that apparently he supplies to the wealthy young Tibetans, so I've asked him to try and get me a list of all those with whom he's connected…commercially.' His white-toothed smile shone out beneath the black moustache as he savoured his own words. 'So, I rather think your theory holds good, Colonel.'

Max said nothing. He was uncomfortable being under an obligation to the man but it was a necessity.

'We will be following it up of course, to see where it leads but the one you described as the knifeman is in a critical condition in ICU at Lok Nayak Hospital.' The smile dropped. 'His neck is broken.' He paused for what he hoped was dramatic effect so that he could increase his purchase on the Irishman. 'The other two know nothing more than their leader told them, which is zilch.' What he would not disclose was that his assets were thinly stretched because of the primacy given to countering Pakistani funded terrorists which left him short handed when it came to the Chinese. But he was damned if he was going to let Devlin know, not now that he had him fully committed to the Sikkim matter.

'Thank you Freddie.' The general supplied the appreciation that he knew the man wanted and topped up his glass himself.

'Enough Sid, thank you.'

'I was wondering, could you locate a Land Rover at a sensible price that Max can buy, one of the old lightweight military models?'

'Not a problem. It'll take me a couple of days or so.' He glanced at Max. 'Can you pay in dollars? We can get a better bargain. The rupee is on the skids again.' Max nodded. He would have it thoroughly checked by Amp Motors in Worli Naka. He had decided to make the journey to Sikkim by road. It would enable him to slip out of Delhi at night and once onto the nightmare that was the Indian road system, it would take a cross between Lewis Hamilton and a surveillance drone to find him.

The Akasi chiya dhokan

New Delhi

The tea shop was almost deserted at this time of the day. Nonetheless they selected a booth at the back. Anjali took their orders of coffee for Geljen and *masala* tea for Max and left them. They had met at a pre-arranged location in the street adjoining the back alley and Max had given the Tibetan a brief account of the attack as they had walked to the tea shop, focusing on the attackers' obvious intention to take him out of the Rumtek equation.

'I'm very sorry about this.' Geljen frowned. 'But how can you be certain that it wasn't just a mugging?'

'Muggers don't kill you, they just beat you up. These guys intended to stop me, permanently.' It was not just the way that Max spoke the words but the look in his eyes that convinced the Tibetan not to pursue this line.

'And before you ask me why I say they're connected to your people and Rumtek, my sources tell me that they were hired by a drug dealer who services some of the wealthier young Tibetans, the connection is too much of a coincidence for anything else. Which means that you have a serious leak in your organisation.' Geljen was on the point of saying that only a small handful of people were privy to Max's involvement when it struck him that this proved the Irishman's deduction.

'If I'm to help you on this, I need your word that from now on you tell no-one else anything about me or the plan. No-one, is that clear?' Max's eyes narrowed. 'Or I'm out, as of this minute.'

'You have it.' Geljen's face was a mask. Max took a small black rectangular device out of his pocket.

'Use this to communicate with me. It's a Thuraya SatSleeve, fits over your smartphone and it gives you access to me by satellite. It only works outdoors, which protects us from being eavesdropped on but it's illegal in India, so I wouldn't advertise it. Remit half my fee to my HSBC account in Hong Kong and send the balance to the same account in one month from today.'

'And if you fail to secure our funds?'

'Send the balance to my HSBC account in one month from today, less the success fee.' Max's face gave nothing away.

'Understood.'

'I will text you the codeword "Slim" once we hand over the funds to your Indian contact and "Wingate" if, for any reason I am unable to make the delivery. That's it then.'

'I understand.' Geljen felt embarrassed. Despite knowing that Devlin's fee was not contingent on success, out of a sense of caution he had posed the possibility of failure with the concomitant thought that full payment might be reduced or deferred pending another attempt. Yet he knew equally well that this was not a no-win no-fee arrangement. Max's unfazed requirement for the full fee less the success element, come what may, made him feel dishonourable.

'I apologise for giving the impression that our payment was contingent on success.' Max gave him an autumnal smile.

'I don't blame you for trying. In your shoes I might well have done the same.' Geljen allowed himself to retrieve his self-respect.

'Thank you.' He gave Max a slip of paper. 'This is Shakti's cellphone number. He's quite old and his memory is not good, so he often forgets to charge the battery.' He smiled apologetically. 'But he is a good man and keeps me informed about what is happening inside Rumtek. Tell him that you have a message from me, then when you meet him, give him this.' He produced a prayer bracelet of polished white stones threaded on an elastic string. 'When you hand it to him, hold it so that he can see the seal inscribed on the largest of the stones, this is your authentication.' Max slipped it onto his wrist.

'I also have a message for you from the Abbot of Shadung Monastery.' In his mind's eye Max saw the wrinkled face of the old monk who had been instrumental in arranging for Tashi to spend time with him whilst he recuperated.

'He wants you to know that the cup of your *karma* overflows.' The last thing that Max was thinking about was his future reincarnation, assuming that there would be one. He was too much of a realist to believe that anyone's perception of the good that he might occasionally do would outweigh the rest of his blighted record. But he had not yet forgotten his manners.

'Please thank His Reverence for me.' He signalled to Anjali for the bill. 'You have the gratitude of the Tibetan government and my personal sincere appreciation.' They shook hands.

'I suggest you leave first, I'll wait here a bit longer.' Geljen nodded, made the sign of namascar, turned and left.

Wrapped up in his thoughts, he drained his tea cup. His gaze fell on a faded photograph of Ganju Lama who had won a VC in Burma during the Second World War. It made him think about the significance of the two codewords he had given Geljen to signify success or failure. 'Slim' after the Field Marshall who had turned the British defeat in Burma into victory, and 'Wingate' for the charismatic Chindit leader who was lost when his plane disappeared on a flight over Burma. His mind was still preoccupied with the high risk of failure as he walked out of the tea house.

He did not notice the young woman sitting alone in a far corner, her face averted from him.

Office of Commissioner for Ethnic Integration

Beijing

Bo was so angry that he was lost for words adequate to get his message across.

'What's his excuse?' His jaw was clamped so tight that his PA had to guess what had been said.

'We are told that he says that he paid one hundred and fifty thousand rupees to a major criminal to have the laowai killed but one of the gang that attacked him died and the other two were badly injured. Our man says that Notebook is shitting himself.'

'I don't care if he's passing blood, he took our money but he failed. It's time to make an example of him.' The PA dreaded contradicting his chief but Notebook was the only agent in Dharmasala they could coerce into doing anything they wanted; they could not afford to prejudice one of their deep cover agents in the Dalai Lama's entourage.

'His failure makes him even more indebted to us.' He observed almost to himself. Bo's eyes flicked towards him and rested there for several seconds, making him hold his breath. The eyes moved away and he pressed his advantage.

'He's done very well to infiltrate himself into the inner circle around the deputy prime minister. It seems that they keep the PM in the dark about their various operations.'

'But we're on the inside?'

'Hm.' He nodded. Bo turned to look at the map, then stabbed his finger on Gangtok. He looked over his shoulder at his PA.

'Tell Chopsticks to prepare to move the funds.'

'Do I tell him where you want them moved to?' Bo shook his head and used his fingers to measure off the distance between Rumtek and the nearest point on the border with Tibet. The Chumbi Valley was like a Tibetan forefinger poked into the Himalayan skin of India: part under Chinese control and part strictly controlled by India. The southern segment was only accessible by Indian nationals and then only if they had a specific pass. But it was porous, veined by smugglers routes and difficult for both sides to control.

'We may need that snatch team after all. Ask General Xi to put one of his special force units into Gala and put them on 12 hours' notice to move.' Xi, he knew, would relish the opportunity for a cross-border infiltration. Some members of the central committee rabbited on about Sino-Indian relations but Xi didn't give a monkey's fart for diplomacy.

'What do we do about the Indo-Tibetan Frontier Force?'

'That's the team's problem. We give them the orders, they execute.' Bo was making contingency plans. He had not yet thought it through. From time to time the PLA made short incursions into Indian territory. It was enough to keep the Indians worried but also to build up a pattern of brief penetrations followed by almost immediate withdrawals. When the time came for a full-scale attack, the Indians would still be thinking it was just another border incident. But if Chopsticks could arrange to have the laowai taken out of the equation it might not be necessary to take any preventive action. They had several agents in Sikkim, no need to employ anyone else to do their work for them.

'Tell Notebook to inform us as soon as the laowai leaves Delhi then instruct Chopsticks to locate him and have our people put him out of the picture – permanently this time.'

Amp Motors

New Delhi

'*Bhaud achar gari hei!*' The mechanic's face was a picture of joy, his hand caressed the carburettor and he itemised every replacement he had made to the Land Rover's working parts. The body work looked decidedly distressed and at first glance Max had been minded to tell them it wasn't worth a fraction of the US$8,000 he had paid for it. He began to change his mind as the mechanic insisted on showing him all the work that had been done to bring it up to scratch. They had started the inspection underneath it with the car raised on a hydraulic lift: new springs, new exhaust, reinforced fuel tank, new all terrain tyres, then it was lowered and he had been walked through the engine. He took out the dipstick and was pleasantly surprised to see that the oil was as clear as water. New hoses, fan belt, distributor, plugs, overhead gasket, Max was impressed. The $64,000 question was whether it would run true.

'*Chalo?*' The grinning mechanic spread plastic sheets over the seats and gestured to Max to get into the driver's seat. Fifteen minutes later he was obliged to agree with the mechanic, it was a damn good vehicle and ran as sweetly as if off the production line. The workshop manager greeted them as they disembarked.

'As good as new, *nei*? Mister Devlin.'

'Apart from the bodywork.'

'Not to be judging a book by its cover.'

'Fair enough.' Max laughed.

'There is a gentleman to see you in my office.' He indicated a flight of external stairs leading to a corrugated iron clad room with metal windows overlooking the yard where they stood. Max thanked the mechanic and gave him a 1,000-rupee note. The man's eyes shone.

The office was poorly lit and even when Max removed his sunglasses he could not see far into the room.

'I hope you're satisfied with your purchase, Colonel?' Fernandes walked out of the gloomy interior.

'Very, thank you.'

'You'll leave tonight?'

'Probably.' Max was disinclined to give more information than was necessary. The man had made it clear that he was on his own and he had no intention of confiding in him.

'Here are all the permits that you need for Sikkim, the Darjeeling District and a small bonus, a permit for the Chumbi Valley.'

'But I'm not an Indian national.'

'We have a large population of Anglo-Indians. This permit is all you need.' Max nodded appreciatively.

'The General asked me to give you this.' He held out an oil-skin wrapped package. 'I cannot begin to guess what it contains.' Fernandes smirked. 'Nothing illegal I hope.' Max took it, his eyebrows flashed up interrogatively.

'I said that I cannot offer you any assistance. Not entirely true. I have had a member of the COBRA team assigned to you, a highly experienced commando, *havildar* Dewan.'

'Thank you but all the same no thank you.' Max had no intention of having his every move watched and reported on. 'I choose my own team members from those I know and trust.'

'As you wish.' Fernandes threw open his hands in a gesture of resignation. 'I shall await your signal and wish you good hunting.' Max suppressed a grin. Where did the man get his vocabulary from? At the same time, he felt that the intelligence chief had capitulated too easily over the rejection of his offer of help.

'Thanks, and also for these.' He indicated the permits. Fernandes nodded, then walked past him and out of the office door. Max unwrapped the oil cloth and picked up the 9mm XDM which the general had been storing for him. They had discussed whether or not Max should carry it with him, Sid arguing that now the stakes had been raised by the Chinese it was essential to be fully prepared and Max countering with out of character caution. In truth, Max's main concern was because he did not trust Fernandes. Given the man's track record, having Max arrested for possession of an illegal firearm would have been all too easy. It seemed that Sid must have been given some personal assurance which was why it had been Fernandes who handed the weapon to him. He checked the loaded chamber indicator before extracting the 20-round magazine and wracking back the slide. With the Armalon modifications that had been effected in London, the XDM was the best handgun in the world: unlike the Glock that the poor bloody British infantryman had to rely on. It was both as accurate and reliable as human ingenuity could achieve. He completed the breakdown and then re-assembled it swiftly and restored it to its oil cloth, wrapping it together with the two extra fully charged magazines. Contrary to all his training and past experience of combat situations in which killing an enemy was an instinctive necessity, he had always been averse to taking a life if an opponent could be effectively put out of action. But the recent experiences of the death of his unarmed friends had activated a previously dormant genetic synapse: in the unlikely event of the Chinese intervening in Sikkim there would be no sense of moral restraint, he would be ready for them.

Office of PA to the Prime Minister

Tibetan government-in-exile
Dharmasala

It was a dilemma. Max had been adamant that no-one else know about his movements but because the prime minister was not aware of what was planned, if Geljen was instructed to leave Dharmasala for any reason there would be no-one to handle any emergency that arose, even his normal work schedule involved frequent flights to the USA. Given the delicacy of the situation, Geljen was convinced that there was a very high possibility of something going wrong and he was too good an administrator not to have contingency plans in place. The government-in-exile's position existed only courtesy of their Indian hosts and despite the hospitality they had been shown to date, one could never be sure that a new set of politicians would not force them to pack their bags so that Indo-Chinese relations could be nourished. He convinced himself that it was within the spirit of his undertaking to Max that where expediency dictated it, even arguably Max's safety, he would not be in breach if there was a backup contact. He toyed with the idea of asking the deputy prime minister to provide the extra cover but rejected it, the man already had too much on his plate whereas Norbu could, if necessary, drop everything else and concentrate on the project. The young man had appeared rather nervous but that was understandable for one of his age and inexperience suddenly finding himself at the political heart of their people. Giving him a specific responsibility would help him to mature into the work quickly and he was his assistant, so it made administrative sense.

They were alone in the room, it was a good opportunity.

'Norbu.' He stood up and indicated that they go outside onto the verandah. Once there, they stood side by side staring out across towards the surrounding hills. 'I'm taking you into my confidence over this Rumtek business. In case I'm called away for any reason I want you to be the point of contact with our friend Colonel Devlin should he need any assistance. But no-one else is to be informed of his commission.' He turned to face the young man. 'Do you understand?'

'Hm.' Norbu nodded.

'Good. We cannot afford to offend the Indian government, which is why this has to be kept secret. It is the deputy prime minister's decision to shelter the rest of the Tibetan cabinet from any knowledge of what is planned. I hope you understand?'

'Of course.' Norbu had recovered from his surprise sufficiently to realise that this could enable him to redeem himself with his controller.

'From now on we will refer to the Colonel by the code name "*Mahakala*" this is just between you and me, understood?'

'Yes *Pembu*.'

Geljen lowered his voice, even though there was no-one within hearing distance.

'Mahakala leaves for Sikkim tonight.' Geljen nodded to him and walked back into his office. Norbu could barely contain his impatience to get the information to his controller. He walked off to the lavatory, entered a stall and tapped out a text message. Anxious though he was to hear something less critical in his controller's voice, he was confident that getting the information out this quickly would help compensate for his failure to have Devlin removed. There was the additional bonus that with the man far away, he would not be called upon to get involved in any further action against him. He felt a rush of relief, tonight he could afford to get really high.

Defence Colony

New Delhi
0335 hours

Commando Havildar Dewan eased the Royal Enfield Bullet 500 off its stand and sat astride it, watching the road out of the Defence Colony. It was a good position from which to maintain surveillance, the overhead canopy of the tree's low hanging branches cast a deeper shadow that would be virtually impenetrable. The same old frisson of anticipation was there, the knowledge that soon the re-modelled vintage motorbike would be carrying its rider through the night and along India's mish-mash of roads, the scarred surfaces transmitting their wounds and botched surgery up through the structure of the machine making the rider's body one with the land. COBRA had been supplied with ten of the 500, each one modified for their special operations: the extra fuel tank giving it double the range, the brilliant muffler that muted the exhaust to little more than a purr and the all-terrain tyres, converted it into an ideal means of transporting a COBRA unit into locations inaccessible to most vehicles. Packed into a helicopter on a cushioned pallet, a team could be dropped into a Drop Zone a few miles from the target, from where they could move up at a speed that no-one would anticipate. But this operation would be quite different: tracking the Land Rover across the breadth of northern India and into the Himalayas without being detected posed a special challenge but one that the commando had met and overcome on a number of previous occasions, shadowing Islamic militants. True it was that this time the quarry was a 'friendly' but the orders had been explicit, unless there was an imminent threat to the target's life, it was imperative that he remain unaware that he had a tail.

The sound of the Land Rover's engine turning over confirmed the commando's acute sense of hearing, the sound of a Land Rover door closing had been distinctive. The vehicle's battered bodywork made it melt into the surrounding area and the headlights were on a dimmed beam but the commando knew that from the rear, it presented a distinctive pattern that would not be confused with anything other than a Land Rover of the same model and vintage. Donning the matt black helmet and lowering the smoked glass visor the Bullet eased out into the night. It would be a long ride.

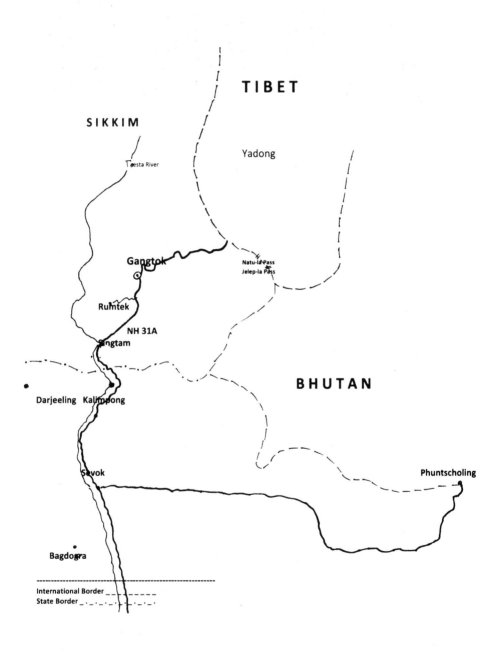

Kalimpong
Darjeeling Gorkha Hill Council

West Bengal

'There's no milk.' Deepraj put the tray of coffee mugs on the table.

'Doesn't matter, we'll get some later.' Max handed a mug each to Nyima and Dendi.

'Sugar?'

'Added.' Max tasted his.

'It's good.' Deepraj acknowledged the appreciation and seemed to relax as he stood next to the table. Max tapped the map spread out between them.

'Assuming that they haven't moved the stuff already, the first task is to get it out of the gumba and then we were supposed to have to transport it to the RV with the Indian in Bhutan.' He pointed to Phuntsholing. Dendi looked at Deepraj and shook his head.

'That's a big risk Saheb. We'll be out of the Gorkha Hill Council area, well into West Bengal, not a lot of friendly faces.'

'That's right Saheb.' Deepraj added. 'Inside Sikkim we can move through the jungle, but once we get down to Siliguri, the West Bengal armed police patrol the road into Bhutan.' Max nodded his agreement.

'What about within the GHC, what's the position there?'

'I've already contacted DK, he says he'll give us as much help as he can but all this agitation for a separate state has made the government bring in more Indian Army units in case the guerrilla movement becomes active again.'

'I'll talk to DK myself, he owes me a favour.' Max had once interceded on behalf of DK Mukhia when DK had commanded the Gorkha guerrilla movement that had fought the West Bengal government for an independent Gorkha hill district. Eventually a very limited degree of semi-autonomy had been granted, the Gorkha Hill Council being the ultimate end product. But the separatist campaigns being waged in other parts of India had reignited the aspirations of the majority ethnic Nepalese people in this section of the Himalayas and more Indian Army units had been posted into the region in anticipation of trouble.

'So, we have to avoid the Indian Army and though we can expect some help within the GHC we'll be exposed once we're into West Bengal?'

'Huzoor.' Deepraj and Dendi agreed. Max studied the map again. In theory they could move through the heavily forested hills in which the state and national boundaries were far from clearly delineated, but once it was known that they had seized the treasure they would have to expect hot pursuit in which artificial divisions like boundaries would be meaningless, added to which they would be burdened with the loads.

'*Dai*?' Nyima gave Dendi a quizzical look.

'What?' Nyima brushed the tips of his fingers across the map from Rumtek to the Sikkim border.

'*Sala*!' Dendi swore at him then laughed. 'Nyima wants me to tell you that there are smugglers routes through Sikkim, Saheb.' Max raised one eyebrow.

'Well, are there?' Dendi sighed and punched Nyima's shoulder.

'There are…but I've not used them myself.' Nyima looked at Deepraj and both men began to laugh.

'Dendi?' Max inquired. The Sherpa traced a line from Gangtok running due east towards the border with Bhutan.

'It's quite a short route but it would be really difficult getting to Phuntsholing.'

Max studied the map again for a minute then drew an imaginary line westwards across Sikkim from Rumtek to the river Teesta.

'What about moving in this direction? Are there any smuggler routes?' Dendi leaned over the map, orienting himself.

'There are a couple of routes out of Nepal through Yuksom and I think there's a narrow path once you cross the Rangpo.' He pointed to the river west of the Teesta. Max nodded slowly. The main highway through Sikkim began to parallel the Teesta from Singtam and ran down into India where it met the road junction at the Sevok Bridge from where the river continued south and a road ran east towards Bhutan. The germ of an idea was growing in his head but there were several imponderables, chief of which was changing the RV with the Indian contact to somewhere far more convenient than Phuntsholing.

'Nyima, you remember Arun Thapa, the white water river guide?' The Sherpa nodded slowly. Max held up his hand to stop any objections.

'Yes, I know he had a reputation for getting smashed.' Max smiled. 'But he's one of the best men on the water. I think he's in Darjeeling, d'you think you could find him and get him to come over here?'

'I know where he lives. Shall I go today?'

'Yes. Don't tell him anything except that I may have a job for him.' Nyima gave a head flick of acknowledgment and left. Max turned to Deepraj. 'I need you to go to Rumtek. Find Shakti, he's expecting me to contact him but tell him I sent you and show him the seal on this prayer bracelet so that he knows you're genuine. Ask him if the Urgen Karmapa camp is doing anything about the treasure, such as moving it. Get as much information as you can about security at the monastery, locks, guards, duty patrols and schedules. Take a copy of the floor plans and put in as much detail as you can get. Do a complete reconnaissance of the grounds and the approach routes and find out where the nearest armed police are stationed, then hurry back. Don't use your mobile unless it's absolutely necessary, find a landline if you have to give me any urgent information.' Deepraj frowned.

'Is that all?'

'No. Steal an armoured personnel carrier and bring it back.' There was a momentary silence as Deepraj digested this before Max let the serious look on his face slip. 'Yes, you *chalak* bugger! That's all, now carry on.' Deepraj grinned and drew himself to attention before walking out of the room. Max smiled at Dendi who was enjoying hearing Deepraj being described as a smartass. 'We'll go down to Gompu's and have some *momos* with the rest of the team.'

The first of the monsoon rains had broken on the previous night but now the sky was crystal clear, the sun drying out the roadside vegetation carried the rich mulch smell of the earth and leaves up into their heads as they walked down Upper Cart Road towards the town. There was almost no vehicular traffic, only the occasional man or woman stepping purposefully uphill, the loaded conical bamboo *doko* on their backs, its weight supported by a Hessian strap that wound around the bottom section and then passed up and across the forehead. Dendi broke into the silence.

'We'll have to carry the loads in *dokos* Saheb. Do we buy them here or wait till we get into Sikkim?'

'Get them here, there'll be a *haat bazaar* tomorrow.' The growling noise of heavy lorry engines filled the night air and a military convoy laboured its way uphill. They stood back to let it pass and Max noted the insignia of a Dogra regiment. When the last vehicle had passed them and the wet silence recovered its hold over the atmosphere, they resumed their walk.

'The Indian Army used to post Gurkha regiments up here.'

'Since the campaign for a separate Gurkha state they've replaced them all with Rajputs, Sikhs, Dogras, anyone except Gurkhas. It's as though they don't trust them.' Dendi's tone was disgusted. Max could see the wisdom in it, in fairness, the soldiers' loyalties would be divided, better not to put them to the test. He decided not to share his opinion with Dendi.

'What about up on the passes into Tibet? Have they pulled the Gurkha *paltans* out of those too?'

'Huzoor, let the Deshis freeze their balls off.' Dendi gave a scornful laugh. Whereas whatever the Indian Army did in the Darjeeling District could be rationalised, Max was firmly of the view that Gurkhas, with their superb ability to adapt, were far and away the best troops to man the Himalayan passes. The Sino-Indian War in 1962 had proved that even the outstanding Sikhs and Jats operated at dangerously low levels of efficiency in the bitter cold at 14,000 feet. Border surveillance would suffer.

Apart from more cars on the road, Kalimpong's main thoroughfare had changed little since Max's last visit. Gompu's showed no signs whatsoever of having changed over the last 30 years. Half a dozen people were seated at different tables and the table at the rear was occupied by five Nepalese, the four whose faces he could see looked to be about in their early 30s but the fifth one had his back to them as they walked in. The four got to their feet, held themselves briefly at attention then made namascar with a short bow which Max reciprocated. The fifth man turned and welcomed Max with a smile that was framed by his shoulder length hair and bushy moustache.

'DK. *Bhai...Arami*?'

'*Arami-ni* Max *Daju*.' He pulled up a chair next to him, indicating for Max to take it. DK Mukhia had been the commander of the guerrilla force that had taken to the hills and jungles to conduct an armed insurrection against the government of West Bengal in support of an independent Gorkha homeland for the Nepalese of the Darjeeling District. Eventually, their nuisance value had won them a seat at a negotiating table in Delhi and though they had not achieved their ultimate objective, they had been given a higher degree of self-governance substantially free of interference from the Communist government of West Bengal. Overnight, DK had changed from being a criminal with a price on his head to a respected political figure, though in the current political climate he would be a marked man. Max had donated generously to their fighting fund when he had been operating his group of travel companies in Nepal and they were fast friends. DK introduced the four men to Max explaining that they went by their nicknames, a simple security device that they had adopted during the insurgency.

'Anda' was big for a Gurkha, about five foot ten and built like a bull: he was ex-1st Gurkha of the Indian Army. Max guessed that his nickname of 'the egg' was attributable to the fact that he was totally bald. 'Beis' and 'Ekeis' were identical twin brothers who were known only by the last two digits of their army service number, so 20 and 21. They had been members of the Indo-Tibetan Frontier Force.

'Beis is the one with the broken nose, claims he got it in a fight with a Chinese patrol on an incursion but we think it was the husband of a Naga girl he was shacked up with.' They all laughed. DK turned to the shortest of the four, barely five foot tall. 'This one is "Paad".' Max's eyebrow shot up quizzically. Why would anyone be called 'fart'? DK grinned, anticipating Max's query. 'He acquired this title in the 5th Gurkhas when they were dealing with the terrorists in Kashmir. His speciality was stealing up on people and overcoming them silently.' He punched the little man playfully and they all laughed.

'Max my friend, Deepraj came to me with your problem. You helped us and now it is my turn.' He gestured towards the others. 'These are my best people and now.' He lifted his hands to indicate that they were now Max's to command.

'I'm very grateful, DK.' He turned to face them. The facial features of the Mongol hillmen are chameleon-like: the dominant expression being a ready smile that mutates into one of ferocious intensity when their blood is up.

The trained soldier acquires an unreadable mien, only the eyes alive and questing. These men all fit the description. As he sized them up, Max was impressed by the quiet confidence they exuded.

'You work as a team.' It was more statement than question.

'Saheb.' Anda responded for all of them confirming Max's guess that he was their commander.

'You know "Indus Kothi" where I'm staying?' They nodded. 'Make your way there this evening but come individually, not as a group. Between 19.00 and 19.30 and we'll eat and talk.'

'Good.' DK clapped him on the shoulder. 'Now let's have some of Gompu's momos.'

As they ate, Max studied his new recruits and reflected on his options. During the drive from Delhi he had gone over the situation from every angle that he could conceive of and had concluded that the whole venture was a nightmare. There was no way he was going to mount an assault on the monastery and even a clandestine burglary was fraught with the risk of triggering violent resistance from the monks with the prospect of them suffering injuries or worse. Despite being committed to restoring the treasure to its rightful owner, he shied away from a physical confrontation with the monks, even those who supported Urgen Trinley. They were entitled to their opinion as to the legitimate Karmapa, whether or not Urgen was a Chinese puppet, and violence was totally anathema to Buddhist philosophy. Yet he had to face the fact that there were people amongst the Tibetan government-in-exile who had no such inhibitions when it came to control over the funds and he had to be prepared for a fight. The major unknown factor was the Chinese. They had already tipped their hand. Unlikely though it appeared, the fact remained that the Chinese border with Sikkim was uncomfortably close and his recent experience in Nepal had demonstrated that the PLA ignored international borders when it suited their purposes. But a deep penetration into Indian territory? The political ramifications would be dramatic. Despite rating it as highly improbable he could not dismiss altogether the possibility that they could get into a firefight: as guerrillas DK's team's tactics would have been fire and flight, always using their knowledge of the terrain to their advantage. Much the same factors would apply if they were bumped by a PLA unit. He took his notebook out and wrote a shopping list of his needs then handed it to DK who read it to himself.

'When do you need them?'

'Yesterday.'

'Do my best.' He tapped the list. 'You're a bit over optimistic.'

'The GPMG?'

'No chance. Best I can do is a Bren.'

'OK.' Max nodded. The good old reliable Bren gun would have to do. DK gestured with his head towards Anda.

'It's his favourite toy.' He pushed his chair back. 'Better get started. Can you collect?'

'Of course.' DK looked at his men and grinned.

'Look after the Colonel Saheb. I don't have many friends left.' He waved at the waiter. 'Put this on my tab.' Then he was gone.

Max turned his mind back to the more immediate threat posed by Rumtek's monk 'soldiers' and the Sikkim armed police. From what Fernandes had told him, Delhi's writ did not run in Sikkim and its current state government was obviously aligned with Urgen Trinley's faction. Even the delicious pork momo was not helping him to resolve the problem that he had wrestled with over the past few days. Short of getting Nyima and Dendi to go and ask for their money back he could see no profit in anything but a clandestine burglary. Despite having the tools for an armed confrontation, this was contingency planning only. They would have to use the minimum amount of force, especially in relation to the monks. He found his mind wandering, the image of Kim was suddenly there. Even if he had harboured doubts about the wisdom of simply disappearing from her life, he was more than ever sure that it had been the correct decision now. Already there were too many imponderables. He cursed Fernandes for the umpteenth time.

Gangtok

Sikkim

Lyangsong loved examining the beautiful gold coins, feeling their weight and admiring the artistry. Every year the pandas were presented in a different pose: the earlier ones only portrayed a single panda but recently there had been pairs, they looked so endearing that they made him smile. But most of all he enjoyed the sense of power that his hoard gave him. Each coin weighed one ounce of 999 gold. He had 95 and Tenzing had promised him five more if he could find out where Mr Devlin was staying in Sikkim. The sound of a door closing downstairs made him touch the plastic box containing the most recent coins to his lips quickly before returning it back into the recess behind the brickwork in the wall of his room. He carefully repositioned the two bricks that sealed the hole and rubbed some loose sand over the joints, nodding in self-appreciation at the skill with which he had concealed his hiding place. He wiped the sweat off his face, Tenzing terrified him, he never smiled, just wore that threatening expression all the time, even when they had been at school together. There was the time when they were teenagers, walking back from classes, Lyangsong had queried Tenzing's use of a Lepcha expression, it did not sound the way it ought to have in *Rong-ring*. To Lyangsong's ears it sounded just like the way that Li Gai the Chinese cobbler said it. Tenzing had been furious and threatened to take him into the forest and strangle him. When Lyangsong burst into tears and promised to do anything the much bigger boy wanted, Tenzing had taken him at his word and from that time on Lyangsong had done the much bigger boy's bidding. The only difference now that they were adults was that he was rewarded for his work. There had been more and more occasions when he knew that what he was instructed to do was illegal but he persuaded himself that each time would be the last time, even though he knew that so long as the gold panda coins kept coming he would continue to obey. It was not as though he was doing anything illegal, merely informing Tenzing of everything that went on inside the monastery at Rumtek, what harm could that do?

'Didn't you hear me call you?' Lyangsong was jerked out of his thoughts.

'*Ahughn...*' He stuttered.

'Why aren't you searching for Devlin?' Lyangsong looked at his watch and started to mumble.

'I'm not interested in your excuses. Find him. Today!' Lyangsong muttered an apology and hurried out of the room.

Tenzing's eye noted the sand on the floor and his gaze traced up the brickwork until it came to rest on the powdery residue around two of the bricks. 'Stupid shit.' His fingers pressed against the bricks and he felt slight movement, confirming his conclusion. Once the Lepcha had served his purposes, he would retrieve his coins. Not now. His instructions were crystal clear. Lyangsong was their best source of information inside the Rumtek Monastery and his superior officers would never forgive him if the treasure trove went out of their control. The instructions he had been given made little sense to him. Beijing regarded the man Devlin as some sort of threat to the treasure but he had been given no specifics. In any event, what could one foreigner do? Even if he was some sort of Rambo character it would take days to search the monastery and then, in the impossible event that he had remained undetected, how would he propose to move it, physically? The office types sending him his orders always thought they knew better than the man on the ground. There could hardly have been a safer cache for the treasure than deep in the bowels of Rumtek. He had considered making the inquiries about Devlin himself but decided that it would draw too much attention to him. It was not even certain that the foreigner was in Sikkim, only that he had left Delhi. His superiors were emphatic, the man had to be disposed of. Tenzing regarded this as overkill, then smiled at his own pun. Once located, any one of a variety of accidents could be arranged, foreigners were always falling off mountains or simply disappearing and Tenzing had at his command a number of *Naxalite* terrorists who had disposed of those who stood in his path; but first he had to find him. No, let the Lepcha bumpkin find him and then he would deal with him, that was the professional way.

Lyangsong was halfway to the ICAR Guesthouse when he remembered that he should have told Tenzing about the monastery's intention to move the treasure to Singtam. He did not know why, only that there had been a heated argument between the senior Rinpoches which had resulted in the decision to locate the treasure away from Rumtek. He pondered whether to call Tenzing on his mobile phone and tell him but resentful of the man's bullying insistence that he search for Devlin he decided to leave it until later. He drew some satisfaction from the thought that had it not been for Tenzing's habitual threatening manner he would have given him the information before he had departed. Serve him right if he had to find out later. Finding Devlin was not a problem, his cousin in the Sikkim state police had promised to inform him as soon as the foreigner was processed through the checkpoint. Even those with a Protected Area Pass had to disclose the address at which they would stay whilst in the state.

Kalimpong

The look on Deepraj's face warned Max that it was not good news. 'Shakti says they're planning to move the stuff out of the monastery but he doesn't know where to.'

'Did he say when?'

'Only that he thinks it will be in a matter of days.' That meant that Max would have to move the team into Sikkim and be ready to move at very short notice.

'The old man took some convincing, even when I showed him the bracelet. I think he either does know or has a pretty good idea of when but he's holding back: he was expecting a foreigner.'

'Yes, I thought about that but the bracelet was supposed to be the identification.'

'If you go Saheb?'

'Looks as though I'll have to now.' Max had wanted to avoid showing his face in Sikkim until the very last minute. Any foreigner stood out a mile, added to which he was a known figure. The others in the room looked at him. He checked his watch again, it was already gone 21.00 he had expected Nyima to be back by now.

'What time's the last taxi from Darjeeling?'

'21.00.' The twins spoke in unison. That meant that Nyima could still arrive before midnight but the critical question was whether he would have the river guide in tow.

'Right, go and collect your kit, you'll have to doss down here tonight, we have to go over the plan and may have to leave early tomorrow morning.' The sound of a motor horn made Max go over to the window and shade his eyes to see out. The chowkidar was opening the iron gates and the beam of the headlights bounced over the uneven driveway. In the dark shadow behind the lights he could only make out two figures alighting from a jeep. He went out onto the entrance verandah.

'I gave the driver a few extra rupees to deliver us to the door.' Nyima grinned.

'Max!' The lined and sun-smoked face of the river guide emerged out of the shadows and embraced Max in a bear hug which also brought the man's alcohol infused breath right up close.

'Arun, you drunken bastard.' The river guide pulled away, his face a picture of contrition.

'Only on special occasions like this.'

'Every occasion is a special occasion for you.' Max shook his head in mock despair. 'Come on in.' He turned and led the way back into the main room. Arun high-fived Deepraj and Dendi.

'*Arey ho*! Now we can have a real party.' Max looked at the grinning expectant faces and knew that he was the only one wearing a grim expression.

'I'm sorry boys, we've no time for boozing. Deepraj, make us all some coffee.' He looked at Nyima. 'Have you two eaten?'

'Huzoor, we had some chilli chicken before we left.'

'Right.' He made the introductions to DK's men, then sent them off. Whilst they were away he would talk through his plan with Arun so that by the time they got back he would know whether or not it was feasible.

Arun heard him out in silence as he had explained what their objective was. Part way through, the river guide started to nod as he saw where Max was going.

'Assuming that we do get hold of the stuff in the first place, I estimate that we will only have a few hours' head start before all hell breaks loose and the world and his wife are in pursuit.'

'So you want to use the river as your escape route?'

'Exactly.'

'How big is the load, one raft, two rafts?' Arun looked at Nyima who glanced at Dendi before responding.

'All the kit plus eight of us, two?' Dendi nodded his agreement. Arun scratched the back of his head.

'Can do.'

'What condition are your RIBs in? Last time I seem to recall you were using one that looked like an advertisement for BandAids.' Arun threw his hands up in feigned dismay.

'You've forgotten that when the Nepal government appropriated your companies you let me smuggle your three best RIBs out down the Sunkoshi.'

'So I did.' Max mused, rubbing his chin. 'Unless you've wrecked them in the meantime.'

'*Moi*?' Looking at Arun's distressed features it was easy to forget that he was a Baccalaureate from the Sorbonne. Max drew them around the map.

'We need the best route from Rumtek,' he said, running his finger across until it touched the river running through Sikkim and out into India, 'to here. Then, if the Gods are kind, we'll run the river down to just south of Sevok or possibly to a point above Jalpaiguri. I'm waiting for a call from the *Bhunnia* we have to deliver it to. He wants to meet us inside the Bhutan border but I'm trying to persuade him to take it off us whilst we're still in India.'

'You're going to trust a Bhunnia?' Arun's voice was incredulous.

'No option, he's the Dalai Lama's choice, at least the Tibetan government's.' He looked at their faces, each man registered the same disbelief.

'The gold and currencies have to be converted into a deposit in a bank outside India, the Bhunnias are doing it all the time.' No-one said anything. 'Anyway, once we deliver it to him our job's done and we all get paid and go home.' Max realised that nothing he said would change their deep-rooted suspicions.

'What happens if the Bhunnia insists we deliver it to him in Bhutan?' Nyima's face was creased with worry. Max knew that though they could probably organise some transport from Sevok or Jalpaiguri they would be at far greater risk, especially if the authorities in Sikkim called for help from the West Bengal government. He made his decision right there and then.

'I'll tell the Bhunnia that we either deliver to him at Sevok or Jalpaiguri or not at all. He won't want to run the risk of losing the commission on the transaction, so he'll have to accept our terms.'

Arun was leaning over the map, he turned to face Max.

'Singtam, you'll have to manpack it to Singtam. There's no point of access to the river before there.'

'What about if we went north to Dikchu?' Arun glanced back at the map and shook his head.

'Too steep for me to get the RIBs into the water. It'll have to be Singtam.' Max nodded his acceptance of the river guide's assessment.

'One small matter.' Arun was scratching the back of his head again. 'The Teesta's not yet in full spate but some of the white water will be…technical.' Max's laugh was grim. Arun's description of the quality and difficulty of the Himalayan rivers was unique. 'Technical' conveyed being tossed around or thrown out of the RIB.

'That's why we have the best river guide in the business.' Arun smiled.

'So long as you stay off the booze.' They all laughed at Arun's hurt expression. Max knew that he could organise the escape route with a large measure of certainty, the real problem was going to be getting hold of the stuff in the first place and even though he had told them he'd insist on the Bhunnia taking delivery close to the river, there was no guarantee that he'd agree or, worse still, renege on the deal and leave them stranded. What he could plan for he would, as for the rest they'd have to play it by ear. He was far from happy about having to move up the trip into Sikkim but once the stuff was moved, finding it again was likely to be even more problematic. The burglary had been jettisoned, now it looked as though they had to plan an ambush.

Yadong, Xigatse Province

Autonomous Region of Tibet

The unit of the 128 Mountain Rapid Reaction Regiment consisted of Captain Wu Zihan, two sergeants and five specialist soldiers. They had only recently been posted to Xigatse, having spent the previous three years on the border with North Korea dealing with defectors. Wu had taken over command three weeks ago, their previous captain having been promoted. Anxious to assert his authority, Wu had put them through an intensive training programme to get them acclimatised to the height above sea level and the challenging terrain of the Chumbi Valley. He was anxious to conceal his own lack of self-confidence and accused the sergeants of a lack of commitment, threatening them with adverse reports. The sergeants, in turn, took it out on the men. It was a tough unit but not a happy one. Wu's orders were that his team had to be ready to make a clandestine cross-border incursion into Indian territory but he had not been told precisely where or the purpose. His study of the maps was not reassuring. They had a choice of three passes: the most accessible was the Natu-la Pass but it was also known to be the most heavily guarded by the Indian Army. His team could cope with the snow and ice at that height but once they descended they would be into the fissile, jungle covered mountains in the monsoon downpour. The contour lines indicated that the mountain sides were almost vertical which would render them treacherous. There would be precious little purchase which would seriously impede their ability to manoeuver. The only comfort was that the Indian Army soldiers would be disinclined to maintain a keen watch whilst the rain was hurling itself out of the skies. The team had trained for snow and ice, not mud. Why was it that their superiors made such flawed decisions and then ordered them to carry them out on pain of dire consequences if they failed? His request for detailed orders had not been met. He fumed at the combination of adverse factors that were piling up against him: how could he advance his career in situations like this? 128 MRR Regiment was a sought-after posting for officers. Only those considered wholly committed to the party were eligible and a successful rotation led to rapid promotion. But failure would hang about his neck like a permanent yoke, dogging his prospects at every turn. He opened the door of the hut and shouted towards the team that were cleaning their weapons.

'Sergeant Xian!' The lean figure of the senior NCO looked towards the hut, appeared to say something to the men around him and then walked across to where Wu stood, his feet planted in a wide belligerent stance.

'Comrade Captain?'

'Weapon cleaning should have been completed half an hour ago.' He looked at his wristwatch. 'Take them on a 10-kilometre run, with full packs.' The sergeant looked up at the heavy snow clouds overhead.

'All the better if you have to deal with a snowstorm, we must be at peak fitness.'

'Captain.' The sergeant turned away and was met halfway by the second sergeant whose eyes queried their orders.

'Ten K run with full packs.'

'Arsehole's not coming?'

'You joking?'

No sooner had they ordered the men to reassemble their weapons than the snow enveloped them. Nobody said a word but their eyes wore murder beneath the darkened glass of their goggles.

2nd Department, General Staff Headquarters Department

PLA

Beijing

The Chinese military intelligence services are distinct from the intelligence services run by the Ministry of Public Security. Adding to the complexity of the intelligence structure, each province has its own organisation which determines its priorities irrespective of the directives from the central committees. The PLA has a dynamic all its own and guards its territory jealously. The Autonomous Region of Tibet presents an almost impenetrable structure over which the PLA exercises its authority almost without interference from the civilian ministries. In relation to the threat of internal dissension, the PLA was embedded with the office of the commissioner for ethnic integration: all and any overt sign of protest amongst the splittist communities was put down ruthlessly. Commissioner Bo Ziling had developed a profitable working relationship with General Wang Gui, commander of the 8341 Unit Central Security Regiment of DGS2 and neither man considered it necessary to involve the Ministry of Foreign Affairs in their activities, even though they both ran agents outside the mainland. Wang had summoned Colonel Ji Guan, the commandant of the 128 MRR Regiment to a conference with Bo.

'We have an opportunity to regain the face we lost when your unit failed to prevent the Dalai Lama from escaping into Nepal.' The colonel bristled at what he regarded as wholly unfair criticism but he said nothing. The blame should have been laid on a poor command structure that had failed to give his unit sufficient advance warning. But if there was a chance to redeem their reputation he would grab it. Wang pushed the map towards him and used a pencil to draw a circle on Yadong then traced a route from the Natu-la Pass, along the highway to Gangtok then through Singtam, Rangpo, Rangli and back across the Jelep-la Pass and back to Yadong. He drew a box around Rumtek.

'That is your route, approximately 100 kilometres from Pass to Pass.' He indicated Bo with the pencil.

'The Commissioner wants us to recover all the bullion and money the Tibetan terrorists stole. Our agent in Sikkim has informed us that it is to be moved from here...' He pointed at Rumtek, '...destined to be stored here.' He indicated Singtam. 'Our information is that it will be transported by road but we have not yet been told when. Your team must seize it somewhere between here...' He pointed to the road junction from Rumtek to the highway, '...and here.' He tapped Singtam. 'Roughly, over a distance of 20 kilometers.' He tossed the pencil onto the map and leaned back. 'It's not my job to tell you how to do it, but we want it recovered. Is that understood?'

Wang Gui was heavily built and his creased jowels and lidded eyes did nothing to soften his facial expression which challenged Ji to say anything against the operation. Yet the special force commander was acutely conscious of the fact that Wang had grossly underestimated the difficulties of such a task. What looked like 20 kilometers on the map would represent at least double that on those mountain roads that contoured the hillsides. They would have to infiltrate and exfiltrate via two heavily guarded Himalayan passes, avoid detection by the Indian Army, the state armed police, ambush the transport at a point they would have little time to reconnoitre and then pass undetected, skirting at least three towns on their return journey. Even assuming that the local agent provided them with accurate information, the window of opportunity would be perilously narrow.

'Can we go in by helicopter?' Even as he asked the question he knew that it was impracticable. Indian Air Force radar detection would pick them up instantly. The General shook his head.

'Too great a risk.' Ji nodded acknowledgment. At that height the air was cold and thin making it particularly challenging for the helicopter pilots. Nonetheless, he could risk an airborne extraction. The gunships could be in and out before the first IAF fighters could respond.

'General, permit me, what happens if they are caught?'

'We will say that they lost their way whilst in hot pursuit of Tibetan terrorists.' What might possibly have been a smile on anyone else's face merely raised the corners of Wang's eyes. 'There are no yellow lines demarcating international borders up in the mountains.' His face resumed its death mask configuration. 'They will not be caught.' Wang struck his desk with his rigid forefinger. Ji concealed his animosity for this armchair soldier who had never had to put his skin at risk in any conditions, let alone in the bitter cold of the high Himalaya and in what amounted to enemy territory. He owed his rank to the fact that he was a princeling for whom arse-creeping with the party cadres was the norm.

'Do we have the latest satellite pictures?' Wang looked at Bo who extracted a slim bundle of films from his briefcase and handed them to Ji who spread them out on the General's desk and examined them without comment before facing Bo.

'Communications?'

'Our agent in Sikkim has a secure Global Star GSP and will provide your team with all the information necessary to identify the target, its route and timing.' Wang gestured to Bo who handed over a sheet of paper.

'The number and identifying codes.' Wang lifted his right hand as if to say 'What more could you ask for?'

'It will be up to you to ensure that this time there will be no clouds concealing the sun.'

'General.' Ji had nothing but contempt for his superior's attempt at the poetic. Who did he think he was, Li Bai?

'How much time do I have to get my team into position?'

'None.'

Wang picked up the telephone on his desk and put it down in front of the colonel. 'Make your call now.' Ji frowned and paused before reaching for the phone. He had to make it look as though he was unprepared when in reality his contact in Wang's office had already given him a heads up about the operation. It was vital to protect his mole.

'Are you authorising my people to kill the Indian Army personnel on the border?' Ji knew the Natu-la Pass well and the chances of slipping unseen by any of the Gurkha soldiers was negligible. They would have to use moderators to take them out but that would make the re-entry 100% more difficult. Wang nodded his approval.

'I shall need your written orders before I commit the team.' Did Wang take him for a complete fool? The General shifted his bulk in his leather upholstered chair and pointed at his military secretary who handed the document over to Ji who studied it carefully before taking out his own mobile and punching a saved number.

'Put Captain Wu Zihan's team on 30 minutes' notice to move.' He closed the clam-shell phone definitively, thrust it into a pocket of his camouflage smock, scooped up the films and drew himself to attention. 'I'll need to scan these films to my unit.' Wang's eyes flicked at his military secretary who took them from the colonel's hand and walked quickly out of the office.

'I shall be monitoring the operation from Yadong, should you need me, General.' Saluting, he marched out of the office with the map in his hand. Bo gave Wang an inquiring look.

'He strains at the leash…but he's my dog.' The corners of his eyes flicked up again. Bo nodded appreciatively then thought for a moment before airing his one concern.

'The central committee…if the Indians give us trouble?' Wang's face clouded in contempt.

'Against the PLA and the PSB?' His shoulders gave a momentary shrug of dismissal. He pinched the top of his nose, screwing up his eyes for a second or two. 'I hope to have those Microsoft shares very soon.'

'Ah, yes.' One million dollars was a small price to pay for recovering the Tibetan treasure.

National Highway 31A

North of Rangpo, Sikkim

Keeping tabs on Devlin's vehicular movements was facilitated by the locator device that had been installed into the Land Rover during its fitting out in Delhi, but keeping him under undetected personal surveillance when he was on foot up here in the hill towns required that combination of tradecraft and stealth which had caused General Ranjit Singh to single out Havildar Dewan for this assignment. It also helped to belong to one of the ethnic groups indigenous to the region. Despite the rains that were crashing down onto the mountain roads making them treacherous for anyone on two wheels and the constant curtain of water washing down the crash helmet and across the goggles reducing vision to a minimum, the havildar was glad no longer to be maintaining watch from beneath the groundsheet piled with dead leaves and rotting vegetation. Whilst in Kalimpong, individual members of Devlin's team had gone off for hours on end whilst Devlin had remained in the town but now in addition to the Land Rover they had acquired a re-conditioned Jeep at the same time that they had taken delivery of some packages that an experienced eye recognised as weaponry. All of this had been reported back to COBRA HQ at Meerut but the orders remained unchanged. The commando was both encouraged but surprised at the breadth of discretion given to someone of such low rank: the briefing had been given by General Ranjit Singh himself. The objective was to restore some valuable property to its rightful owner, the Dalai Lama. Execution was to be carried out by an unauthorised group of ex-Gurkha soldiers led by a foreign national with the tacet but entirely unattributable approval of the secret Intelligence Department working in tandem with the commander of the Commando Battalion for Resolute Action. The havildar's unquestioning loyalty was confined to COBRA, none of the battalion's members looked beyond it. The 'Action' element of the order was 'Use your discretion, render assistance if it becomes necessary, stay undetected if you can.' The several cross-border operations that the havildar's team had carried out into Pakistan Kashmir had been more precisely restricted; alone, the havildar had complete discretion. It was not for the havildar to question superior officers.

Negotiating a blind hairpin bend the havildar suddenly caught sight of the brake lights on the Land Rover and had to drop back again. It was all too easy to allow the focus of concentration to narrow on just navigating through the torrential rain, the tracking system made it unnecessary to get this close.

Gangtok

Sikkim

Max pulled into the forecourt of the Denzong Inn to let Deepraj and Nyima alight.

'Check in, then see if there's any chatter in the bazaar. Meet me in the bar of the Nor-Khill at 1800 hours.' Max drove out of the forecourt and headed for his hotel. He had decided not to draw attention to themselves by having them all staying together. Arun had a brother who would put up Dendi and the twins in his apartment on the south side of Gangtok and both 'Egg' and 'Fart' had family with whom they could stay. The latter two would also harbour the weapons. Not knowing when the treasure was to be moved was the major complication which he intended to resolve by talking to Shakti himself. But, as he was acutely aware, he could not risk making a move until he had his people in place. Arun had promised to call him as soon as he had the RIBs at the RV close to Singtam. He checked his watch as he drove into the forecourt of the Nor-Khill Hotel. Once upon a time it had been a residence of the Sikkimese royal family but now it provided a cosy retreat which managed to combine the gentle warmth of the hill people with a measure of quality hospitality. He could not help smiling to himself at the kaleidoscope of garish reds, yellows, blues and greens that infused the décor, but it was a part of what made Sikkim so delightfully otherworldly. The broadly grinning faces welcomed him back and escorted him to his room on the top floor with its wonderful view. Once alone, he called Ashok Dariwallah's number yet again and this time the Bhunnia replied. Max had made it clear the previous evening that he could not make delivery in Bhutan but that Dariwallah would have to receive the goods in the vicinity of Sevok. The Bhunnia had protested long and loud that this was impossible whereupon Max had called his bluff and told him that the transaction would be given to someone else. This had brought the man's wailing to a sudden halt.

'You cannot be doing this.' The tone was part disbelief and part indignation.

'I not only can but shall.'

'But you are not having the authority…' Max cut the line. Moments later the Bhunnia was calling him.

'Please, Colonel Saheb, allow me some time.'

'Midday tomorrow. I'll call you.' He cut the line again. Max pondered whether to call Geljen to explain the problem and ask if they had an alternative broker to handle the deal. Time was running against him, Dariwallah must have organised the onward remittance, it was only the transportation through West Bengal into Bhutan that needed to be arranged. Without knowing what the Bhunnia's commission would be on the deal Max was confident that it would be sufficiently mouth-watering to cover the cost of carriage over a relatively short distance, including any bribes along the way. Nonetheless, Max was sweating on the man agreeing.

'Ashok *bhaia*?'

'*Ha ji*.' Max thought he detected a note of resignation in the response. 'Transport all arranged?'

'Oh my Gods, what are you doing to me?' A sense of relief coursed through Max as the response could only mean that the Indian would take delivery as he had demanded.

'Making you a very rich man, I suspect.'

'Nai, nai I'm just a poor man.'

'You will have six hours' notice.' Max interrupted him. 'I will call you six hours before I deliver to you 500 metres downstream from the Sevok Bridge on the east bank of the Teesta. Repeat that to me.'

'You are killing me Saheb, killing me…'

'Repeat my instructions.' Max commanded. There was a pause, some unintelligible muttering and then with studied reluctance the Bhunnia complied.

'Don't turn off your phone, Ashok.'

'*Tik hei* Colonel Saheb.'

'Good. I'll be seeing you soon. Thank you.' Max ended the call and shoved the phone back into his pocket. He still felt uneasy about the arrangement; it all depended on the man's cupidity which should have been a given, but for a reason he could not put his finger on, the part of the whole operation that ought to have been the simplest nagged at him. Every rational argument pointed to the Bhunnia carrying out his part of the operation, otherwise how would he get paid? Men like Dariwallah had been operating the *hundi* transactions in foreign exchange for generations, it was as normal for them as drinking *chai*. He made a positive effort to push it to the back of his mind. There were far more urgent matters to attend to…except he did not really believe it. The phone started to vibrate again, he checked the display: Arun.

'The river's rising Max.'

'But it's still doable?'

'Mmm…tomorrow…the day after? Yes. In a week's time? Not if you value your cargo. When do we go?'

'Can't say yet. I'll have a better idea tomorrow.'

'I think you'd better have.' Arun gave an empty laugh. 'Call me. We'll be at the RV by tomorrow evening.'

'*Merci mon vieux*.' Max rang off. The whole operation was threatened by the known unknowns, how the hell was he supposed to plan for contingencies when the only thing he was certain of was the uncertainties?

Gangtok

Sikkim

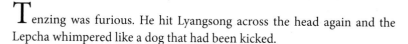

Tenzing was furious. He hit Lyangsong across the head again and the Lepcha whimpered like a dog that had been kicked.

'So you knew this morning but you waited until now to tell me!' He hit him again. Lyangsong cowered against the wall making wounded animal noises.

'Go to Rumtek now. Find out when you're expected to move the treasure, not just the day but the time.' He slapped the side of Lyangsong's head on the words 'day' and 'time' to reinforce his orders. 'You're the truck driver, they have to tell you. Have you spilled the paint on the front?'

'Yes.' He cowered, his arm raised defensively, even more terrified because he had not splashed the paint on yet.

'Now get out.'

'But...' The Lepcha snivelled.

'But what?' He shouted at him.

'I found Devlin for you.' He made it sound like 'devillin'. Tenzing grabbed him by his hair and pulled his face up close to him.

'But you didn't tell me about the treasure, you useless piece of dogshit!' He shoved him towards the door and Lyangsong fled. Tenzing checked the time, 06.10, he had to tell the Naxalites where to find Devlin and order them to get rid of him as soon as possible but first priority was to pass the latest information to his control officer. There was no time to go down to Siliguri where the signal was strong enough for his Nokia. He'd have to use the Satcell, something that always made him nervous. His superiors had warned him that Indian intelligence had positioned a formidable array of dishes along the border to monitor all radio traffic; the one event he really feared was being discovered. He could hear the rain drumming on the galvanised iron roof as he shrugged himself into his waterproof cape and headed out to distance himself from the house. He had a few more choice curses on his lips for the Lepcha who could have given him the information earlier in the day then comforted himself with the prospect of winning praise for disposing of the foreigner. That was a foregone conclusion with Amir Ali's Naxalite thugs.

Max's team had carried their drinks up to his hotel room rather than sit in the bar and were standing around the table studying the map.

'All we know at this moment is that the treasure will be moved from the gumba to an unknown destination in Singtam. We don't know precisely when or what sort of escort they'll provide. It depends on what transport they use, though my guess is that they'll pack it into a small truck and cover it with something to conceal it from the police at the checkpost. Our plan is to ambush them once they're on the 31A.'

'A *pukka* ambush Saheb?' Anda the Egg frowned. 'They're only monks.' Max gave a dismissive wave of his hand and smiled.

'No, we're not out to kill anyone, just frighten them into abandoning their load. We fake an accident so as to block the road and force them to stop.' He pointed at Deepraj. 'I want you to get a motorbike. Follow their vehicle when they leave the gumba at Rumtek then overtake them once they pass through the police checkpost on the 31A. I need you to get sufficiently ahead to give us a couple of minutes' warning.'

He pointed at Anda. 'You drop a tree across the road behind them to block any following traffic.' The big man nodded. 'Set up the Bren so that you can cover the back of their vehicle.' Anda nodded then asked.

'Could we block them on the road with a tree as well?'

'Good idea but we can't delay our own escape. When they stop, order them out at gun point, handcuff them with plastic ties.' He indicated Beis and Ekeis. 'Then get them off the road and into the trees. Make them lie face down and bind their ankles together then get back to the vehicles. I'll take Nyima, Dendi and Paad in the Land Rover. Deepraj will drive the rest of you in the Rumtek vehicle.' He paused and smiled. 'Then we go like a bat out of hell for the RV with Arun.'

'What if they start firing?' This was the contingency that troubled Max most. It could not be discounted that there would be some form of armed escort. He was banking on their overwhelming show of firepower to awe the monastery party into submission.

'Rules of engagement, if and I emphasise if they open fire, I'll take out the shooter, that ought to stop them. If any of us gets hit we bundle him into the Land Rover. If I'm knocked out, Deepraj takes command.' It was not the greatest plan but it had the merits of being simple and Max put a high premium on simplicity.

'Have you got balaclavas for everyone?' He questioned Anda.

'Huzoor.' The big man pulled one out of his jacket pocket and handed it over. 'Yours, Saheb.'

'Good.' He looked at the four guerrillas. 'Stand down until I call you, don't leave all together.' His left eyebrow twitched up. 'Don't drink too much or call attention to yourselves.' They grinned back and left the room. 'Deepraj, keep an eye on them whilst they're in the Dragon bar.' The instruction was acknowledged with a slight shrug of the shoulders as he followed them out. Max turned to Nyima and Dendi.

'You two don't have to take any part in this. I shall be happier if you get yourselves back to Nepal.' Nyima shook his head and frowned.

'We have to finish the job huzoor.' He looked at Dendi. 'Isn't that so?' The Sherpa gave a little sideways flick of his head.

'It is. We took our pay in advance huzoor, now we have to earn it.' He gave a wry grin.

'OK. But if the shooting starts, you two keep your heads down.' They both looked amused. 'Oh, and Nyima?'

'Huzoor?'

'Be careful with your kukri...don't want any arms separated from their owners.' Max clapped him on the shoulder and herded them both out of the room.

128 MRR Regiment Forward Base

Yadong, Autonomous Region of Tibet

The overhead light swung slightly as it was caught by the draught that penetrated between the wooden slats of the hut's walls. Colonel Ji reached up and grabbed the edge of the enamel lampshade, steadying it over the aerial photographs. He traced a line with his forefinger along the southernmost track to the Sinchei-la Pass into Bhutan, then west just on the Bhutan side of the Indian border and back up to the Batang-la Pass.

'It's a longer route, much harder going but it's thinly guarded.' His eyes read the captain's discomfort.

'The Indian Army guards the Bhutan border as well.'

'It's a Madras unit, southern Indians. They'll be paralysed with cold.' Wu nodded, unconvinced.

'You go in tonight.' Wu tried to conceal his surprise and failed. Ji was already regretting having given him this command. The men were good, very good but their leader was unimpressive. Too bad, it was too late to change the orders now. The clock was already running against them, in any event both the sergeants were seasoned veterans, which was why he had included them in the briefing.

'Our contact hasn't given us the EDT of the package from Rumtek, so you take the team in, recce your ambush position then dig in and wait for his signal. The vehicle will be a small truck with a canvas cover over the tray. The near side front mudguard will have white paint splashed on it and there'll be a red rag flying from the radio aerial. Our contact will give you an estimate of when it should reach the 31A, so you calculate the extra time depending on your position south of the junction with the Rumtek Road.' Wu was writing hurriedly in his notebook. Ji handed him a card.

'These are your radio frequencies, A is to command control, codeword "Foxden", B is for your contact in Sikkim and X is for emergencies. Don't write this down, contact's call sign is "Chopsticks".' Wu nodded and handed the card over to sergeant Xian. 'Your exit route is back through Gangtok to the Jelep-la Pass.' Wu's face creased, his eyes opened in disbelief.

'But that's back through the town...'

'The opposite way to the one anybody would expect.'

'But...'

'The town.' Ji stared him down. He knew it was a risk but it was well calculated. Even if anyone raised the alarm, which he doubted, the assumption would be that they'd head for Singtam and the southerly route out, always assuming that they were identified as PLA.

'Once you're in position the contact will call you on your cellphone. In case there's no signal, you'll also have to keep radio watch for two minutes on the hour every hour; one or the other, the contact will raise you.'

Wu was scanning the photographs again, trying not to show his doubts about the whole operation. Getting in was not his main worry, it was getting out again laden down with the packages and the distinct probability that the border forces would be on the alert or even on their tail. He looked up at the colonel.

'Helicopter extraction?' Ji shook his head.

'Not in the plan.' In fact Ji had already spoken to his opposite number in the PLA Air Force, an officer he worked with on a regular basis but he wasn't going to disclose this to Wu. A flight of Z-10 gunships was on standby if he found it necessary. Ji was confident that if he had to pull his team out, the Z-10s would deal with whatever the Indians had. These weren't the crappy Russian-built death traps they had had to put up with before but the latest piece of hi-tech equipment designed and produced by China. He smiled as he checked his watch.

'Move out in one hour's time.'

'Colonel.' Both sergeants stood to attention and saluted. As Wu shovelled the aerial photographs into his satchel, Ji caught the eyes of both Xian and Xu and the fingers of his right hand tapped the pocket containing his satphone. Not a word was spoken but they both understood that the colonel was counting on them to see this operation through. They were both seasoned cross-border infiltrators, hard men who could be trusted to use their initiative and, perhaps more to the point, directly answerable to him. Wu, busy zipping up his camo, missed the almost imperceptible nods that his sergeants gave the colonel, saluted and led all three out of the hut.

Ji reached into his hip pocket and pulled out a leather-covered hip flask. Unscrewing the silver top he let a gorge of XO slip down his throat. One advantage of a duty trip to Beijing was the opportunity to top up. He savoured it for a little longer then popped a couple of peppermints into his mouth. Time to make contact with Chopsticks for the latest info. He still had one more player in deep cover in Sikkim, though he'd been instructed not to use him unless it was an emergency. Civilians, he shook his head disparagingly, they never grasped the vital importance of contingency planning. If he really did need to use 'Night Owl' in an emergency it would be too late to bring him up to speed. What was the use of having these people on the ground anyway? No, the Night Owl would have to be warned that he might have to fly at a moment's notice. If nothing came of it, no harm would have been done.

Gangtok

Sikkim

Next Morning

'I'll go to Rumtek and find Shakti.' Max drained his coffee cup and replaced it in the saucer.

'Saheb?' Deepraj frowned.

'No need for both of us, I don't want to frighten the old bugger.' Max smiled.

'No, I mean…going alone.'

'It's broad daylight.' Max pointed up at the lightening sky. 'Not to worry, they're not going to have a go at me amongst all the tourists at Rumtek, even if they know where I am, which I very much doubt.' He smiled.

'They found you in Delhi.' Deepraj bit back.

'I can't have you riding herd on me all the time, old son.' Max reasoned. 'I want you and Anda to go and recce the A31 from the junction with the Rumtek Road down to Singtam, find the best spot for us to ambush their vehicle.' Deepraj stood looking at him in silence for several moments before he gave a disgruntled sigh.

'Huzoor.' It was said with bad grace then he got up and left the breakfast table and stalked out of the dining room. Max continued speed-reading the Sikkim Express and then scanned the previous day's Times of India for any news items that could have a bearing on his plans.

'Hello.' He looked up and it felt as though all the air had been sucked out of his chest in one go. Instinctively he got to his feet.

'No, don't stand up. I just wanted to confirm my worst fears.'

'Kim…I…' She held up both hands.

'Don't.' It was the scathing bitterness of tone that arrested him.

'Damn you to hell Max Devlin, you're an ace shit.' She turned away, the sweep of her body conveying utter scorn as she left the dining room. Even as he considered pursuing her he registered that this was precisely what he had intended. There was no way in the world that he wanted her caught up in this madness. But the sight of her…she had been so close to him that her scent was in his head.

'More coffee Saheb?' He managed a mechanical nod and sank back onto the chair. A kaleidoscope of options tunnelled their way through his brain until, quite suddenly, they hit the buffer of Sid's question: no, he didn't have any 'Fuck off' money and he desperately wanted to continue working in the Indian subcontinent, all of which led inexorably to his current, distinctly questionable assignment. Ambushing a bunch of monks and grabbing the Dalai Lama's trove was in the same league as stealing sweets from a baby or should be, always providing that the Sikkim armed police or their Bengali counterparts didn't get in on the act.

Someone with perforated eardrums put some execrable Hindi-pop music on which drove him out of his reflections. Time to go.

Her tears blurred Kim's vision as she propelled herself out of the dining room. Just hearing him call her name nearly made her abandon the anger that she had been husbanding since learning that he was in Gangtok. But she held on to her self-discipline and let the hurt and the fury carry her through the confrontation. She told herself that she could have accepted being informed that it had been great fun but it was just one of those flings but she knew that it wasn't true, she still believed that he had been as genuine as she still was, which made it all the more unacceptable. Steve Manthos' nasty jibe about Max only being interested in tits and ass had led to her storming out of their Delhi apartment, her furious retort left hanging in the air.

'There's more man in his little finger than in your crabby little body, wanker!'

She left her car in the car park and walked down the drive, trying to make sense of it. Despite the fact that they had only faced each other for a matter of seconds she had sensed the same warmth in his eyes, his body language was awkward but not repelling her. She had wanted to reach out to him and yet hit him at the same time…it was incomprehensible.

She was unaware for how long she had been walking until she found herself in the flower show centre facing a rhododendron, its trumpet-shaped vermillion flower drawing her attention. She relaxed. This was the image that she summoned for herself when she meditated. Perhaps such a fortuitous event was telling her to be patient.

The urgent beeping of the locator drew the havildar's eye to the LED screen: the target was moving.

'*Ke ho?*' The teenager who had been admiring the Bullet 500 pointed at the screen.

'Just my GPS.'

'Magic.' The youngster enthused, his eyes glowing. The havildar started the engine and eased the machine through the little crowd of admirers in the car park of the supermarket. With one last friendly backward wave the bike cleared its audience. Ordinarily the havildar was happy to explain the finer points of its design features but too close an interest was to be avoided at all costs and duty called. The screen showed the target travelling south on the 31A heading for Upper Tadong, a 500 to 750 metre gap was comfortable, no chance of being spotted. The havildar would have loved to see just how fast the Bullet could travel on these mountain roads but discipline won out. Apart from the time spent maintaining surveillance in Kalimpong which had involved concealment in a shallow earth body cavity under a loose canopy of leaves and twigs, this mission was proving to be a non-event of boring proportions. Going through the weapon check drills was automatic, even on the bike. Leaning back a little brought the top of the KA-Bar against the spine, the MP7A1 had been cleaned and cleared immediately upon waking and now rested in its clip under the false top of the fuel tank. It was the havildar's favourite weapon, light enough to use in one hand with remarkably little recoil, it was accurate and its 4.6mm rounds provided all the penetration necessary. It was a mark of the Commander's recognition that the havildar had one of the only four MP7's in the unit. Typical defence ministry parsimony, denying the country's elite special forces a general issue. General Singh threatened to buy them himself to shame the government into purchasing them. The havildar grunted contemptuously. The sudden directional change of the cursor showed that the target had left the 31A and was travelling west on the Rumtek Road. Two minutes later the havildar took the same turning. The rain that had started on leaving

Gangtok now increased in intensity. It was time to close the distance to the target. In these conditions with the limited visibility a one-minute gap was appropriate.

Kim's sudden appearance was still preying on Max's mind as he drove the Land Rover along the winding road to Rumtek. The early monsoon rains were already gaining intensity and he examined the hill face on his nearside for any early signs of slippage. A torrent of water was cascading onto the wide road over a culvert just ahead of him, bouncing off and rushing down the mountain on his offside. An air horn blasted immediately behind him and a battered Tata Safari SUV bulled its way alongside him, forcing him almost into the nullah next to the cliff face.

'Bastard!' Max felt his nearside wheels dipping and wrenched the Land Rover back onto the road. The Safari had no lights on but that was not unusual, despite being dangerous, it probably didn't have any lights anyway. But he chided himself for allowing his attention to wander. Having overtaken him the Safari did not appear to be in any great hurry and was now travelling more slowly than Max had been. The rear window had some sort of screen across it, he could not quite make out whether it had been boarded over but he could not see inside it. The Land Rover's windscreen wipers were thudding away aggressively but visibility was erratic. The road widened temporarily as it met another culvert. Suddenly the rear of the Safari loomed right into his path and he had to stamp hard on the brakes, coming to a halt no more than four feet behind it. The doors of the Safari opened and three, no, five men climbed out. Even if he had not seen that they were all carrying weapons of some description he could not have failed to register the threat. Throwing the Land Rover into reverse he started to back up the road but even as he did so he knew there was no way he could drive out of the situation on these roads in these conditions. He was virtually blind to the road behind him. But he had created a bit more space for himself. He left the engine running and pulled the handbrake on. They had not even broken into a run, so confident that he couldn't get away. He cursed himself for leaving the XDM in his gun case back at the hotel. Max unlatched the driver's door but didn't open it. Reaching up with both hands as though he was surrendering his fingers eased the pickaxe handle out of its retaining clips in the roof and he twisted his body partly towards the driver's door.

The nearest man was carrying a length of chain and he swung it at the radiator and grinned at Max with betel-stained teeth, shouting something unintelligible at the one who had got out of the Safari on the same side as himself. This one laughed as he approached the Land Rover driver's door leaning forward a little and smacking a machete into the palm of his left hand. The laugh was swallowed as Max's bunched legs kicked the door straight into his face, the top of it caught him across the eyes and he staggered back, his arms windmilling as he lost his balance and fell off the road down the mountainside.

Max knew that he had only seconds to exploit the element of surprise and shot out of the vehicle using the pickaxe handle as though it was a bayonet. He lunged the end of it into the chain man's midriff and swung the end round as if he was delivering a butt stroke to the head. It connected with a satisfying crack of bone. Out of the corner of his eye he caught movement behind him and guessed that some of them had circled around the back of the Land Rover. Instinctively he swung the pickaxe handle backwards like a club but it only connected with the upper structure of the Land Rover. Pivoting round to his right he was faced by a heavily built man as tall as himself who swung a baseball bat at his head. Max took the blow on the shaft of the pickaxe handle. The force of it was like an electric shock in both hands which momentarily slowed his reaction so that the jab he aimed at the man's eyes lacked full strength. Nonetheless it made his attacker step back a pace and lose focus: not so his companion who shouldered his way forward. Max's eyes were half-closed against the driving rain but his gut clenched as he saw the barrel of a gun pointing straight at him. He heard the muffled crack.

The dot on the LED suddenly stopped. The havildar frowned and increased speed. Inexplicably, it started to move backwards. Intuitively, the havildar gunned the motor and lay into the curves of the road with a silent prayer that the tyres would retain friction on the rain slicked surface. Nudging the release catch on the gun box cover with an elbow the havildar's eyes were covering the road and the LED and silently praising the designer of the goggles that retained almost clear vision against the curtain of water through which the machine cut. Judging to a nicety the proximity of the dot on the screen to the target's location the engine was throttled back rounding a bend in the road and the situation was starkly clear. Despite the fact that the rain washed a uniform shapelessness into the figures the victim was unmistakably the target, surrounded by attackers. The havildar braked to a stop, both boots on the ground, reacting to the immediacy of the attacker who was bringing his weapon to bear on the target. Well-honed intuition laid the MP7's sights into the mass of the attacker as the trigger was squeezed, the shot felling the man in a half-spin. The scene froze for a second, possibly two before the target was defending himself against the big man swinging a baseball bat. A man wielding a machete was manoeuvring for an attacking position and a figure suddenly appeared standing on the bonnet of the Land Rover, coming up behind the target with a weapon in his hand. The havildar sighted reflexively, squeezed the trigger and watched him collapse onto the roof. Eyes back on the target as he traded blows with the big man wielding the baseball bat. Running forward the havildar registered that the target was driving the big man back with short fast swings and jabs, keeping him off balance without space to swing the bat. What the target could not see was the man coming up behind him, holding the machete above his shoulder. It was only at the last second that this one saw the havildar. He tried to bring the machete down towards the havildar's head but re-directing it made it lose force before it glanced off the crash helmet and the havildar smashed the stock of the MP7 into his jaw. The man staggered back towards the open side of the road and the havildar kicked his feet from under him. Momentum did the rest and he disappeared down the side of the mountain.

A gasp of pain made the havildar swing round, the baseball bat hit the ground and the big man turned and started to run back up the road. The MP7 was back up into the shoulder and was coming to bear when the target shouted.

'*Nagara!*' The havildar's eyes flicked across.

'*Bhayo, bhayo!*' It was a command and the havildar obeyed then pointed at the two dead men.

'*Naxalites.*'

Max nodded. His chest was heaving as he took in the scene. Whoever his rescuer was clearly had no compunction in killing his attackers. Pointing at their vehicle, he gestured towards the open side of the road with his head then jogged up the slight gradient to the Safari. The steam coming out of the exhaust pipe told him that the engine was still running. Reaching in through the driver's door he released the handbrake and the vehicle began to roll slowly back towards the flat section of road over the culvert. Walking beside it with one hand on the steering wheel he angled the rear towards the open side of the mountain, then when the rear wheel was no more than two metres from the edge of the road, he jumped away and watched it gain momentum then go crashing down the mountainside.

'Saheb.' Holding the feet of one of the remaining attackers, the havildar was dragging the corpse towards the edge. Max grabbed the wrists and together they swung it out into the void. The havildar kicked the gun across the road and sent it after its owner.

Max grabbed a handful of clothing and slid the body on the roof of the Land Rover onto the road from where they dragged it to the edge and then shoved it after the car. With the sweat and rain running into his eyes, Max had to screw them up to see. The motorbike laid flat on the road and the crash helmet told him how the stranger had arrived. His commands in Nepali had been followed and the spoken accent pointed to a Nepalese. Introductions were overdue. But not here.

'Get your bike and follow me.' The havildar came momentarily to attention, the MP7 held tight into the side of the body before walking quickly back towards the Bullet. As Max climbed back into the Land Rover he had no doubt that he was dealing with a soldier and it was not rocket science to guess on whose orders.

A few kilometres further along the road towards Rumtek Max pulled in beside an empty road maintenance hut. He stood in the open doorway until the soldier dismounted and followed him inside, out of the rain.

'You've been following me on the orders of Mr Fernandes.'

'No Saheb.'

'Alright, but you are acting on the orders of a superior officer.' Max had no intention of playing games.

'Saheb.' The havildar nodded.

'But you're not permitted to tell me who?'

'Huzoor.' Grateful though he was for the timely rescue, Max was irritated by the official stonewalling. There was also something not quite right about the soldier but he couldn't put his finger on it.

'Look, you're armed with an MP7 which means that you probably belong to COBRA or the Black Cats. You're a first class shot and,' he pointed his finger at the visor of the helmet, 'your rules of engagement give you authority to shoot to kill, which you just did, twice, knocked another one over the side of the *khud* and helped me dispose of the evidence.' Now that he was close up and there was no rain masking his vision, he could see the eyes and suddenly he knew what it was that had been troubling him.

'And you're a woman.' He could not keep the surprise out of his tone. The helmet was lifted up and the short hair shaken loose as she stood to attention.

'Havildar Dewan of the National Security Guards, Colonel Saheb.'

'The Black Cats.' Max nodded slowly, his suspicions confirmed.

'Saheb.' The response was mechanical, strictly regimental. She could not be more than in her late twenties, had just shot two men and helped him dispose of the evidence but gave no sign of having been affected. Not surprising that she was a sergeant. He offered his hand.

'I'm indebted to you, Havildar.'

'It's my duty, huzoor.' She shook his hand without removing her glove.

'In the circumstances, I think I'd better know what your orders are.' The havildar was silent, her eyes measuring him, calculating whether and if so what to disclose. He decided to ease the tension.

'I know your name and rank and your unit: you don't have to tell me anything more.' He allowed himself a faint smile. 'But now that you've shown your hand.' He left her to draw her own conclusions. She compressed her lips for a second.

'My orders were to keep a watch over you and take whatever action I thought necessary.' She paused, a slight frown passed across her face like a passing cloud. 'It was necessary.'

'You're damn right it was necessary.' Max was irritated that she should think she had to justify her actions. 'But now that we've disposed of the *badmas* what happens to you?'

'I have to report back and wait on my orders.' He was tempted to say that this was a statement of the obvious but held his tongue.

'Stand easy.' He chided himself for having kept her at attention. 'Alright. I'm going to the Rumtek Monastery, then I'll go back to the hotel. You have my mobile number?'

'Huzoor.' She probably had his inside leg measurement too but he needed to know if they were to open a channel of communication.

'Yours?'

'9535587.'

'Call me after you've received your orders.' He nodded a salute and walked out of the hut. Though he was loath to admit it, Fernandes had assessed the situation accurately. The Chinese were intent on having him removed from the equation. So, what else might he expect? If, as he felt confident, the treasure was to be moved in the next 36 hours, could they summon up another gang of murdering hoodlums that quickly? Perhaps it had not been a good idea to let the big guy run away. Well, he surmised, it was highly improbable that any further attack would be made in the time it would take to get to Rumtek and back. As he hauled himself into the seat of the Land Rover he registered that he was soaking wet: not the ideal image to present to Shakti.

The old man had been easy to locate and was patently relieved, quite apart from the exchange of passwords, he was dealing with someone who answered the description of the person he had been told to expect. Bald and with a face like a dried prune, his eyes lit up when Max spoke to him in Tibetan and the smile, albeit revealing no more than a few discoloured teeth, was genuine. He gestured towards a roofed over walkway beside what appeared to be a series of rooms and spoke quietly as they walked, gesturing from time to time as though pointing out features on the temple compound.

'*Dasho* Geljen appointed me to look after His Holiness's interests at Rumtek.' The old man's pride filled each word. 'These people…' He made a dismissive gesture towards the monastery buildings and spat onto the wooden floor, '…they do not follow the true path.' He angled his face up towards Max. 'All they think about is the money but it isn't theirs, it doesn't really belong to the Dalai Lama either. It belongs to Tibet.' His voice dropped and he mumbled incoherently. Max had been loath to interrupt him but felt that he was drifting.

'When are they going to move it?'

'Eh?'

'The treasure.'

'Yes, they will take it away.' Max began to worry that the old man was havering. He put his hand gently on Shakti's shoulder.

'When? When will they take it away?'

'Tomorrow. I told you already.' Now was not the time to argue.

'Morning, afternoon, night-time, do you know when?'

'After nightfall.'

'How can you be sure?'

'"Don't take it out of the vaults until it's dark", that's what I heard the Rinpoche say.' They had reached the end of the walkway and the old man gestured with his head for Max to follow him. They walked quickly through the narrow passages between the buildings, Shakti's gait suddenly made Max think of the Gollum and he had to restrain his smile. The path became increasingly muddy and there were furrows carved by vehicle tyres so that they had to step from the top of one ridge to another to keep their boots out of the puddled mud. The old man turned back, grabbed hold of Max's arm and put his finger to his lips, then pointed into what appeared to be some sort of makeshift garaging. There were a couple of Toyota 4×4s, an elderly Safari and a Tata half-truck with a canvas cover over its rear.

'That one.' Max bent down so that he could hear the man's whispers. 'The one with the white splash on the front. That young fool Lyangsong knocked a pot of paint over it. They told me to clean it off but I didn't do it, let the fool do it himself, he's the driver.'

'OK. Let's go.' Max had made a mental note of the registration number of the truck.

'This way.' Shakti pulled him towards a different alleyway which soon led to the open apron in front of the monastery buildings. Max put a folded wad of rupee notes into the old man's hand.

'No, I don't...' Max cut him off.

'Yes, I'm paying you for guiding me around the monastery.'

'Ah, yes, I understand.' The old man pocketed the notes inside his shapeless robe.

'I want you to do one more thing. Tomorrow, when the truck leaves here, call my mobile number. Don't speak, just call the number.' The gnarled features took a few seconds before comprehension registered, accompanied by a rasping chuckle.

Watching the access road to the monastery from a concealed vantage place amongst the trees the havildar reported in directly to General Singh by her TS2.

'You should have disposed of the one that ran away.'

'Yes, General.'

'But the target ordered you not to fire?' It was difficult to be sure over the satellite line but the havildar thought she detected a note of amusement in her commander's voice.

'General.'

'Well, a colonel outranks a havildar but a brigadier has the final say.' There was a moment's pause before a gruff acknowledgment. 'It was his call, man on the ground. We'll find the fleeing Naxalite anyway. Our people will clean up the mess. I assume you collected your spent shells?'

'Huzoor.'

'Good. Stay with the target, and continue to use your discretion. Out.' The line went dead. The havildar hoped that the target would take tonight off. She needed a few hours' uninterrupted sleep to allow her equilibrium to cope with having killed the two men. She had no doubts that it had been necessary but retaining an objective frame of mind drew on her inner resources. People thought that just because you were a soldier, killing was part of the job. Facing an enemy who was intent on killing you, as she had in Kashmir, was a question of survival but Sikkim was not a war zone, even if the Naxalites had meant to kill the target. Though she had stuffed away her Buddhist upbringing into a distant corner of her mind, she could still hear her master's teachings whispering to her about the sanctity of all living beings. How her thoughts travelled from this to a sudden awareness of how attractive she found the target she could not recall. Though he had spoken softly, his voice had a mesmeric quality. She shook her head, sending the rain flying, as she reminded herself that he was the target, nothing more.

Gangkok

Sikkim

It was a shallow cave on the reverse slope from the road running south from Gangtok towards India, ideal for their purposes: part way up the hillside and concealed from curious eyes by the vegetation that spilled down from the overhang and more or less dry. Better still, it was no more than a 15-minute hike to the ambush position that Sergeant Xian had reconnoitred. Wu had checked on it and could find nothing to criticise, yet he was still uneasy. That they had eluded the Indians patrolling the border had been a great relief but Ji Guan's orders to return via the same route struck Wu as incredibly stupid. Driving a stolen truck full of PLA special forces on the main road through Gangtok which would certainly involve negotiating their way through at least two police checkpoints was tantamount to suicide. His problem was that both the sergeants had been present at the final briefing when Colonel Ji had spelled out the orders for the re-entry routing. Ji had made it sound like a sightseeing visit.

'This is a snatch. These are monks, not soldiers, so just bundle them out of the vehicle, truss them up and leave them well off the road. It'll be hours before they either free themselves or anyone comes looking for them, by which time you'll all be safe back in barracks.'

Unless it didn't go according to plan. In which case Wu would have to make a decision as to how best to extricate themselves. He had already varied the operational plan by ordering Chopsticks to travel in the truck so that he could SMS him the truck's progress, that would enable them to set up their ambush at the last minute. Colonel Ji should have thought of that but he hadn't. These hard men had their limitations. Well, he, Wu Zihan, was in command of this operation on the ground and the decisions were for him to take and he had no intention of providing a target for the filthy Indians or worse, spending time in an Indian prison.

Max knew that he was not being honest with himself. Operationally, his team was more than adequate for the task in hand: though they were not ex-soldiers, Nyima and Dendi were almost as totally dependable as Deepraj and both were as tough as old boots. His locally acquired troops were all ex-army and highly experienced guerrillas, exactly what he needed for this operation. So, why involve the havildar unless his motives were ulterior? He had rationalised briefing her on his plan simply to keep her in the picture. Clearly, she had been shadowing him since Delhi, so there was little point in leaving her in the dark about their plan. God forbid that her shooting skills would be required against the monks, but his predeliction for contingency plans was nudging him to manoeuvre her into providing a backup role. It would also enable them to leave the hired motorbike in Gangtok, so avoiding another loose end. He hit the pre-dial button.

'Colonel.'

'Meet me at the entrance to the *Gurudwara* at 08.15.'

'Saheb.'

She waited in the shadows until she was sure that no-one was paying him any attention, then fell into step quietly beside him.

'What I'm going to say will not conflict with your orders.' She gave a non-committal 'Hmm'. He gave her a sideways glance.

'You know what I intend to do?'

'Saheb.' She nodded.

'The treasure will be moved from the Rumtek Monastery tomorrow after dark, my team will move into position tonight.' He gave her a detailed account of the plan and the map reference of the location for the interception. 'I expect to receive a signal when the truck leaves Rumtek.' He paused. 'But I'm not entirely confident that it will be sent. You could remove the element of doubt.'

'You want me to signal you when it leaves the monastery.' It was not a question.

'Exactly.' She was silent for a little while and he decided not to push it.

'Whilst I am keeping watch at Rumtek I shan't be maintaining surveillance on you.'

'But you will know where I am.'

'True.' Again she paused in thought. 'Why not have one of your men keep the watch on Rumtek?' She looked up at him from the corner of her eye. He smiled.

'I don't know how many people will be on the truck and I need to overwhelm them with numbers. You can free up one of my men.' She digested this for a moment then gave a little nod.

'*Hunchha*, huzoor.' Good. He really wanted Deepraj to drive the Land Rover as backup for the job. Under other circumstances he would have invited her for a drink to give him an opportunity to get to know her but this only existed in his mind.

The rains had cleared the air which was sweet, the scent of the water on the trees and buildings seasoned it and he breathed it in. He struggled a little with his conscience: he had only told her of getting the treasure to the river, not about what happened after that. Caution dictated that she only learn what was immediately necessary; whether or not her orders came from Fernandes he had no doubt that the intelligence chief was behind this and bitter experience had taught him never to trust the devious bastard. Still, he did not doubt her intelligence, she would follow them to the river RV and draw the obvious conclusion.

'We're going to ship the cargo down river, it'll avoid being intercepted on the road.' She nodded.

'Thank you for telling me.'

'I appreciate your co-operation.'

'*Tik chha*.' He smiled to himself, her use of the ubiquitous Nepali expression meant everything and nothing.

'Thank you and good night.' Facing her he was struck again by that elusive quality of something he could not put a name to but which he found curiously attractive. There was a certain contradiction between the soft voice and the ruthless efficiency that he had observed.

'Goodnight, Saheb.' She turned away and moments later she had blended into the shadows of the night. He shook his head disapprovingly. 'Mind on the job Devlin.'

Rumtek Monastery

Sikkim

1940 hours

Persuading Shakti to let him drive the truck had been easy; though the old man had grumbled, Lyangsong got the impression that in reality he was relieved. What really frightened him was when Tenzing said that he had to be on the truck and it was up to Lyangsong to fix it. Even without knowing why, he could think of no legitimate reason for his presence. Fortunately, the Rinpoche was so preoccupied with getting everything loaded onto the truck that he had given him a cursory wave of acknowledgment when Lyangsong had asked if his 'cousin' could accompany him on the journey. It took longer than expected to load the wicker baskets into the rear of the truck and the two soldier monks who were guarding the consignment were in a foul mood which was not improved when they discovered that Tenzing was already in the driving cab next to Lyangsong.

'My cousin will help us unload at Singtam.' He volunteered in the hope that this would take some of the anger out of their faces. Both monks clutched a shotgun which Lyangsong found incongruous against their robes and only served to make him sweat more.

'*Kham-n.*' Tenzing greeted the older of the two monks as he swung himself up into the cab and threw himself onto the bench, shoving Tenzing hard against Lyangsong. Muttering to himself, the monk held his shotgun across his lap with his elbow digging into Tenzing's side. Leaning slightly out of the window, he shouted at his companion.

'You'd better get in the back.' This was acknowledged with an angry grunt. A minute later a loud bang on the rear panel of the driving cab that gave Lyangsong a shock signalled that he was on board.

'Drive.' The monk ordered him. He could sense the anger in the two men sharing the cab with him and tried to concentrate on getting the truck out of the yard, a task rendered even more difficult because the gear lever was tight up against Tenzing's thigh and perilously close to the end of the shotgun barrels. Keeping his eyes firmly on the road ahead he heard the metallic snap as the monk closed the gun though he didn't see the cartridge that had been inserted into the breech of the shotgun. Nor was he aware of the fingers of Tenzing's right hand tapping out a brief SMS on his mobile.

As the truck swayed a little on the uneven road and its tail lights receded into the night, Shakti dialled the number he had been given, listened for it to ring twice then disengaged.

'Why are you here?' The monk's voice sounded over the labouring engine's clattering growl as it tractored its way along the mountain road. His shaved head was half-turned towards Tenzing, his tone matching the angrily puckered skin of his forehead.

Tenzing was ready with his answer.

'My cousin,' he said, indicating Lyangsong with his head, 'suggested I offer my help to the Rinpoche and I was very happy to be of service to the monastery.'

Now that they were well on the road, there was no realistic chance that the monk would query it. This was received with a dismissive grunt. Lyangsong gripped the wheel more tightly and hoped that the monk's curiosity had been satisfied. Had the Rinpoche not been so preoccupied he doubted that he would have agreed to allow Tenzing to come. He slowed the truck down as they approached the junction with the N31 highway. There was no other traffic on the road and he turned right for Singtam. After a couple of minutes the monk began to hum tunelessly to himself. Tenzing glanced at him out of the corner of his eye, assessing whether it was safe to tell Captain Wu that the monk had a weapon. Crushed together, he realised he'd never get away with it, sending the SMS had made him break out into a sweat. To hell with him, Wu was a soldier and supposed to be able to handle himself. Despite his anxiety, the twists and turns of the road as it contoured the mountainside made him feel sleepy and his head kept dropping forward. A sudden harsh application of the brakes shook him awake.

'Don't stop!' The monk shouted at Lyangsong.

'But...'

'Drive! Go! Keep driving!' Armed figures in camouflage uniform stood in the middle of the road waving them down with torchlights. Two of the soldiers now pointed their weapons at the windscreen. Lyangsong had heard too many stories of trigger happy Indian Army soldiers so he ignored the monk's order and stamped on the brakes causing Tenzing and the monk to lurch forward violently. A torch light appeared beside the open window on the driver's side.

'Out!' His hand found the door handle as he moved to obey the order. A massive explosion filled the cabin deafening Lyangsong; his entire system shut down but his eyes registered what he could not hear. The monk's face was contorted in rage, his mouth working manically and Lyangsong knew that it was directed at him but he was paralysed. Then, as though he was watching one of those silent movies that the teachers at school had once shown him, the monk's head exploded. He felt the wetness slap into his face and suddenly he was lying on the road beside the truck. As though from a distance he began to hear voices screaming though he could not make out what was being said. What made him do it, he could not tell, but he rolled away from the truck until the road fell away and he was falling, bouncing off rocks and trees, then he was swallowed by a black hole.

Wu Zihan could hardly believe his eyes. Sergeant Xian took the force of the shotgun straight in his face and was knocked backwards. Without waiting for orders Sergeant Xu shot the monk in the cab and another man beside him. He had the impression that there had been three in the cab but there was no sign of a third man. Following the plan Wu had made, four of his men ran towards the back of the truck, two on each side. Two more shotgun blasts preceded the dull reports of his men's AK52s. Wu ran towards the back of the truck following Sergeant Xu. A monk lay over the tailboard, blood dripping down from his fingers and one of his own soldiers sat on the road being attended to by two of his men. He nearly tripped over another inert figure on the ground before recognising yet another soldier. One of his men appeared out of the interior of the truck.

'No-one inside, just this one.' He slammed the butt of his rifle down on the lifeless head of the monk.

Wu's mind was racing, what about their contact, had Xu shot him? He was certain there had been three men in the cabin.

'Sir.' Wu looked down at Xu who was checking on the man on the ground. The sergeant looked up. 'Dead.'

Wu pointed towards the driver's side of the truck. 'Xian?' Another soldier appeared beside him. 'Head's blown off.'

'Load our dead and wounded into the back of the truck, toss the bodies in the cabin and this one down the mountain side and let's go.' He turned to Sergeant Xu. 'There was a third man in the cab, the driver, where's he gone?' Xu shrugged.

'Do you want us to look for him?' Wu shook his head. If he was gone, he was gone, speed was what mattered. As if to reinforce this their heads turned as they heard the sound of a vehicle engine approaching them from the direction of Gangtok. Xu glanced at Wu.

'Take it out?' Wu nodded and Xu signalled to the others to spread out. The headlights swung around the bend and Xu watched the driver as he braked to a stop to avoid colliding with the truck. It was an easy shot and the man slumped into his seat as the jeep rolled into the back of the truck. He ordered two men to dispose of the driver down the hillside and looking at Wu, made a head movement to ask whether the jeep should follow him.

'No. Let's go. We'll drive south through Rangpo then back up to Rangli, dump the truck about 1,000 metres from the border and exfiltrate through the Jelep-la Pass.' Xu's face was impassive but his eyes closed down to slits.

'Colonel Ji ordered us to go north through Gangtok to the Natu-la Pass.' His tone was neither questioning nor critical, simply a restatement but Wu bridled at what he read as insubordination. He waved his rifle towards the cab of the truck to lend force to his words.

'I have changed the orders.' With Xian and another man dead, another wounded, his force was reduced to seven fully effective. He checked his mobile once more in case their contact had messaged him: nothing. They had what they had come for, now it was his responsibility to get them back across the border. Xu held his eyes for two or three seconds then turned away and issued the orders. In less than three minutes they were on their way, two men in the jeep, Wu with Xu in the cabin of the truck and the fifth member of the team with the dead and injured in the back. He used the butt of his rifle to knock out the rest of the shattered windscreen as he decided not to report yet; having disobeyed Colonel Ji's orders the best plan was to keep radio silence until they were close to the border.

The havildar had been following the truck closely and heard the tyres screeching on the road. She switched off the ignition and coasted forward silently until she had sight of it. As it came into view she heard the crash of the shotgun followed moments later by muzzle flash from a position ahead of the truck. She registered that whoever was attacking was using moderators, that signalled professionals. Dropping the Bullet into the nearside nullah, she slipped forward, hugging the hillside. Armed figures in camouflage dress ran down either side of the truck and she heard shouting in what she recognised as Chinese. As the first two figures rounded the back of the truck a figure rose up and both barrels of a shotgun were discharged before there was the flash of shots fired from the right-hand side and the man in the truck fell forward, the shotgun spilling out of his hands.

She felt momentarily exposed. She could drop flat in the nullah but if anyone caught a glimpse of the bike it would give her position away. If they turned the truck around, the chances were that they would see her. She looked back up the road for better concealment, conscious that she would have to wait for them to fire up the truck's engine to camouflage the sound of her own motor starting and then retrace her route until she found somewhere. Her thoughts were interrupted by the sound of a vehicle engine approaching from the direction of Gangtok. She pulled up the hood of her camo jacket and threw herself into the nullah. With her face pressed into the damp soil she held her breath as the vehicle passed her position then slowly raised her head in time to see the jeep's brakes being slammed on. She saw the flash and heard the dulled double tap, then the jeep slid slowly into the back of the truck. She heard what sounded like orders being shouted out then what appeared to be a lifeless body was dragged out from the driver's side of the jeep and tossed down the side of the mountain. Further shouting resulted in two men getting into the jeep and starting it up. To her relief the truck resumed its journey south closely followed by the jeep. She thumbed the target's pre-set mobile number.

'Speak.'

'Your truck has just been grabbed by what I think are Chinese soldiers. They've also snatched a jeep. All the civilian occupants appear to have been killed and the vehicles are now heading in your direction.'

'How many bandits?'

'I saw five plus one wounded, two in the jeep, the rest in the truck.'

'Weapons?'

'AKs, silenced.'

'Estimate their ETA my position?'

'Ten to twelve minutes.' There was a pause before he responded.

'Can you take out the two in the jeep?'

'OK.' She had no difficulty in reconciling that with her orders or simply to exact retribution for the murder of the jeep's driver.

'Can you watch my back?' She decided that this was precisely what she was doing and ended the call. Motoring forward in pursuit of the jeep she hit another pre-set.

'Singh.'

'Commander, call sign 65.'

'Go ahead.'

'I think a PLA special forces unit has just ambushed the truck and a civilian jeep and is headed towards the target's position.'

'*Eh Bhaguwan*! How many?'

'I make five effective. They've probably killed the occupants of the truck and the driver of the jeep. I'm following. What are my orders?'

'Stay with the target, give him backup as necessary, can't have the bloody Chinese army playing around in my backyard and getting away with it. Give me a SITREP as soon as you can.'

'Commander.' The havildar guessed that she was their force's only asset within several hundred miles, which left her commander with no options. Hers were the only boots on the ground and she found this entirely satisfactory.

Lyangsong felt as though his face was on fire as his consciousness returned. His fingers went to his cheek and the fire spread to his hand and was alive. He opened his eyes and screamed as the red ants burned their way across his skin. Still half-dazed he shook his hand violently and swept his face with his sleeve, knocking the vicious insects away. Disoriented, his head aching enough to make him want to retch he looked about him trying to make sense of where he was. A trickle of blood ran down his forehead from a gash on his scalp. He brushed it away from his eye, then everything came back to him in a rush and he threw up. Dragging himself upright, he grabbed hold of a thick bush to steady himself. There was sufficient moonlight filtering through the low canopy of trees for him to realise that he must have tumbled 50 or more metres down from the road. His ribs hurt when he breathed in but his arms and legs were all functioning. Slowly he began to scrabble his way back up the hillside. He paused, suddenly terrified in case the attackers were waiting for him above. Listening intently and straining for sight of any movement above him, he stood silently for what he estimated to be about three minutes. Then neither hearing nor seeing anything untoward, he began to climb cautiously; halfway up he was suddenly aware of a body sprawled diagonally across the hillside. He thought his heart would stop with fear and he froze. The figure was motionless and as he stared at it, there was a frightening familiarity about it. He eased himself forward, inch by inch. Reaching out he realised that his hand was trembling as he pulled the shirt tails away from where they had been caught up in the bushes and concealed the head. The sight of what was left of Tenzing's face made the bile rise in his gorge and he fought it down out of sheer terror that the noise would give away his position. Though he tried to keep still, his whole body shook for what must have been eight to ten minutes and there was neither sound nor movement above him, then he recommenced his climb. By the time he reached the road he was gasping for breath, the pain in his chest was sharp enough to make him whimper. Pulling himself painfully onto the macadam he wiped the sweat out of his eyes with his sleeve and as he did so he caught sight a mess of blood, bone and brain on the road. He retched violently and his head spun. As he staggered to his feet he wondered if he was the only survivor. It dawned on him that somehow he had to make a report to the police before anyone thought to blame him for what had happened.

'Change of plan.' Two precious minutes had been lost as he called everyone in for an emergency orders group.

'The Chinese Army has snatched the truck, killed the monks who were guarding it, grabbed a jeep that happened on the scene, killed its driver and they'll reach us in about eight minutes. Recovering the treasure means taking on professional Chinese military. We have to take them out before they shoot us. It's not what we planned so, if anyone wants out, go now.' He paused for a couple of seconds as he scanned their faces. No-one moved.

'Good. Anda.' He faced the big man. 'Drop a tree across the road, then go back to where you've sited the Bren up there.' He pointed to a position on the south side of the bend in the road some 45 metres distant. 'Whoever is in the back of the truck, they're yours, go.' He turned to Deepraj. 'Shoot the driver as soon as he stops, not before, we need the truck.' Looking at the twins, Max pointed to an elevated slab of rock some 30 metres back up the road on the mountain side. 'If anyone survives, it's your job to take them out.' They nodded and jogged back up the road. Max took out a stun grenade from the bag hung over his shoulder and handed it to Paad.

'I want you to lie in that nullah next to the mountain side. When the truck stops, pitch this into the back.' The little man grinned and walked away. Nyima frowned.

'What about us Saheb?' He indicated Dendi.

'I want you two out of the line of fire. Once we take control of the truck I'll need you to clear the tree off the road and then follow us in the Land Rover to Singtam.' He gave them a wry smile. 'I think you've had more than enough experience of being shot at by the PLA.' The Sherpas both managed to look disappointed. 'Now get yourselves round the next bend, out of sight.' As they trotted down the road Max joined Deepraj in the position they had prepared for themselves earlier.

'What if there is more than one man in the cabin?' Deepraj was adjusting the sling of the rifle and sighting it to where he anticipated the cab would be. Max laughed.

'You're the marksman.'

'Well, huzoor, I thought you said that the XDM was the best handgun in the world.'

'Just consider me as backup, you've got the L42.'

'Prefer the LWM, there's no suppressor on this.'

'You don't need anything fancy over this short distance, you could have used a short Lee Enfield.' This was greeted with a laconic 'Huzoor'. The buzz of the chainsaw sounded extraordinarily loud in the still night air. Max peered through the camouflage of bushes that concealed their position and breathed more easily as he heard the crack and rush of the tree's branches as it fell at a neat 90° angle across the road.

'I think he's done this before Saheb.' Deepraj murmured. Max heard the sound of Anda's boots on the road as he ran to where his Bren gun was positioned. He glanced down at his wristwatch, if the havildar's estimate was correct, they would hear the truck within the next minute. He hoped to God that there was no traffic between them and the oncoming PLA, that would really stuff their ambush plan, Paad would be too far forward and the chances of collateral damage would increase dramatically. Apart from his XDM and Deepraj's L42 his team's weaponry was inferior to whatever the PLA carried. He was relying on the element of surprise and their choice of terrain. He turned his head fractionally towards the bend in the road, there was something coming.

'Safari.' Deepraj said softly.

'Heads up.' Max spoke into the microphone taped to his head.

Captain Wu saw the tree across the road but he failed to notice that its base was cleanly cut, no roots. The specialist driving the truck beside him knew what it was.

'Ambush! Ambush!' He yelled as he tried to calculate his chances of crashing straight through but he realised that he didn't have enough speed and the tree was too big.

'Out! Out!' Gripping the steering wheel with one hand as it fought against the brakes and went into a skid he banged his fist against the back of the cab to drive home his message. Wu was not reacting. The truck came to a violent halt as it hit the tree, then suddenly lurched to its right. The driver was in the act of opening his door when the shot smacked his head against the cabin's rear wall. Wu snapped out of his shock, grabbed his AK52 and threw himself at the door but in his panic he grabbed the window lever. Max's shot entered his cheek and took off a large part of the left side of his face.

Xu saw the truck's brake lights come on as he heard the tyres burning their way to a forced stop. Instinctively he shouted 'Ambush!' as he rolled out of the open side of the jeep fractions of a second before he heard the *tung-ki-tung* of a semi-automatic weapon and the windscreen shattered. Caught between the side of the jeep and the face of the mountain he knew he would be an easy target. He rolled under the jeep just as the concussive sound of the grenade hit his ears. Despite being under the jeep the blast deafened him momentarily. The jeep had swung out wide as it came round the bend so that its offside was no more than half a metre from the edge of the road. He knew it was his only chance. Clutching his rifle into his body he half rolled, half threw himself over the side of the mountain. Bursts of gunfire covered the sound of him sliding erratically down the steep slope until he arrested his fall by grabbing hold of the bole of a bush. He strained his ears for the sounds of a firefight but all he could hear was that cursed LMG, whoever was firing it knew what he was doing. Now everything was a matter of survival. He hugged the earth, moulding himself into its contours.

Paad saw the driver of the jeep roll out before it collided with the back of the truck and dart forward bent double.

'*Sala!*' Paad raised himself up on one arm to toss the concussion grenade into the back of the truck then sank back into the nullah. The thump of the grenade puffed out the truck's canvas sides and he looked for movement on the offside of the truck. The jeep's driver was in a firing position flat on the road, facing away from him. Easing himself out of the nullah he snaked his way under the truck keeping his hunting knife parallel with the surface of the road. Either there was a sudden lull in the firing or the jeep driver's sixth sense kicked in and he turned his head just as Paad drew level with him. Beneath the truck there was little room for manoeuvre and Paad's knife hand shot out, straight into the man's neck. His face registered surprise as the blood pumped out of his carotid artery. Paad's free hand grabbed the rifle and he hauled himself on top of the man, pulling his knife free before stabbing it into the top of the cervical spine. There was a convulsive jerk and then all resistance collapsed. Paad withdrew his knife and wriggled back slowly listening for any sign of resistance. He could see Ekeis' boots approaching the rear of the truck on the hill side of the road. He rolled out carefully and rose into a crouch just as Ekeis reached the corner of the truck and spoke into his microphone.

'Anda, anyone left inside?' He couldn't hear the response but Ekeis pulled himself up the nearside of the truck and swung over the tailboard. As he did so, Beis mounted the rear offside, swinging his rifle with its barrel mounted torch across the interior. A muffled shot punched the silence and Ekeis fell back. Beis caught the shooter in his sights, stretched out across the top of the wicker baskets, blood on a face which jerked as the first round hit it. Systematically he worked the bolt and shot everybody he could see.

'Ekeis is hit!' He shouted as he fired the last round and changed magazines. Sweeping the interior of the truck he counted six bodies.

Satisfied that they were all dead, he moved across to where his brother was slumped against the side wall. Max climbed up over the backboard as the torchlight fell on Ekeis' face. The dark stain spreading across his shirt front indicated internal injuries. He gave his brother a crooked smile.

'Get the bastard, *bhai*?'

'Of course.' Beis moved to open his brother's shirt, then angrily. '*Murka!* Why didn't you wait for me to cover you?' Max put a restraining hand on his arm as he opened Ekeis' shirt and examined the wound. The entry wound was small, but he knew that the damage would be extensive if the 7.62 round had hit bone or muscle. He applied a field dressing then lifted one of the man's hands and placed it across the dressing.

'We'll get you to a hospital. Hold this on.'

'No Saheb.' His eyes closed momentarily. 'I'm gone...' Anda swung himself over the tailboard.

'We have friendly doctors who'll ask no questions.'

'The nearest one?' If he wasn't dealt with quickly his chances of survival were paper thin, he was all too well aware of Gurkhas' tendency to give up if there were internal injuries. They were unutterably stoic with damage that was visible but what they couldn't see assumed overwhelming dimensions and they had a tendency to give up on their resistance.

'Singtam.'

'Right.' He gripped Ekeis' shoulder. 'We're taking you to hospital and we'll get you fixed. So, stay with us.' It was an order, something more likely to achieve results than words of comfort. He spoke to Anda who was standing on the road looking in. 'Carry him carefully. We'll transfer him to the Land Rover, it's a better ride.'

'Here Saheb.' The big man passed up the medical kit. Max gave Ekeis a shot of morphine. Deepraj swung himself up onto the tailboard and Max pointed to the wounded man.

'I'll take him with Anda and Beis in the Land Rover, Anda knows where to go.' A sudden surge of drumming on the canvas roof signalled a monsoon downpour, rain sheeted onto the road and he had to raise his voice to be heard.

'Drive the truck with Paad, Nyima and Dendi and RV with Arun.' Deepraj surveyed the carnage in the back of the truck, glanced out at the rain that curtained them off then looked at Max.

'We can't afford to delay Saheb, Arun was worried about the river being in spate.' He jerked his head towards Anda. 'Can't he take care of him?' Max shook his head.

'No, he's my responsibility, more important than the treasure.' Deepraj held his eyes for a moment and then shrugged acquiescence. He understood Max's refusal to abandon any of his men but that left him with the responsibility for a stolen truck loaded with gold, cash and several dead Chinese soldiers.

'What about the bodies?'

'Load them in the truck and their weapons in the Land Rover.' Max clambered out over the backboard.

'What'll I say if we're stopped?'

'You'll think of something.' Deepraj saw that Max was smiling, the water streaming down his face.

'Don't stop but don't kill anyone…unless there are any more PLA bandits.'

'Huzoor.' In his mind's eye he saw the old *Subadar* who had instructed him on his senior NCO's course. 'All sahibs are mad but they're *our* sahibs.' This had been a crazy job from the beginning but it had just got worse and their chances of success were getting smaller and smaller, as was their chances of receiving the reward for pulling it off. They covered Ekeis with a ground sheet and manhandled him out of the truck and into the Land Rover, an operation that Max was encouraged to note caused him to cry out on a couple of occasions: if he was still in pain he was still alive.

'Dendi, move that jeep so it doesn't block the road.' He swung himself up into the Land Rover checking his watch before shouting to Deepraj.

'We'll probably reach the RV at more or less the same time.' A quick look into the back seat showed him that Anda had wedged himself sideways on with Ekeis' head pillowed on his lap. It was the best they could do. He knew he'd have to balance speed with as smooth a ride as possible but speed would be the priority. He gave a sympathetic glance towards Ekeis.

So far they had been lucky, there had been no traffic or people to come and gawp but it couldn't last. He put the windscreen wipers on 'fast' and set off down the road. So far he had not disclosed the havildar's existence to anyone else but time was running against them. Driving one-handed in these conditions was imprudent, to say the least, taking your eyes off what could be seen of the road was bloody stupid. He was imprudently stupid. She answered on the second ring.

'I watched what happened. One of your men shot?'

'Abdominal wound, looks bad. I'm taking him to a friendly doctor.' She knew this meant one of the medics sympathetic to the Gurkha independence guerrillas and wondered whether to suggest that she accompany him to the nearest military hospital but the target anticipated her.

'Have to keep this off the books.'

'OK.'

'I'm going to abandon this truck with its full establishment of dead PLA soldiers on the Singtam-Rangpo road. Your people can take over from there.'

'Huzoor.' She paused. 'Are you going to tell me what your plans are?'

He knew this question was inevitable. It was obvious that she could follow them and would find out soon enough.

'I'm taking the load down river. I'll RV with the Land Rover near the Sevok Bridge and since you've obviously got a locator bug on my vehicle, you'll know where I am.' He paused then added as an afterthought. 'I'd appreciate it though if you can make sure that my wounded man isn't troubled by the authorities, if that won't clash with your orders.'

'Hmm.' He decided to interpret that as a yes.

'Thanks.' He ended the call.

The havildar called in and her commander picked up immediately.

'What's happening?'

'The target has done our job for us. The infiltration group are all dead. They're loaded onto the monastery's truck which will be abandoned on the Singtam Road. One of the target's men has an abdominal wound but they're looking after their own wounded.'

'Alright.' She thought she detected a grudging note of respect in his voice. 'Leave the *bahinchut* Chinese to me. Stay with the target.'

'He asked if we can keep his wounded man out of the hands of the local authorities.'

'*Acchibad*.' She was momentarily tempted not to mention the target's plan to use the river, she had begun to admire what he was doing and no-one had told her what her superiors intended to do with the man. Discipline won out.

'He's taking the treasure down the Teesta by boat, there's an RV just south of the Sevok Bridge.'

'How do you know he isn't fending you off with a story?'

'I don't, but they'd never make it down the road and it's imaginative.'

'Hmph.' She could tell that her commander was uncomfortable. He had to trust her judgment. When he replied, it was reluctantly condescending.

'It's your responsibility.' He mumbled something she did not catch.

'Say again.'

'I said it's on your head. Are you sure they got all the infiltrators?' She heard the doubt in his voice.

'It was a firefight in the dark but no-one was firing at them when it finished.'

'Fucking Chinese.'

'General.' It was the privilege of rank to shift the weight of responsibility down the line and the gap between a havildar and a general was a lot of privilege. He made his point by ending the call. She was philosophical about it; genuinely happy at having been selected for the task, she also acknowledged that Ranjit Singh was not some IT whizkid general, he was a decorated veteran who'd earned his position in the field. In any event, what choice did she really have? She wondered whether the Chinese had shot their bolt by now: infiltrating a special forces team had been an incredibly risky undertaking and it had ended in disaster. What else could they do?

Colonel Ji woke with a start. He had been watching his team's progress, its movement traced by the GPS in the sat-phones of Wu, Xian and Xu displayed on the LED map on his screen. It had been simple to interpret them having selected their ambush position and then they must have sprung the trap and started back except that Wu had disobeyed his orders and was heading south. Ji ground his teeth together but decided to give Wu the benefit of the doubt as the commander on the ground. Wu's options were limited, he'd have to exfiltrate via the Natu-la or Jelep-la passes. Silently cursing the man he set about alerting the border units to watch out for an incoming team. Satisfied that he had covered the contingencies, he had stretched out on a camp kot in the communications room and fallen asleep instantly.

'Sir?'

'What is it?' He shook his head clear.

'I think you should see for yourself, sir.' The screen showed the Sikkim road system in diagram format and next to it was a satellite photo of the same area. A pulsing pinpoint was stationary whilst two such pinpoints had separated and were moving south; he estimated that they were already about five kilometres apart. The stationary signal was a good 20 kilometres south of the ambush position, so whatever had happened was not directly related to that. He questioned the signals lieutenant sharply.

'After they left the ambush position did they stop anywhere before here?' His finger stabbed the stationary signal that pulsed at him as if offering a direct challenge.

'No, Colonel. All the signals stopped at this juncture for…' He consulted his notes, '…12 minutes. We maintained signal silence, as you ordered. It was when the LED locators separated by about 2.5 kilometres that I thought it necessary to inform you.' Ji could think of no good reason to leave one man behind, not at such a distance.

'What about the speed, has that accelerated or slowed?'

'Not noticeably Colonel.' If they had hit a police post, even if one man had been hit, he would have expected them to speed their way out. But that still left the unacceptable fact of leaving a man behind, that would be contrary to every rule in the book.

'Shit!' There was no way to avoid raising them on the satnav.

'Who is it?'

'Xu Xiping.'

'Call him for me.' Ji's eyes were glued to the LED screen, willing it to give up its story.

'Fox three.' Xu's voice was clear, his tone flat.

'Control, situation report.' There was a pause before Xu came back on the line. Then in short sentences he told Ji what had happened. The colonel's fingers gripped the handset, his knuckles turning white. Xu continued without interruption until he said that he was in covert pursuit of the truck. Momentarily, Ji's throat seemed to close off his airway. He swallowed to gain control of his vocal chords.

'Call in a SITREP every hour.' He closed the line and then remembered that he had not asked Xu if he was injured. He knew the man's character, he wouldn't mention it unless asked. He reasoned that anything that would have prevented Xu carrying out his orders would have been stated. Pulling the padded coat closely around him he stepped out into the refrigerated night air. It was a question of priorities: he had to recover Xu and the bodies, General Wang's bloody gold didn't begin to measure against the political leverage the Indians would acquire if any of them were left behind. He let the numbing wind blow onto his face, anaesthetising it as he grappled with the potential disaster to the PLA and the guaranteed disaster to his career. There was not a second's doubt in his mind, he'd have to put another team into the gunships for the fastest possible extraction. General Wang would have to be informed but the key question was when? He knew perfectly well that he should report to Wang immediately but the General was a political animal who had no sense of the responsibility that a commander owed to his men in the field. No, wait until the extraction was fully committed and then tell him. He managed what would have been a smile had he been able to move his facial muscles. He turned back into the command centre, called his opposite number in the PLA Air Force and gave him a quick run down.

'*Bushiba*! What a cock-up.' There was a pause as Air Force Colonel Zheng digested the ramifications. Ji's voice was controlled and peremptory.

'We'll have to go and pull them out, bodies and all.' Zheng paused before answering.

'I can get in under their radar but they'll soon pick me up…narrow window before they scramble out of Bagdogra. We'll know the minute they take off but that will be the cue for us to get the hell out of there…think you can do it?'

'No choice.'

'OK. I'll stand by a flight and wait on your call.' Ji heard a long intake of breath. 'Have you informed Confucius?' They shared a hearty contempt for General Wang who commanded the sector.

'What d'you think?'

'Wait until we're committed. He'll have you boiled into *maotai*.' It was dark humour and Ji knew that he'd be lucky to survive, whatever the outcome.

'*Xie xie* my friend.' They were both career military cadres who held their posts because they were highly regarded professionals but their links with their respective party cadres were tenuous. Ji was realist enough to know that he would be the scapegoat, the party could not abide failure. Might as well make his exit worthwhile and get his men back. He enjoyed a moment of professional pride that two officers were prepared to put their own careers or more on the line in the interests of their men. He speed-dialled his B team leader.

'Guo, stand by your team and get up here for a briefing in 10 minutes.'

'Sir.' Captain Guo had come up through the ranks, minimal formal education but totally dependable unlike Wu; too late to regret not having sent him in instead.

'Wu's team are dead, all except Xu. We're going in to bring them back. I'm coming this time.'

'Sir.' No surprise, no queries, Guo was old school.

'The Z-10s will take us in.'

'And out, sir?' The grim humour was not lost on Ji.

'If the blackies don't get us.'

Rumtek

Sikkim

As Sergeant Xu drove into the almost deserted main street of Rumtek the rain stopped as suddenly as it had started. He had not been able to catch up with the truck on the road but he could see approximately where it was located from the LED screen on his GPS which was tracking Captain Wu's mobile locator. The truck had been stationary close to the river for about 15 minutes but now it was on the move again and heading in his direction. The side streets were either in darkness or ill-lit. He stopped the jeep and reversed into one that afforded him a view of the road to his left then switched off the engine and killed the lights. He watched Wu's signal travel towards him then suddenly it moved off left at 90° to its track, travelled a distance he estimated could be no more than 100 metres then turned 90° again and took an erratic course before stopping. He zoomed in for an aerial view of Rumtek and identified the position of the truck. It was no more than 400 metres from his position. He swung himself out of the jeep, concealed his weapon under his camo jacket and keeping close to the buildings lining the street he set off towards where the truck had stopped. With his hood pulled over his head he was indistinguishable from the few people out at this time of the night. He had memorised the street plan and following in his head he soon reached the junction where the truck must have turned off. The houses were more thinly spaced here and petered out, giving onto a broad flat area of open ground surrounded by trees. About 150 metres towards the direction of the river he could just make out the shape of the truck which was parked close against a thick stand of trees. He cocked his rifle and hugging the trees at the perimeter of the area, advanced cautiously, stopping and listening for any sound that would indicate that the truck was guarded. By the time he was a few metres away his senses were telling him that it had been abandoned. He reached the back of the truck, hauled himself silently up so that he could see inside. There was no movement so he eased himself back down and slid along the side until he reached the driver's door. Keeping himself below the level of the window, he took hold of the handle then in one movement swung the door open and thrust the muzzle of his rifle into where the driver would have been. Nothing.

He wiped the sweat out of his eyes and moved quickly back and up into the rear of the truck. The narrow beam of his torch swept over the lifeless bodies of his comrades sprawled haphazardly on the planked bed of the truck. His anger was selective; he grieved for Xian with whom he had shared so much, worked to suppress the fury working its way up his chest at the waste of the other team members for whom he felt responsible, but he felt nothing but contempt for Wu who had led them into this trap. He brought himself under control and checked the map reference on his LED screen for the position at which the truck had been stationary before it had been driven here and abandoned. The cursor had been hard against the line of the river. It was time to call Colonel Ji.

East bank of the Teesta River
South of Rumtek

Arun wiped the sweat and rain off his face and surveyed the RIBs through part-closed eyes. The gold and currency packs had been loaded into big waterproof barrels and the lids sealed. If they went overboard they were designed to float but given their weight Arun thought it more likely they'd sink. He took in the state of the river which had already risen and broken bits of trees were being carried wildly along; as the level rose so whole trees would be wrenched from their roots and if one of them was thrown against a rib it would almost certainly capsize. He pulled back the sleeve of his anorak, 27 minutes past midnight, where the hell was Max?

'*Dai.*' Deepraj held out a mug. 'Jungle tea.' He grinned. Arun inhaled the aroma of the rum which heavily laced the dark condensed milk tea before taking swallowing a mouthful.

'What have you done with the truck?'

'Left it on that open area behind the houses at the river end of Rumtek, tucked under some trees. It'll take some time before they find it.' Arun nodded. That was not his immediate concern. He indicated the river with his head.

'This is going to be…interesting.'

'I was glad I wasn't coming with you but if the Saheb's not here soon I'll have to go.' Arun nodded. Deepraj continued.

'He says we have to meet this Bhunnia.' The contempt in his voice left no room for doubt as to his take on the the wisdom of this course. Though Arun shared this view of dealing with the moneylenders, he also knew that their capacity for risk was in direct proportion to the amount of the financial reward in it.

'Should be OK.' He drained his mug and handed it back. 'Thanks. I'll just check on the RIBs.' Not that anything needed to be done, both the RIBs were firmly anchored to the river bank in this little hyphen-shaped pool which provided a relatively safe harbour from the rushing water. But activity was an antidote to anxiety. He stepped up close to Gokul, the other river pilot, the sound of the river loud in his ears.

'Double check the lashings, we'll put the passengers for'ard of the barrels, that will help to keep the nose down.' The instructions were not necessary, Gokul was as experienced a river pilot as he was but they were both on edge; the river and its dangers even in normal times was their familiar but embarking in these conditions went against the grain. The cargo was another matter. If they were caught they'd be treated as armed robbers and the news about the dead Chinese soldiers added a whole new dimension to the operation. Deepraj came up to him and pointed at his watch.

'How *interesting* is it going to be?'

Arun waved towards the river that was rushing beside them so that the RIBs were straining against their mooring ropes.

'The two hours we've already lost have allowed the river to rise.' He left it to Deepraj to draw his own conclusion.

'Still a go?'

'Mmm.' Arun nodded but his expression registered his concern. He looked up towards where he expected Max to come from, willing him to appear.

'*Bhayo*.' They couldn't wait any longer. There was no point sitting there with their thumbs up their bums and their minds in neutral.

'We'll have to go. Max Saheb will let the twins stay together. That leaves those of us here to go by river. So let's get on.' He counted them off on his fingers. 'Anda and Paad go with Gokul, you take Nyima, Dendi and me.'

'Exactly what I would have organised.' Max emerged from the boulders lining the river bank. 'But I'm sending Dendi in the Land Rover with you and I'll go with Nyima in Arun's RIB. Now, have you got any more of that hot brew that I can smell on Arun's breath?' Deepraj emptied the thermos into Max's mug.

'You've got the map reference and Ashok's mobile number. If you get there before me, call him up and get him to the RV. Make sure he has transport. I think you'll get there before us, if we don't drown first.' He laughed.

'Huzoor.' Deepraj held out his hand and for a second Max looked perplexed.

'The key Sahib.'

'Oh Christ, yes.' Max found it in his pocket and handed it over. 'Talk your way through trouble, don't let Anda get into a shooting match.' Deepraj braced momentarily to attention, turned and together with the big Gurkha set off up the bankside. Max surveyed the river that was thrashing itself into turbulence as he stepped into the leading RIB.

'Let's go and for God's sake keep these bloody things upright.' Arun waved to Gokul to follow and undid the mooring ropes.

'It's going to get a bit technical.' This was delivered in a flat tone.

'Well you're the bloody technicians, so just keep us afloat.' Arun paused a moment before smiling silently. The rains suddenly started to pour down over them and they pulled up the hoods of their parkas.

300 feet above Rumtek

'There.' The Z-10 pilot pointed to the open area of ground behind the buildings closest to the river bank. Colonel Ji signalled to the men standing in the space behind them then spoke into the pilot's ear.

'Take us down.' He used the helicopter's searchlight to look for the truck but almost immediately picked out Sergeant Xu waving them in with a fluorescent cloth.

'Got it.' The pilot nodded and banked the helicopter hard in towards a spot some 50 metres from the truck. The second Z-10 followed them down and parked 100 metres away. Both teams were out before the wheels hit the ground, half of them formed a defensive semi-circle and the rest converged on the truck. Ji noted the time 03.12, he had given them a maximum of five minutes to be in and out. Sergeant Xu jogged up to him.

'They must have taken to the river, Colonel.' Ji returned the salute and nodded his agreement.

'They can't be that far away.' Ji knew what Xu was thinking and he had been turning it over in his own mind during the course of the inbound flight. He would dearly have liked to recover the money but if as seemed a virtual certainty it was on some sort of craft going downstream, operationally that would be incredibly hazardous, even if they did not come under fire. The constraints of time dictated that the only option would be to kill the crew and sink the craft. General Wang and the commissioner would be furious at the loss but fuck them. He checked his watch, two minutes were gone. Captain Guo ran up to him.

'We'll be loaded in two minutes, sir.'

'Pull in the security now.' Guo acknowledged the order with his head and spoke into his radio. Ji waved Xu to accompany him and they ran back to the command Z-10 and climbed in under the revolving rotors. Ji tapped the pilot on the shoulder.

'Clear?' The pilot nodded. Xu was helping to load the bodies as Captain Guo launched himself up, clapped him on the shoulder and shouted 'Go. Go.'

Xu turned trying to catch the colonel's eye but he was bent over the pilot as the Z-10 tilted forward in the ascent. The pilot pulled one side of his headset away from his ear.

'The river?'

'Slight deviation.' The pilot tapped his wristwatch anxiously. Ji had to shout to be heard above the noise of the engine.

'Break off the second you get the signal.' The pilot shrugged and steered a course out over the river as he ordered the other Z-10 to follow. Ji beckoned Guo forward.

'We're going to sink them…if we have time. Put a man on the machine gun.'

Guo's smile was grimly satisfied. Ji stared out of the cockpit window, scanning the rushing water below. He gripped the pilot's shoulder.

'Can you take her up a bit more, give me a longer reach.' The pilot eased the aircraft up muttering.

'Radar…'

On the Teesta River

With the drawstring of his hood pulled tight around his head and the crashing of the water around them Max was deaf to any extraneous sound but his sixth sense made him turn and look back up the valley. He shielded his eyes with his hand, squinting through the driving rain.

'Shit!' The RIB was bouncing violently in the water's race so that extracting his night glasses from under his parka one-handed was clumsy. Holding the lenses against his eyes he adjusted the focus. The image shifted in and out of his vision but he'd seen enough. Arun was holding the tiller of the outboard, facing towards him. Max waved the binoculars up towards the sky behind them.

'Helicopter.' Arun gave a quick backward glance, not comprehending.

'Z-10, bloody Chinese!' Max yelled as he recognised the tapered rear of the fuselage. He turned to scan the route ahead, looking for a rocky cleft or some protective overhead cover on either bank. Nothing.

Max found that climbing to the back of the RIB whilst it was being thrown around in the water was even more difficult than he had expected. Holding fast to the rope that ran along the top surface of the inflated side, he stumbled into Arun, caught his balance and then shouted into the hood of his parka.

'Got to dance the boat around on the water…make a difficult target… the Chinese are bound to try and shoot us…puncture the RIB.'

The look of incomprehension on Arun's face shifted to one of alarm and he began to jig the RIB across the waves. Max gave him a ferocious nod and then crawled back to the front, casting a frequent backward glance up at the sky to their rear. He gripped Nyima's shoulder and pointed up towards the approaching helicopter.

'Get down. Chinese.' Nyima scowled and pushed himself into the narrow space between the side of the RIB and the two storage barrels that were lashed lengthwise in the centre. Max took hold of the waxed bag holding the Bren gun, opened it and extracted the gun and three magazines. Clipping one magazine into the breech he cocked the action and set it at automatic then took a quick sighting of the angle. Resting the bipod legs on top of the nearest barrel he lowered himself so that his back was wedged into the 'V' of the RIB's prow. There wasn't a snowball's chance in hell of hitting the Z-10 which he knew was armoured against 7.62 ammunition so that .303 ball was never going to penetrate, but there was no way he was going to present a sitting target to the bastards. Arun's zigzagging made the bipod slide over the top of the barrel but by now he didn't give a shit. It reminded him of the helmsman's all too fragile vulnerability. Cupping his hand over his mouth he roared in Arun's direction.

'Get low...get your arse off the edge of the RIB!' This was acknowledged with a dismissive wave of the hand.

'Can't control it that way.' Obstinate bastard, there was no point in arguing with him. Max tried to take a bead on the aircraft as it closed in on them. No point firing too early, he needed the shots to hit something so that the pilot would know he was taking fire. It was at this moment that he realised there was not one but two helicopters.

'Shit a brick!'

'Saheb?' Nyima looked up at him, the rain streaming off his face.

'There are two of the bastards.'

'*Arey-ho!*'

Calculating the distance as best he could through the thick veil of rain that partly obscured his vision, Max decided to open fire at about 1,000 yards. God help them when the Z-10s opened up with their 14.7mm Gatling guns and even God wouldn't be able to help if they used their 30 mm cannon. The RIB lurched and the bipod slid to the left, stopped by the raised ridge of the barrel's lid. He heaved it back into alignment and pulled the legs of the bipod so that they rested against the ridge nearest to him. So, he thought to himself, this is how it's going to end. The rain was streaming down his face and had penetrated the collar of his parka, soaking him through. The thought flashed through his mind that they should all dive overboard and leave the fucking RIB as the soft target but he let it die as quickly. When they killed the monks and shot up Ekeis they had pissed him off right royally and there was no way he was going to abandon ship now. Still, he told himself, he'd been an idiot to get involved in the entire bloody enterprise, so he only had himself to blame. He squinted through the back sight, that was about right: the underbelly of the leading Z-10 presented itself and he squeezed the trigger.

'Hey!' The pilot automatically adjusted the Z-10's path as he saw the flash from the boat. 'We're under fire.'

'Give us a firing platform.' Ji shouted into the pilot's ear and the helicopter tilted at an angle that gave him a view of the river. He waved towards the gunner anchored in the open door.

'Got it?' The man nodded and Ji switched his attention back to the rubber raft that was tossing around in the swirling waters below. There was a brief hammering as the gunner opened fire. The pilot's expression was one of satisfaction as he angled his machine in an approach that put it broadside to the raft.

'Break away! Break away!' Suddenly his ears were hit with sound that tensed his entire body. He swung the machine hard to the east.

'What are you doing?' Ji grabbed his shoulder and shouted against one side of his headphones.

'Escaping...' A stream of information was pouring into his ears.

'No, you're not! Not yet!' The pilot shook his head.

'They'll lock on to us, Mirage Mark IIs, less than two minutes away, we're ordered back to base.'

'But we have them...' The anger in Ji's voice was threaded with frustration.

'Sorry.' The pilot gave him a brief apologetic wave as the instrument panel started to ping. 'He's locked on, I'm releasing chaff.' Half turning in his seat he gestured at the open door. 'Close it!' Ji fell violently to one side as the helicopter was thrown into a series of erratic avoiding manoeuvres. Misfortune was fast turning into disaster.

The squadron leader of the leading Mirage was smiling behind his oxygen mask as he closed on the Z-10s.

'Blue leader, are we cleared to fire?' The voice of his wingman was full of anticipation. Ah, he thought, the zeal of youth.

'Blue 2, no. I say again, no. Our orders are just to chase the buggers out of our airspace.'

'Roger that Blue leader.' Disappointment carried through the air. The squadron leader surveyed the Z-10s, nodding appreciatively to himself. Nice kit.

At first, Max thought that the Z-10s were manoeuvring for a better approach angle but as they bounced away he heard the sound of the approaching Mirages and offered up a silent prayer of thanks to the Indian Air Force. For a few seconds he was reminded of a similar escape when USAF F16s out of Bastion had broken up a large concentration of Taliban that threatened to overrun his patrol in Helmand. He had become superstitious to the extent that he had stopped counting whether or not he had exhausted his nine lives. Whatever it was, he had used up one more. He removed the magazine and cleared the Bren, shoving it back into its bag, nearly being pitched overboard as he did so.

'Hang on!' Arun yelled.

'Bit bloody late.' Max shouted back, relief at the removal of the Z-10s replaced by anxiety as the RIB seemed to skid uncontrollably over the water, pitching and tossing like a ping-pong ball.

'White water.' Arun's free arm described a semi-circle in front of them. Holding on for dear life, Max was blinded by the combined effect of the rain and the water breaking over the prow of the RIB. The river suddenly washed the RIB up until it was almost standing vertically on its left bulwark.

'Go right! Right!' Arun commanded as he threw himself astride the right-hand bulwark and the outboard motor screamed as it was lifted clear of the water. Max levered himself up against the side of a barrel, launching himself bodily across the inflated bulwark. Their combined weight made the RIB right itself and the propeller dug into the water, propelling them forward as Max slid back inboard.

'I told you it was a bit technical.' Arun chuckled.

'Technical my arse, you nearly had us over.' Max's tone evinced a sudden loss of humour.

'*Pardonnez-moi, mon Colonel.*' Arun threw him a mock salute and Max gave him a reluctant nod. He peered through the rain for sight of the second RIB and was relieved to see that it was no more than 10 metres behind them.

'How much more of this stuff?'

'A lot.' Arun shrugged. 'But if you and Nyima follow my orders quickly, we can anticipate most of it by co-ordinating our body weight to keep it in balance.'

'OK. Where do you want us to stand?'

'Where you are, until *I* tell you to move left or right.' Max grabbed hold of Nyima's jacket.

'Did you get all that?'

'Huzoor.' Nyima grinned. 'It's worse than the mountains.' Max nodded. It was all proving the old adage that leadership is just a question of who knew best what to do in a given situation. There was a curious sense of liberation that he didn't have to take the command decisions over the coming hours. But that only affected the river: the rendezvous with the Bhunnia was far less certain than he had led his men to believe. A *Marwari* who had to choose between risking his skin and making a small fortune could normally be relied upon to follow the money, but the fact that he'd had to more or less threaten Ashok introduced an extra dimension into the equation. On the strength of Arun's estimate, it was now time to make the call to the money changer.

'*Ji-ha.*'

'I need you at the meeting point by 0600 hours this morning.' There was no response. 'Ashok, are you there?'

'Ji-ha Colonel Sahib.' Max waited for what he was sure would be a 'but'.

'It is being impossible...' Max switched to Hindi.

'*Nei mera dost*, if you renege on this deal I'll make sure your name is shit in your business and then I'll come for you myself.' The Marwari went into a litany of begging on behalf of his wife, his children, his aged father and countless relatives all of whom would starve to death if he was arrested. Max turned the screw.

'What the police will do to you in the *thana* will feel like Mother Teresa's blessings compared to what I'll do.'

'Nei...nei...Colonel-ji.' Max heard theatrical sobbing coming down the line and let it exhaust itself. He let the silence weigh the man down.

'For the sake of *meri beti* let me meet you inside the Bhutan border, please *burra Saheb*.' Max was as angry as he was disgusted. His plan had relied on the Marwari providing transport from the river, a quick handover and his work would be finished. The RIB bounced up in the air and he nearly lost his grip on his phone. He was cold, wet and still had hours of risking having his brains dashed out on a rock or tree trunk or the cargo and crew drowned and this arse-wipe was only aggravating his problems.

'Is it worth you gaining a point in your commission?' The tone of the response was revealing.

'A full point, *saheb-ju*?'

'A full point.' Max could almost hear the man calculating it in his head.

There was another lengthy pause.

'Colonel Saheb, I'm just a poor man trying to make a small living.' The wheedling tone and the absurd lie made Max want to spit but he let the Marwari bleat on. 'I'm not doing this for the money, Colonel-ji, but for His Holiness.' Max felt his eyes roll up in his head. 'I can meet the Colonel Saheb at the border but it is more than my miserable life is worth to be caught in India with such a commodity.' The wheedling tone had gone, replaced with a desperate determination which Max realised was not going to be changed by anything he said. He was so furious that had he spoken it would have been a tirade of the richest abuse he was capable of. A strong wave hit the RIB and struck his face, time to recalculate. In his mind's eye he pictured the interior of the Land Rover, trying to calculate whether he could get the entire consignment in it. It would mean leaving all but three of the team behind, even then they would be packed tightly together in the front and it was long drive at the best of times.

'OK. Listen. I'm going to deliver this to you in Jaygaon and you're going to get it over the border, do you understand?'

'God is great, Colonel Saheb. This I can do.'

'Not can, will.'

'Ji-ha.'

'I'll call you just before we reach Jaygaon,' Max had to pause to get his voice under control. 'But if you're not there I'll hunt you down and I will kill you.'

'*Nei nei*, Colonel Saheb, you have my word.' Max was tempted to say that this was just what was worrying him but he felt a heavy silence spoke more effectively. He ended the call. The whole plan was going from bad to worse. He was wet through, cold, tired and already on to plan B which had a poor prediction.

Teesta Bazaar

0215 hours

As the Land Rover started across the bridge Deepraj saw an armed policeman step into the middle of the road signalling for them to stop. He was in a foul mood because the road had been awash and slowed them down significantly.

'Oh oh, what do these bastards want?' He stuck his hand out of the window and waved acknowledgment before exiting the bridge and parking in the main street, just south of the police office.

'Stay here, I'll find out what's up.' Dendi sat silently. The policeman jerked his rifle towards the wooden hut. Deepraj noted that he was a Bengali and ignored him. Entering the hut he was not surprised to find the office unoccupied but there were sounds coming from behind a curtained door that indicated activity.

'Hello.' He did not expect any response but wanted to ensure that the duty officer was aware of his presence, then he sat down on the only chair on his side of the desk. A few more minutes passed and he was about to call out again when the curtain was pulled aside and a middle-aged West Bengal Armed Police inspector emerged into the room still adjusting his uniform. He spoke in Bengali.

'Where have you come from?'

'I don't speak Bengali.' This in Nepali. The inspector sat down and surveyed Deepraj across his steepled fingers.

'You are speaking English?'

'A little.' The inspector nodded.

'You are coming from Sikkim?' The momentary fencing with languages had given Deepraj time to consider his answer. Max had dinned into him never to tell an outright lie if he could avoid it. He shrugged and nodded.

'Going to?' Now was the time to lie.

'Nepal.'

'You were having no troubles on the road?'

'The rain was very heavy and slowed us down.'

'Us?' Deepraj kicked himself.

'My friend and I.' The inspector shouted an order for the sentry to tell the man in the vehicle to come into the office. Deepraj decided it was time to ask some questions himself.

'What's all this about?' This was ignored as the officer aligned the pens and pencils on his desk until Dendi walked in. There was nowhere for him to sit so he just stood inside the door. Deepraj saw the inspector's expression change and he took a quick glance at Dendi who remained blank-faced.

'I'm knowing you.' The tone was less than friendly. 'Come over here.' He pointed to a spot beside the desk where the light was brighter. Dendi complied with a quizzical frown on his face.

'I arrested you for smuggling last year, isn't it.' The Sherpa leaned forward a little peering into the half shadow.

'Yes, sir, you did.' The inspector's face was triumphant. 'But your superintendent-saheb released me when there was no evidence, sir.' The light in the inspector's face died. His features contracted in malevolence.

'Stand there.' His lips quivered as he pointed to the spot that Dendi stood on. Deepraj willed Dendi to keep his mouth shut and with an obvious effort the Sherpa set his mouth in a line, staring back at the police officer.

'Keys.' This to Deepraj. 'Car keys.'

'They're in the ignition.' Deepraj cast a quick look at Dendi for confirmation and got a nod.

'You sit here until I return.' They watched him jam his uniform cap on his head and stalk out into the street.

'What the...?'

'Probably thinks we're smuggling something in the Land Rover.'

'Not his lucky day.' Dendi grinned.

'Nor ours.' Deepraj looked at his watch. 'The saheb's expecting us to get to the RV before him and sort out this Bhunnia, we're not going to make it.'

'But there's nothing to find.' Dendi's exasperation was already on parade.

'Take it easy, *Daju*, let me handle him.' The Sherpa shook his head.

'Fucking Bengalis.' Deepraj put his finger to his lips.

'Shhh.' There was nothing in the vehicle to justify detaining them but if they could be connected with the murdered monks and the stolen truck not only would they not make the RV with Bhunnia, they would probably spend the rest of their days rotting in some foul Bengal prison whilst the ruptured Indian legal system sucked away their lives. He fought down the temptation to just cut and run, even if they abandoned the vehicle and took to the jungle they'd become permanent fugitives. He shook his head at the irony, to be stopped on one of the rare occasions over the past few days when they were not carrying weapons or escorting a fortune in gold and currencies was bizarre.

The havildar stood sipping a mug of *chai* in the shadow of a building opposite the police hut, watching the inspector and a police sergeant searching the Land Rover. It did not require vast powers of deduction to conclude that the target's men were being detained on suspicion of something related to the vehicle. She wondered whether the Sikkim state police had been in touch with their colleagues in West Bengal, that would certainly stir things up. Aware that the Land Rover was meant to make a RV, she called General Singh and requested orders.

'Just observe. If they've not been released in one hour's time, get down to the RV and cover the target.' Irritation coloured his words. He ended the call and speed-dialled Fernandes with the latest report.

'We had to chase the buggers out of our airspace, I hadn't anticipated it ballooning like this. Now we have the turnips sticking their noses in too.'

'Will you get the commissioner to order their release?'

'No.' Fernandes's exasperation blew down the line. 'They'll have to take their chances.'

'Won't Devlin need the transport?'

'Probably, but I'm beginning to think we ought to have stayed out of it altogether. I've got the home minister and the defence minister breathing down my neck, politicians, why don't they stick to lining their pockets and leave us to run the country.' Singh gave a disgusted laugh. There was a pause before Fernandes sighed.

'Ranjit, I think maybe you're right. Devlin's had the luck of the devil so far but I'd better give the devil a hand. I'll have his men released.'

'You want us to continue to track him?'

'Please.'

The jangling of the ancient Bakelite telephone on the inspector's desk startled Deepraj out of his depressed thoughts that were going nowhere. The officer stalked back into the room ignoring them and snatching up the phone. The angry looks that were flashed in his direction suggested that their fate was being determined elsewhere. Maybe it would be best to make a run for it after all. He caught Dendi's attention and swivelled his eyes towards the open door. The Sherpa registered momentary surprise before giving an almost imperceptible nod. The sound of the telephone handset being crashed down onto its rest made him look towards the inspector.

'Go. Get out!' The officer pointed towards the door, his face taut with anger. Deepraj tried to keep the smile off his face and asked politely.

'We may go?' The inspector just made a dismissive wave towards the door.

'Thank you.' He could see Dendi winding himself up to express outrage so he grabbed his arm and pulled him out into the night and hustled him towards the Land Rover.

'Let's go.'

'But…'

'No buts, we're seriously behind schedule.' He started the motor and pulled out into the road looking up into the sky as he did so. 'At least it's stopped raining.'

East bank of the Teesta River

1km South of the Sevok Bridge

The monsoon rains had sheeted down on them over the last hour of the journey but his faith in the skill of Arun and Gokul had been amply vindicated. On one occasion the massive roots of a huge tree that had snagged on some projecting rocks had missed his head by a whisker when it suddenly broke free and swung violently across their path. Arun made it look as though the RIB was flying, maybe it was, Max could not imagine how the river pilot had got them out of that one. He also had to rely on Arun's navigational knowledge to tell them when they had reached their RV. When the RIB ran part way up the sandy beach his first thought was that they had foundered until Arun shouted.

'All ashore!' He scouted their immediate surroundings looking for shelter.

'Over there.' Arun pointed into the land that rose behind them. 'There's a cave.' Leaving Nyima to help pull the RIB further up the beach, he struck off, torch in hand. No more than 40 metres away the rocky shoreline gave onto what turned out to be a spacious cavity; though the walls were heavy with the smell of damp soil, the ground consisted of smooth pebbles, the surfaces of which were, he was happy to note, dry. He punched in Deepraj's number.

'Huzoor.'

'Where are you?' The Gurkha gave him a milestone that he estimated made the vehicle about one hour away. He was on the point of asking what had kept them but decided against it. If they had arrived on time the Bhunnia wouldn't have been there anyway.

'Everything OK?'

'OK.'

'Call me when you're 5 minutes out.' He ended the call and walked back towards the RIBs almost colliding with Nyima.

'I'll get some tea brewed up, Saheb.'

'Hot and sweet. Get everyone into the cave and dry out a bit, I'm going to recce the area.' They had to get the loads out of the RIBs and up onto the road so that they could be transferred into the Land Rover. Ideally he wanted to get that done before dawn broke but that now looked like another dead duck.

The night had bled out of the sky leaving an anaemic cover that threatened more rain. They had manhandled the barrels off the beach and up onto the partly wooded scrub that paralleled the road by the time that Deepraj and Dendi arrived. Max winced as he made a visual assessment of the size of the barrels and the capacity of the Land Rover. He and Deepraj stood beside the lowered tailgate measuring the interior visually.

'We'll have to empty the barrels and pack the stuff into the space.' He looked up at the sky. 'Better do it now before the heavens open on us again.' He turned and beckoned Nyima over.

'You're the expert on packing, can you stuff all this gear in do you think?'

'*Kunni Saheb.*' Max curbed his tongue. It was a less than respectful response but men were apt to give ill-tempered answers when tired and stressed. Deepraj was not so inhibited.

'Well, don't just stand there, find out, *murka!*' There was an awkward moment as the two men stared at each other then the Sherpa's face cracked.

'Sorry Saheb.' Max waved acknowledgment and nodded Deepraj to walk a little away.

'What kept you?' As he listened to the events at the Teesta checkpoint Max wondered why they had been stopped in the first instance and equally how they had suddenly been released. Obviously someone higher up the command chain had intervened. Fernandes or the havildar's commander?

'The bloody Bhunnia isn't coming. We'll have to make for the Bhutan border. He's to meet us at Jaygaon.'

'That's five or six hours' drive.' Max nodded. Deepraj's face showed the strain.

'If he doesn't?' This was the non-existent plan C conundrum. Much though he wanted to share the problem, Max knew that morale would sink if he admitted that he had no solution.

'He'll be there.' Said with a conviction that he didn't have, it was accepted. Not for the first or last time, Max marvelled at the innate trust. The Gurkha could be obtuse and sometimes just plain contrary but the basic truth was that they relied on each other and ultimately it was Max's responsibility.

'Can we cram Anda in the front with us?'

'He'll have to sit astride the gear lever.' Deepraj grinned. Max's phone vibrated. Pulling it out of his pocket he saw the havildar's number.

'The fan's hit the shit.' She spoke in English.

'You mean the shit's hit the fan.' He corrected her.

'No, Saheb, you're already in the shit.' She paused then continued in Nepali. 'The Sikkim police have put out an alert for you, they say you killed the monks and stole their money.'

'What about the Chinese?' Max was trying to make sense of it even as he recognised that deep gripe in his guts that told him he was being suckered.

'I think...' she began as though she was holding back, '...I think the government doesn't want to admit that they ever infiltrated.' He heard the hesitation in her voice. His mind was calculating all the arguments to contradict the official version but he acknowledged that the witnesses were all in government service and there would be a blanket denial.

'It's only the impression I got from my commander, nothing specific.' Max wanted to know just how far the Indian government would distance itself from him.

'You've been recalled?'

'Not quite.' Again the hesitation. 'I'm still to keep tabs on you.' Max interpreted that to mean that it would make it easier for them to arrest him whenever they decided to do so. 'And to help if I think it's necessary.' Now he did not know what to believe. She sounded genuine, as far as one could judge over a mobile phone.

'OK.' He ended the call. There had to be a homing device somewhere in the Land Rover but there was no time to search for it now. They'd just have to take their chances. He had a terrible sense of *déja vu*, it was Chakrata all over again and this time round he was the expendable figure in place of the Tibetan Dapon. Yet there was something still not right, surely it was way above Fernandes' pay scale: carrying off this operation successfully would have benefited the intelligence chief enormously whereas the political ramifications for him now looked poisonous. There was no question but that the Chinese incursion was linked to the Dalai Lama's treasure and Max's involvement could be traced with relative ease. He called the team together and spelled out the bad news. Their expressions looked grim.

'It's time to pull the plug.' He pointed at Nyima and Dendi. 'You two find your way back across the border into Nepal.' Turning to Anda and Paad he gave them a dark smile. 'You boys get lost, quickly.'

'No-one has anything on us.' Arun interjected, Gokul nodded. Max shook his head.

'The Black Cats commander does.' Arun's eyebrows asked the question. 'We've been tracked since I left Delhi.' He waved an apologetic arm. 'I made contact with their…man.' The word got stuck in his throat. 'He helped us, in fact that's where the news about me being a fugitive came from; but he's not sworn to secrecy. I'm afraid you're tarred with the same brush. Your best bet is to get back into the Gorkhaland admin area and keep a low profile. You too.' He swung round to face Deepraj. 'Your brush with the inspector at the Teesta bazaar links you to me through the Land Rover. Best tag along with Arun and get back to Darjeeling.' The Gurkha pointed at the loaded Land Rover.

'What about the *paisa*?'

'I'll try and bluff my way through to Bhutan.' Deepraj shook his head.

'It won't work.' Max felt the same way but he had run out of options. It was a case of *sauve qui peut*. The chirruping of his satnav interrupted him.

'Colonel?'

'Yes.'

'I need to get that parcel delivered, can you do it?' Fernandes's voice sounded strained.

'Hmm.' Max fought down the instinct to tell him to go and fuck himself, and contented himself with a non-committal grunt. Where this was going?

'I can buy you three, perhaps four hours, no more. Can you deliver?' Four hours to do a five or six hours' journey in the monsoon, he was tempted to say 'you have to be joking' but something stopped him.

'What choice do I have?'

'The clock is ticking.' The line was cut. It was madness but no more crazy than the entire enterprise had been from the beginning. He rounded on Deepraj.

'Tank full?'

'Nearly.' He opened the door and turned on the ignition, the needle indicated a full tank. They stood around him in a rough semi-circle, their faces uniformly showing concern. He pointed at Anda and Paad.

'DK is holding your pay.' Turning to the rest of them he said, 'You'll find your pay already in your bank accounts. Now get out of here and if anyone asks about me, give them the simple hillman's response *kunni*!' As he pulled the driver's door open he felt his arm grabbed.

'I'm coming too, Saheb.' Deepraj's expression bordered on anger. Max always knew that he'd refuse to leave him but it had been important for his own peace of mind that he gave the man the option.

'Well why are you standing there, we're already late.' He caught a glimpse of the smile of satisfaction before the Gurkha turned and ran around to get into the passenger seat. Hauling himself up, Max called to the little knot of men.

'Plaster some mud on the registration plates.' A knock on a rear panel signalled that it was done just as Nyima waved to tell him that the front plate was also finished.

Max had been driving like a madman for half an hour before Deepraj broke the silence.

'What do we do if you hit someone?'

'I'll tell you if and when it happens.' Max felt the muscles in his neck tightening under the strain. There had been two very near misses already, one old woman who changed her mind as she crossed the road and nearly had them into the nullah and a buffalo that took off like a bullet as the Land Rover slid along its flank.

'How are we doing for time?' Deepraj had a map open on his lap, ran his forefinger along the road and checked his watch.

'Another four hours and five minutes at this speed.' Max factored in the distance and the 35 minutes they were behind the clock. The Land Rover had the speed and the road was fairly straight until they hit the incline as they got closer to the Bhutan border but the human and animal traffic on it meant that he was constantly braking and swerving, all of it slowing them down. He'd have to take more care, Deepraj was right, driving like a maniac was more likely to lead to a disaster.

'You take over in half an hour.' He was tempted to tell the Gurkha to get some sleep but he needed the extra pair of eyes on the road.

Max started awake, momentarily disoriented. He checked his watch, 08.25, he'd been asleep for almost half an hour. The map had slipped off his lap and he reached into the well to recover it then waited for the next milestone before he found their location.

'You've made good time. We're nearly two-thirds of the way there.' When there was no response he looked at Deepraj's face. It was set in a mask of concentration, his eyes closed to narrow slits as he fought fatigue.

'Pull over, my turn.' There was no argument. No sooner had he got them back on the road than the Gurkha was slumped against the side window, out to the wide. Max smiled to himself, the men had a remarkable knack of falling asleep at every opportunity and usually in the most curious of positions. His own neck ached and his eyes felt as though they were bathing in ash. It had started to rain but only a light shower: he stuck his head out of the window and let it wash his face. It felt good and he allowed himself a flicker of optimism.

Ordinarily, he would have been drinking in the stunning forest clad foothills of Bhutan and the undulating terraces of the tea gardens which filled his horizon with shimmering greens but this was no ordinary moment: not only was he dog tired, the rank stench of his clothes stuck in his nose, he was driving a shitload of gold and currencies like a bat out of hell to make a rendezvous with a man he doubted would be there when he arrived and to top it all he was now wanted by the police for the murder of some Buddhist monks who had been killed by a PLA special forces unit that the Indian government in its infinite wisdom were pretending never existed.

'Shit!' He hit the brakes and swerved to his nearside to avoid a *goru gari* that had suddenly pulled into his path, wrestling with the steering wheel as the Land Rover careered wildly from side to side of the road. He snatched a glance at his watch: the maximum grace time Fernandes had granted him was now exhausted but there was still another half hour or more of this hopelessly potholed road and if the monsoon rains decided to throw the heavens down on them, God alone knew how much longer it would take. They could not take the risk of just driving into Jaygaon and relying on the inefficiency of the West Bengal police not to have received notification that they were wanted. As each minute passed he became more and more cagey about the dodgy Ashok who, if anything, compounded his fears. Bearing in mind the depth of trouble that he could bring, he was loath to involve anyone else, but he had run out of options. He shook Deepraj awake as he slowed down and pulled to a halt.

'Take over.' The Gurkha's movements were slow and deliberate and Max wanted to chivvy him along but he knew it would be counter-productive. There was still some tea in the flask so he removed the cap and passed it across, reflecting as he did so on the irony that they had run out in the middle of one of the most productive tea growing regions of the world.

'*Hawas*.' Max found it reassuring that the basic courtesies were still observed, Deepraj had developed the surly habit of retreating into himself when things stacked up against them.

He shook his head involuntarily, it simply did not add up. Why would the police connect him with the murdered monks? True, he had the Tibetan treasure but to the best of his knowledge there was no witness to their ambush of the Chinese special forces. Even as he reached that conclusion it hit him that the havildar was the link. Had he misjudged her? He did not read her as two-faced but if he was right there was one man at the centre of this spider's web: Fernandes, the same man who had played him for a fool years earlier. Yet it still made no sense: it was Fernandes who had manipulated him into the job, if the Indian intelligence chief pulled the plug now not only would the total enterprise have failed but Max would be a very dangerous songbird, liable to disclose politically explosive matter in his defence. The reality hit home in a cruelly cold shaft, he was only dangerous so long as he was alive to tell the tale. He scrolled down his list of contacts then hit the pre-set. The whine of the distant ringtone toyed with him and his finger was over the disconnect when a voice barked in Tibetan.

'Speak!'

'Wangdi…Max.' There was a slight pause, then the response came in English.

'Whey! You bastard, where've you been?'

'No time to explain now, I'm on the 12C about ten clicks out of Jaygaon. Can you smuggle me across the border?'

'Bloody hell, what did you do to her?'

'No joke my friend, the Bengalis want my guts for garters. You're our one hope of getting out of this in one piece.'

'Our?'

'Deepraj is with me.' Max glanced sideways at the Gurkha. 'It's serious stuff, we're transporting a mass of Tibetan treasure.'

'If this is your idea of a joke Max, it's in poor taste.'

'Sorry Wangdi, it's for real and we're on the side of the angels.' There was a reflective pause.

'How did you know I'm commanding the Chukha district?'

'Didn't, just had to play my "Get out of jail" card.'

'Jammy bugger, I'm actually in Phuntsholing. What's your transport?'

'Land Rover, old military model.'

'Good, same as ours. Hold on.' Max heard a muted conversation. 'Max, stay on 12C, come in to Jaygaon and take the left-hand fork immediately after the Dooars Welfare Society, go on for about 500 yards then park and open the bonnet, make it look as though you've got engine trouble.'

'Roger that and thanks.'

'Don't thank me yet, we're not out of the woods.' Max briefed Deepraj and was rewarded with a grunt of acknowledgment.

Now for the Bhunnia.

'*Sar sahib...*' Max cut him off.

'Ashok, listen. Don't come into India, I'll meet you in Phuntsholing.'

'Oh Colonel Saheb, God is great!' The relief in the man's voice flooded over the line. 'Wait for my call.' Max hit the end button.

The tension inside the cab of the vehicle increased the closer that they got to Jaygaon. What he most feared was a West Bengal Armed Police roadblock which would force them either to turn around or run the gauntlet, either of which would almost certainly result in a chase, let alone killing the prospects of making the RV with Wangdi. Fatigue and sleep deprivation were leeching his ability to devise a solution and recognising that as a fact only served to aggravate the situation.

'Saheb.' Deepraj pointed through the windscreen at the ornate Tibetan-style pergola-shaped arch that welcomed visitors to Jaygaon. 'How would it be if we just parked the vehicle somewhere and escaped on foot?'

The temptation to dump their incriminating load and leg it until they bumped into Wangdi was overwhelming. It was as though they had tempted fate to its extremes and pushing their luck just that bit further would end in disaster. But he had accepted the commission and command had its obligations as well as its prerogatives.

'No. You bail out here and I'll make the RV. No need for both of us to get caught.' Deepraj's twisted grin of disdain registered 'We've been here before.'

'*Hut terigar*! Who'd watch your back?' They drove in tense silence for some minutes.

'Turn-off coming up.' Deepraj made the left-hand turn and Max registered the 500 nail-biting metres then indicated a parking space. The street was fairly crowded with people taking advantage of the break in the rains to do their shopping or move across the town. Deepraj was out of the vehicle quickly, lifted the bonnet, removed the points from the distributor and stuffed them in his trouser pocket. Max nodded his approval; it would fool anyone who lacked a basic knowledge of the combustion engine, which he guessed would include most members of the West Bengal police, armed or otherwise. Nevertheless, it was not long before they had attracted a small crowd of curious people who volunteered their diagnoses of the problem, all of whom Deepraj treated with an irritated grunt. Max looked around him, the crowd had grown, they were exciting too much attention: either they would have to solve the problem or make a show of seeking a mechanic. With the number of heads now under the bonnet Deepraj would have to be a magician to spirit the points out of his pocket and replace them without being observed.

'*Kya hogia*?' Uttered more as a command than a question, the crowd parted and a smart West Bengal police inspector using his swagger stick rather like a conductor directing an orchestra walked up to Deepraj.

'The engine died, it won't start.' Wearing an expression that indicated his low opinion of the mechanical skills of the Gurkha, the inspector climbed into the driver's seat and turned the engine over. After several attempts, he got out and rapped on the open bonnet.

'You're obstructing the road, move it.' Max read the riposte that was in Deepraj's eyes and hailed the policeman, forcing a smile to soften his words.

'We'd very much like to do that inspector saheb, but I think we need to get it towed to a garage.' The officer's eyes narrowed, forming a neat line parallel with his moustache and the peak of his uniform cap. Whatever he was saying was drowned by the roar of three vehicles' engines approaching them at speed and then braking violently to a stop beside the Land Rover. Max registered the Bhutanese pennant on the front wing of the leading vehicle just as Wangdi swung himself out, quickly followed by several Bhutan army officers. The police inspector stood to attention and saluted.

'General Saheb.'

'Inspector.' Wangdi acknowledged the salute with an airy wave of his hand. 'My apologies, this is one of our vehicles.' No sooner had the inspector turned away from the Land Rover than several Bhutanese soldiers surrounded it and Deepraj fished the points out of his pocket and fitted them back into the distributor. A Bhutanese sergeant in khaki overalls leaned over the engine and indicated to Deepraj to get into the driver's seat.

'Do you want to take a note of the registration number inspector?' Wangdi inquired solicitously. Max's face was signaling urgently 'No'.

'That won't be necessary, General.' The inspector was magnanimous and Max breathed a sigh of relief. The sound of the engine starting and then being revved up was followed by the bonnet being slammed shut. Wangdi thanked the inspector, turned away and signed for Max to join him in the back of the long wheel based army Land Rover.

All four vehicles moved off in convoy.

'Reminds me of some of the things we got up to at Sandhurst.' Wangdi's grin relieved a little of the tension that had Max as taut as a bowstring.

'Why'd you draw attention to the registration plate, it must have been circulated as a wanted vehicle?' He could not keep the irritation out of his tone.

'We'd snapped on Bhutan army plates, dammit, you think I'm that dumb?'

'No.' Max shook his head in apologetic appreciation. 'You're an ace mate.'

'That was the easy part. Now we have to get back over the border without arousing suspicion.' Wangdi reached behind him, took out a Bhutan army officer's cap and handed it over. 'Put this on, wear your dark glasses and pull the collar of your camo up high, that should be sufficient.' He leaned forward and spoke softly to the captain driving the vehicle. Max had an overwhelming desire to just let go and leave it all to Wangdi but anything could go wrong and he needed to be alert to any possible hiccup.

Wangdi's was the lead vehicle as they approached the border crossing. The pole barrier on the Indian side barred their path. The captain braked beside the sentry, lowered the window and ordered him to bring his commander. Moments later an Indian army lieutenant emerged from the wooden guardhouse, cramming his hat on his head as he did so. The captain, leaning half in and half out of the driver's side window blocked the view into the interior, whilst Wangdi positioned himself solidly against the rear door window. The Bhutanese captain exchanged pleasantries with the lieutenant and to Max's intense relief he saw the barrier pole raised. He willed the vehicle forward, silently urging the captain to wrap up his conversation. The sentry was staring into the interior of their vehicle, squinting as he tried to make out the other occupants.

'Come on, come on.' Max muttered softly.

The vehicle began to inch forward as the chatting officers tailed off their remarks. Max's entire body was rigid as they passed beneath the raised barrier. Now they were into the strip of No-man's land between India and Bhutan, he peered out of the rear window for sight of his Land Rover and Deepraj.

'Relax, my old mucker, relax.'

'Can't. Not till Deepraj is through.' It seemed to him an age before the first vehicle came clearly into view. Now he saw the changed registration plate and the Gurkha's grinning face. Wangdi punched him on the shoulder.

'Welcome to Bhutan you Irish bastard!'

Counting the currencies and weighing the gold took nearly three days. During the counting process Deepraj sat like a cat ready to pounce as the Bhunnia and his assistant fed the notes into a counting machine. A dispute arose over the carat rating of the gold. Dariwallah pointed to the neatly stacked ingots.

'Colonel Saheb, some of this is only 22-carat.' Max glanced briefly towards Deepraj who shook his head.

'Well then, we shall have to have it independently assayed.'

'But there is no-one qualified in Phuntsholing.' The Bhunnia's head was rocking from side to side.

'Lock it all up.' This to Deepraj. 'I'll get an assayer in from Siliguri. Till then it will be guarded by the Bhutan army.'

'No, no Saheb.' The man's face was twisted in apparent pain. 'Not from Siliguri, my reputation.' He wrung his hands before adopting a prayerful pose.

'It is only about 20%, the rest is 24-carat. The difference is only about…' His fingers drummed and clacked over his calculator then he looked up with a hopeful expression. '…only about US$330,000.' He waggled his head and smiled. 'I can make it US$329,000 for you Saheb.'

'Lock it up.' Max turned to leave but the Bhunnia caught the leg of his trousers.

'Alright, US$328,000 Saheb?' Max pulled away and gestured to Deepraj to remove the bullion as he stalked out of the room.

'Why are you cheating?' The Gurkha frowned.

'I'm not cheating, it is you and your Saheb who try to cheat me.' The Bhunnia's tone matched the contempt in his face. He pointed a quivering finger at the bullion. 'You are the thieves!'

'Really?' Deepraj's disdainful response seemed to exacerbate the man's fury.

'You killed the monks and took their gold and money and now you accuse me of cheating.' His face contorted into a snarl as he delivered his punchline triumphantly. 'It is in the newspapers.' Deepraj stood up and looked down at the Bhunnia who was seated cross-legged on a low dais covered with a soiled cotton sheet.

'All this,' he said, sweeping his arm to indicate the piles of currency and bullion, 'belongs to His Holiness the Dalai Lama.' Then pointing his finger at the man's eyes, he added, 'And you agreed to remit the value to the Dalai Lama's bank account in Hong Kong.'

'But I did not know the monks would be killed…'

'Shut up!' Deepraj's hand reached for the hilt of his kukri.

'No!' The man's eyes bulged out of their sockets and he cringed backwards.

'It was the Chinese who killed the monks.' The Bhunnia nodded spastically.

'Then,' the Gurkha spoke slowly and softly, 'we killed the Chinese.' His hand left his kukri and he pointed his index and middle finger between the man's eyes, like a gun. 'So do your job. The Dalai Lama's gold isn't for making jewellery, it's all pure 24-carat.' He took a handful of the Indian's shirt and pulled forwards until their faces were centimetres apart. 'And you know that, don't you?'

'*Tik hei, tik hei.*' The head bobbed spasmodically. Deepraj picked up the prepared receipt and tossed it beside the Bhunnia.

'Now sign for the full value.' Dariwallah's hand trembled as he signed a receipt for currencies and gold bullion to the value of US$51,320,800. Deepraj picked it up without another word, turned and left the room.

Max was sitting on the verandah of Wangdi's bungalow when Deepraj handed him the receipt. He read it and raised one quizzical eyebrow.

'The dhoti-wallah said that according to the newspapers we killed the monks. I corrected him.'

'I hope you left him in one piece.' Max smiled.

'I told him we killed the Chinese. He got the message.'

'Well done.'

'But I don't trust him.'

'Neither do I. We don't have much choice with the hundi system but his base is in Bhutan and now he knows we have powerful connections here.' Max had sent the codeword 'Slim' to Geljen soon after depositing the treasure in Dariwallah's office and had been requested to email a scanned copy of the receipt. The arrangement was that US$1.2 million was to be remitted to Max's personal account and the balance into an account in the name of Victor, also at HSBC in Hong Kong.

'So it's true that the Indians want to arrest you, Saheb.' The Gurkha's expression was puzzled. 'But I thought they were the ones who insisted on you carrying out the operation? Of course they must know about the Chinese, they sent their Mirage fighters to chase them out.'

Office of PA to the Prime Minister

Tibetan government-in-exile
Dharmasala

'We have a problem.' Geljen Ladenla's normally impassive features now bore deeply ingrained anxiety. The deputy prime minister's response was a slight flick of his eyebrows. Geljen handed him a sheet of paper.

'This is a scanned copy of the receipt for all the bullion and currencies.' He tapped the figure with his forefinger.

'51,320,800.' Then he pointed to the printout of their HSBC USD savings account.

'1.2 million US. That is what we agreed to pay Devlin-la.'

'It's a mistake. What does he say?'

'I can't reach him, his mobile is off.'

'Do you doubt him?' Geljen shook his head slowly.

'If he was going to steal it, he could have told us that the Chinese captured it when they attacked His Holiness's escorts in the mountains or that it had been stolen by the Sherpas anywhere en route. We would never have been able to disprove it.'

'What about Dariwallah, what does he say?'

'I'm waiting for him to call me back, I left an SMS for him.' The deputy prime minister's fingers tapped rhythmically on the desk top then he stood up.

'Keep me informed.' He managed a slight smile. 'I'm sure there is an explanation.' Geljen retrieved the receipt and nodded gravely as the deputy prime minister left the room. Turning to Norbu he handed over both pieces of paper.

'You chase up the Indian, I'll keep on trying to raise Devlin-la.' Norbu gave a little bow and walked into his adjoining office. This was information that would be significant for his controller; but should he wait until they found out where the missing 50 million had gone? He could almost hear the contemptuous tone ordering him to find out the whereabouts of the missing money. But supposing they couldn't discover where it had gone? Then he'd be criticised for not having passed on the information as soon as he'd been made aware of the problem. No, he couldn't afford to wait. In the frail hope that he could put off the call to his controller he decided to try and raise the Indian himself.

Office of Commissioner for Ethnic Integration

Beijing

'*Xie xie*, General.' Bo resisted the urge to slam the receiver down onto its cradle. Wang's fury at the loss of virtually an entire unit of 128 MRR Regiment was understandable but certainly not Bo's responsibility anymore than exposing the PLA Air Force to the risk of having its Z-10s downed over Indian territory. Nonetheless, he had barely slept for three nights in anticipation of an ugly international incident blowing up in his face. The Indians were playing an even more devious game than usual; the fact that they had neither shot the Z-10s down nor gone public about the infiltration meant that they intended to use it as a bargaining counter on some unspecified future occasion. When they did – and he did not fool himself that they wouldn't – the entire mess would home in on him with potentially disastrous consequences. His only solution was to recover the money. He slammed his balled fist down onto his desk top. It was beyond belief that this laowai Devlin could have done so much damage without the help of powerful backing. He opened his desk drawer and stared at the grainy photograph of the man who had wrecked his plans to date. He would not stab it with his paper knife, not yet, he was saving that for when he had the man completely in his control, an event that had unexpectedly become imminent. He shut the drawer as his PA came into his room.

'Our man in HSBC headquarters has confirmed that just over US$50 million has been credited to Devlin's personal account and it has been reported to the Independent Commission Against Corruption who will arrest him for money laundering. The account will be frozen and the liaison office in Hong Kong will apply to the court for the return of the funds to

Beijing.' He allowed himself a little smile of encouragement knowing how welcome this news would be to his chief.

'But we can't rely on the Hong Kong judges to act in our interests, they're so full of their own importance, strutting around in their stupid colonial costumes and mouthing all that crap about judicial independence.' Bo stood up but gripped the edge of his desk to channel some of his anger. His PA lost the smile and took a step back.

'But we have well-placed party members within the judiciary who can engineer the right result.' He nodded encouragingly. 'And once Devlin is within the prison system, we can arrange for him to be silenced – permanently.'

'You're sure?' Bo distrusted everyone who was not under his immediate control, even more so after the series of disasters that had tracked his every endeavour.

'Our people in the judiciary are trusted and their party allegiance is secret, no-one would ever suspect them. As for Devlin, it's a simple case of paying some triad prisoners to deal with him, they're cheap and dispensible.'

Bo hesitated to comfort himself on a successful conclusion, he was superstitious about making any such assumption. Given the trail of damage so far he was relying on a favourable outcome to armour himself against being purged. Power in the central committee of the Communist party was being exercised to root out anyone who had been appointed under the previous regime and he was conscious of walking a political tightrope. He glowered at his PA.

'So, our people can engineer the outcome of the court case?'

'I am assured that this is so.'

'Well, I want to be kept informed of every step.' It was no longer a question of promotion or satisfying his wife's demand for a BMW, it was survival.

'If we have to bring pressure to bear on any of these *judges*…' He infused the word with a deep measure of contempt, '…just do it.' He pointed his finger straight into his PA's face.

'And I want Devlin dead.'

General Chopra's House

Defence Colony, New Delhi

The general jerked his head towards an armchair as Fernandes entered the room. As he was sitting down the intelligence chief began to speak.

'I can guess…' The general shook his head and held his hand up to stop any further speech, then leaned towards an impressive array of audio equipment next to his chair and pressed a button. The room was filled with the sound of Queen blatting out 'We are the Champions'. He stood up and strode purposefully across to sit beside Fernandes whom he addressed in tones that would never have carried more than a foot or two.

'I have this place swept regularly but what we have to discuss must be for our ears only.' Fernandes blinked in silence.

'It seems to me that our beloved government have dropped my Irish friend in the shit and, unquestionably, you know what the hell's going on.' He tried to keep his anger under control but he was seething. Fernandes raised his palm in a sign of peace.

'I'm indebted to you for the precautions, most thoughtful, even though I can't stand this western style of…music?'

'Western? Freddie Mercury was a Parsi, born in Tanzania, didn't you know?'

'Wherever.' Fernandes waved his hand dismissively. 'You didn't ask me here to discuss the cultural merits of music.' The general gave an exasperated grunt.

'You know what happened in Sikkim?' Though Fernandes asked the question he already knew that the general had been briefed secretly by the commander of the Black Cats. The general guessed that he knew and had no intention of playing games with him.

'Yes, Devlin and his little band of irregulars wiped out a PLA special forces unit that had murdered some Buddhist monks and stolen the assets that they were transferring. Brilliant counter-insurgency action for which they should be highly commended, instead of which you…' He pointed his finger between Fernandes eyes, '…put the blame for the civilian deaths on Devlin and for reasons which are totally beyond my comprehension, concealed the truth about the Chinese. If they'd been Pakistanis I suppose you'd have had the newspapers hailing Devlin as a true son of India or some such rubbish!'

'Please.' Fernandes held his hands up penitently. 'As you General are aware, I persuaded Colonel Devlin to help the Tibetans recover their assets, as you so delicately put it.'

'No, you blackmailed him into it.' The general's words rasped against Fernandes's ear.

'Let us not quibble.'

'I'm damn well not quibbling, I'm stating the truth that you want to skate round.' Fernandes gave a short head gesture that indicated he would concede the point.

'All that you say is true.' His eyes narrowed and he lowered his voice to a virtual whisper. 'But there are much greater stakes involved now.' He raised his hand to stop the general interrupting him. 'I should not be telling you this but it is my belief that the prime minister wants to keep this card up his sleeve in negotiations with the Chinese leader. That is why we have put a blanket news shutdown on the PLA's incursion.'

'This is ridiculous. It will all come out in the courts in Hong Kong. Devlin will have to give his side of the story now they are charging him with laundering the money through his account.'

'Not necessarily.'

'Hah!' The general's mouth twisted in scorn.

'Allow me?' Fernandes raised his eyebrows interrogatively. 'My people in Hong Kong tell me that the prosecution's case rests on the theft of the currencies and gold from Tibet. They're not relying on anything that happened from the time that the treasure was stolen from the Potala Palace treasury to the time it arrived in Devlin's account. Everything in between is irrelevant. Think about it.' He numbered off on his fingers: 'One, they will produce evidence from the Tibetan administration to say that both currencies and gold were government property. Two, Devlin has to prove that he did not believe that it was stolen. Three, the Dalai Lama's people will not be granted visas for Hong Kong, so it will just be Devlin's word. Four, if he says that he seized it from Chinese military personnel in India, the circumstances will only aggravate his crime.' He frowned. 'So, your friend is snookered, whichever way he wants to handle it.' There was a horrified expression on the general's face.

'You make it sound as though you find this disgraceful mess satisfactory.'

'No.' Fernandes held up both hands in surrender. 'I'm just facing the uncomfortable facts.'

'From the comfort of your seat in our civil service.' The general shot back contemptuously.

'I cannot be connected with anything to do with him but,' Fernandes said, holding up his index finger in an admonitory gesture, 'I am not abandoning Devlin.' The general's left eyebrow rose quizzically.

'The people in Dharmasala need to know that Devlin did not steal their money; then I believe that they will finance his defence.'

'So, you'll sort them out.'

'I will arrange for that to be done.' The general considered this for a moment.

'*Achibad*…but you'd better move quickly. He's on the Chinese's home ground, anything could happen to him.'

'I would not describe Hong Kong precisely as Beijing's home ground, though I concede that it's alien territory for our man.' Fernandes considered for a moment or two.

'Have you spoken to General Wangdi Lama in Bhutan?' The general shook his head angrily.

'You bastard, you know damn well I have.' He jerked his thumb towards the amplification system. 'I can't drown out a telephone conversation you've hacked into.' Fernandes gave a dismissive wave of his hand.

'It might be helpful if he could arrange for that man of his to fly into Hong Kong.' The general nodded grimly.

'Not much help if they get to him whilst he's in a Hong Kong prison.' Fenandes lifted his hands a little to indicate that it was not within his power to do anything about that.

'How soon can you get the Dharmasala people mobilised?' Fernandes gave a quick waggle of his head.

'It's in hand.'

'And you'll keep me informed?' Fernandes smiled slowly.

'General Saheb, you have a network of informants that my department would give its eye teeth for, but yes, I'll keep you abreast of developments from my side.' His expression hardened. 'I expect you to do the same for me.' The general had no intention of providing any information that could possibly harm a friend and fellow soldier but the rules of the game demanded that he exhibit co-operation. Fernandes, he knew, was too smart to be fooled, nor did he want to make an enemy of the man. His assent was given in the knowledge that the intelligence chief would automatically discount it. Max Devlin was in grave trouble and it grieved him that there was so little he could do to help.

Gangtok

Sikkim

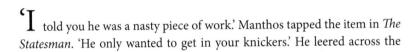

'I told you he was a nasty piece of work.' Manthos tapped the item in *The Statesman*. 'He only wanted to get in your knickers.' He leered across the breakfast table.

'Steve!' Jessica shook her head disapprovingly.

'It doesn't matter Jess, but I can't for the life of me understand what you see in your jerk of a husband.' Kim got up from her chair and started to walk towards the door.

'Hey, I thought you'd be pleased the cops want him, he dumped you, didn't he?' Manthos made no effort to disguise his satisfaction at her discomfort. She shot back at him.

'Even if he killed a monastery full of monks he'd be a better man than you.'

'I told you, your sister's a nut case.' He grinned at Jessica as Kim slammed the door shut behind her.

A few minutes later she was driving angrily out of Gangtok, her emotions in a whirl of conflict. Above all else she just did not want to believe that Max would have killed innocent monks. She recognised that this was a purely emotive reaction for which she had no concrete evidence whatsoever and simultaneously she was asking herself why she should care after the way he had treated her. 'Dumped!' She hadn't even had the satisfaction of a kiss-off, he'd simply disappeared only to reappear, of all places, in Gangtok. Without knowing why, she had the feeling that his abrupt disappearance had something to do with whatever he had been up to in Sikkim and if it was criminal, she reasoned, that would have been ample justification for not wanting to involve her. Yet again, she had not a jot or tittle of evidence to substantiate this line of reasoning but her gut instinct told her that Max's feelings for her went far deeper than his behavior indicated and she found comfort in resurrecting him in her mind. Maybe Manthos was right and she was crazy but she was convinced that she wasn't. The signpost for the turn off to Rumtek came into view and suddenly she knew what she had to do.

By the time she had parked her car outside the Rumtek Monastery she had begun to have doubts about her plan. Uncle Shakti would undoubtedly tell her everything he knew but it was not likely to be much. He wasn't a real uncle but he had worked for her father until he died after which the old man had been taken on by the monastery. She found him watering some plants in a desultory fashion.

'*Kaka?*' He turned and the moment he registered who it was his face lit up.

'Kim *nani*.' He still called her a child and she clasped his hands warmly. They chatted for a while, talking about Jessica and mutual acquaintances until Kim brought the conversation round to the murder of the monks.

'Ah…' He put his head in his hands. 'Devil's work.'

'Who would do such a thing?' Shakti's attitude changed suddenly and he looked about him nervously. Then, pointing towards a stone seat under a wooden arbour of *gogi chaap* he took her hand and led her over there. The sensuous scent of the great white flowers enveloped them in its beauty. Once seated, he spoke so softly she could barely hear him.

'The war between the Karmapas…you know about that?' She nodded.

'The *Bhotia* in Dharmasala…the *Sarkar*…?' He glanced up to see whether she was following to whom he was referring.

'The Sarkar in exile?' He nodded quickly.

'They pay me to tell them what is going on.' She pressed his hand to reassure him.

'They sent a *gorah* Saheb to me, he wanted to know which truck the treasure would be carried in.' He looked into her face and there were tears in his eyes.

'I told him.' Though she was certain it must have been Max she desperately did not want to believe it.

'What did he look like?' Shakti's description was vague enough to fit any number of Caucasian men of roughly Max's age. Then he added, 'He spoke Nepali like an educated *Pahari*, close your eyes and you wouldn't guess he was foreign.' Whimsically, he said apologetically, 'I liked him.' It was the worst information that she could possibly have been given. Now she had no reason to doubt that Max had been involved. For want of anything better to say she asked him.

'Do you think he killed all the people in the truck and stole the money?' The old man's answer made her think he had misheard.

'No.'

'No?'

'They weren't all killed, Lyangsong escaped.' The surprise on her face prompted him to explain.

'The boy, Lyangsong, he's an orphan, used to help out around the monastery, he was driving the truck that night, brought a friend along to help him. I didn't like the look of the friend.' He began to describe the friend but Kim wanted to get him to tell her about Lyangsong. She took one of is hands and held it between hers.

'Poor boy, it must have been a terrible shock, if he's an orphan who's looking after him?' Shakti shook his head.

'Don't know. I think he lives on his own in Upper Tadong, close to the government college. Sometimes he mentioned a *mithai dhokan* he liked to visit in the morning.' The evidence was mounting inexorably against Max but Kim had to follow every possible lead. She took her leave of Shakti as soon as decently possible and headed back for Upper Tadong. Just this once she was glad that Gangtok was a parochial little town where everyone knew someone who knew someone you needed to find.

Tracking Lyangsong down was so easy she became superstitious lest it all prove to be a wild goose chase. The old woman who ran the sweet shop knew exactly who she was talking about and wanted to share the gossip surrounding him.

'The police brought him back this morning. He hasn't left his house since then.' She pointed across the road to a traditional two-storey building. 'He used to live there with that Tenzing *goonda*, I'm not sorry he's gone.' If she was referring to the friend that Lyangsong had brought along that fatal night, no-one had a good word to say for him. Kim thanked her, crossed the road and knocked on the door. No-one responded so she knocked again and again until a voice inside shouted.

'Go away.'

'Lyangsong, I'm a friend, I'd like to help you.' It was a half-truth: she was genuinely sympathetic but helping him could also possibly help her. She spoke gently, coaxing him to open the door. After a few minutes she heard the bar being lifted on the inside of the door and it opened a few inches.

'Who are you?' There were dark pockets under his eyes which were bloodshot and his face was drawn and exhausted looking.

'My name's Kim Namgyal, I heard about your frightening experience from my Uncle Shakti at the monastery. You look as though you need some food and a good sleep. Let me bring you some *thukpa*.' Lyangsong's face relaxed and he managed a suggestion of a smile.

'Thank you, but no.'

'I'll be back in 10 minutes, is that alright?' She ignored his response and he nodded slowly and waited until she was back on the road before he closed the door.

Half an hour later they were seated facing each other across the wooden table, Lyangsong had almost finished eating the thick noodles and meat soup and Kim was nursing a glass of masala tea. She took in the general air of neglect in the room which had minimal furnishing, the table, two chairs and in the corner of the room a clay *chula* with a blackened kettle on the unlit fire. A cheap paper calendar advertising pot noodles was the only decoration on the walls. She waited patiently for him to finish eating before explaining that she sometimes worked for an organisation that counselled people in trouble and that they had discovered that it often helped the victims of violence to be able to describe the event to someone who was prepared to just sit and listen.

'The police don't listen, they told me what *they* said happened and then tried to get me to sign a statement which they had written. When I refused they threatened to beat me up.' He started to cry. 'I didn't want to sign but they made me.' Kim smiled encouragingly.

'Don't worry, everyone knows that's what they do. You don't have to feel guilty.' He wiped his eyes with his sleeve, then in a small voice he said,

'You're nice. I'll tell you what happened.' She nodded her appreciation. He began talking about Tenzing and she had to rein in her impatience until suddenly he told how he had been ordered to find the foreigner 'Divillin'. Kim felt her entire body go rigid and she had to fight the urge to ask questions. It was almost as though he read her mind.

'I think Tenzing wanted to hurt Divillin but I don't know why.' Then he recounted how Tenzing had forced him to splash some paint on the monastery's truck and persuade the monks to allow Tenzing to accompany him in the cabin of the truck that was intended to take the treasure to Singtam.

'Did Tenzing know what the truck was carrying?'

'Yes.' He looked shamefaced. 'I had to keep him informed about everything that happened at the monastery.' Abruptly, Shakti's comment about Lyangsong's 'friend' swam back into her mind and she regretted not having let the old man explain himself more fully. Already it was apparent that Tenzing had engineered himself onto the truck carrying the treasure which he had compelled Lyangsong to mark distinctly. What legitimate purpose could that have served?

'Was Tenzing working with this Divillin?' She pronounced it the same way he did. Lyangsong shook his head.

'I overheard him talking to someone on his mobile, he gave them the number of the *farang*'s car, I don't remember what he said but I think he wanted something to happen to him.' He looked her in the face but his eyes were not focused. 'Tenzing was always hurting people.' Kim still couldn't work out who was doing what but as between Max and Tenzing, the latter was far more closely associated with whatever happened to the truck and its occupants. Minimally, there now appeared to be another and possibly closer contender for the role of murderer.

'I drove the truck from the monastery, Thobten, the monk who was in charge of us, didn't like Tenzing and I felt he blamed me, so the mood in the cab was very uncomfortable. Then there were soldiers on the road ordering us to stop. Thobten shouted at me "Don't stop!" but the soldiers had guns pointing at me so I stopped. One of them came to the driver's door and told me to get out.'

'Indian Army soldiers?' Kim queried.

'Well, they were all carrying rifles and wearing the uniforms that soldiers wear, you know, the patches of green and black and brown.'

'You're sure?' She tried to keep the incredulity out of her voice, mindful of his recent experience at the hands of the police.

'That's what I saw.' A tiny hesitation in his tone emboldened her.

'The one who ordered you to get out, could you describe him to me?' Lyangsong pinched the bridge of his nose, she could see that he was trying hard.

'He looked very frightening, something about his eyes.' He scratched his head. 'Funny, he had sort of…Chinese eyes.'

'Not Nepalese?'

'No.' He was adamant. 'Theirs are more like ours, this man had Chinese eyes.' Kim made a mental note and smiled encouragement.

'I think the monk in the front passenger seat fired his shotgun at this man. It was such a bang, I went deaf and...' He slumped down in his chair, his head bowed as he muttered, 'I don't remember much after that until I woke up on the side of the hill.' She patted him on the shoulder.

'It doesn't matter, it's good to talk.' He looked up at her, she smiled. 'Thank you for sharing it with me.' She took out her notebook and wrote her mobile on a page, then tore it out. 'Here, if you feel you need to talk with someone, just call me.' He nodded silently and took the proffered piece of paper. She stood up to leave and his head jerked up quickly.

'I remember.'

'Yes?'

'The uniform, it wasn't an Indian Army uniform, we see those all the time. It was…different.'

'Don't worry, I'm sure it doesn't matter. I'll let myself out.' He joined his palms together in namascar which she echoed.

New Delhi

Geljen Ladenla walked along Janpath, ignoring the stalls of the Tibetans selling what they purported to be memorabilia of their homeland but were, in fact, fakes. He was not quite sure why he had chosen this route save that it served to remind him of his countrymen and women who scrabbled a living in their adopted homeland with precious little prospect of ever returning to the Tibetan steppes. The meeting that Fernandes had contrived with him in the Intercontinental had created even more problems than he already had to deal with. Despite the fact that Dariwallah claimed that he had executed Devlin's instructions about which accounts had to be credited, Geljen was still inclined to regard it as an error rather than a deliberate misallocation of funds. But none of that was of any assistance now that Devlin's account and the Dalai Lama's money in it had been frozen. The Hong Kong government's involvement meant that a formal application would have to be lodged on behalf of His Holiness to claim the funds. To date, there had been no restrictions on various Rinpoches visiting Hong Kong but he knew that the Chinese embassy would never grant a visa to any of the Tibetan government-in-exile's representatives. Prior to the discussion with Fernandes he had planned to approach one or both of the Karma Kagyu sect leaders to apply for release of the funds to them for onward transmission to Dharmasala, assuming that they would co-operate. But the Indian government's insistence on there being no mention of the ambush in Sikkim meant that neither Dorje nor Trinley's people could be involved. That meant that the claim would have to be made on behalf of His Holiness and so far, Beijing had not indicated what its attitude to the infant Dalai Lama would be. Very clearly, no-one in the government-in-exile could be involved. As if that was not enough, Fernandes had made it crystal clear that it was Geljen's responsibility to get Devlin out of trouble.

He kicked an empty bottle of Thumbs-up out of his path and glared at an elderly Tibetan shopkeeper, then felt guilty. It would have to be managed through one of their sympathisers in Hong Kong.

Lai Chi Kok Reception Centre

Hong Kong

Escorted by a Correctional Services officer out of his cell block and across the concreted yard that was divided into areas by tall wire fences, they walked towards the building that held the interview rooms. Halting outside a metal door, his escort nodded at the face that appeared in the inspection window. The ubiquitous sound of yet another lock being turned heralded the door opening and he was led inside where he stood in a confined entrance lobby whilst his name and prison number were checked against a list on a millboard. Max's curiosity was only thinly veined with a strain of hope. All he had been told was that it was 'a legal visit'. He had few expectations that his visitor would be other than some devious lawyer anxious to promise him deliverance via legally aided representation. Such information as he had been able to glean from his fellow inmates had reinforced his opinion of the quality of counsel he would be assigned if he applied for legal aid, which he declined to do. Nonetheless, even a visit from a lowlife legal clerk offered a welcome break from the crushing tedium of prison life.

'Room number 3.' The CSD officer pointed down the narrow corridor and he paused in the doorway, recognising the young barrister who had represented him in the magistrates' court.

'Colonel, this is Mr Peter Rougier QC,' Annie Xu said, before motioning towards a short attractive Chinese woman standing beside her.

'And this is Miss Anita Seto, our instructing solicitor.' The solicitor shook his hand and indicated the chair on the other side of the table from the lawyers. As he sat down Max switched his attention to the tanned, grey haired barrister who, though formally dressed, wore a colourful yellow silk tie which Max found oddly comforting. The solicitor began speaking in a warm chocolate-toned voice that seemed a little at odds with the serious expression on her face.

'Colonel Devlin, I have received instructions to represent you.' Max interrupted.

'That's very kind of you, Miss Seto, but I regret that I'm not in a position to pay for your services.' She smiled as she reached across and patted the back of his hand.

'We know, sir, but we have been put in funds, we assume on behalf of your principals. However, we do need your instructions to act for you.'

'My principals?' The solicitor nodded.

'A very wealthy businessman here who is an ardent supporter of Buddhism approached my firm and asked us to represent you. He wishes to remain anonymous but he told me to give you the message from "Slim" and that you would understand.' Max laughed involuntarily. So, Geljen still believed in him, or, the thought struck him simultaneously, they needed his co-operation if the money was to be restored. Whichever way, it was a lifeline he was not about to ignore.

'So, Colonel, may we act for you?' She looked apprehensively at him.

'By all means.' He managed the whisper of a smile as he turned towards the young barrister.

'Does that mean that I'm now your client?' She grinned and it lifted his spirits.

'May I get a word in between these two gracious ladies?' The QC interposed. Max looked him in the eye.

'Can you get me out of here?' To Max's ears his question struck him as rather gauche but it was too late to retract it. Rougier's expression suggested that he was not impressed.

'I can well understand your desire to find more salubrious accommodation but I don't intend to raise false hopes.' He gestured towards the young barrister. 'Annie, here, retailed your account to me and the odious manner in which the magistrate dealt with your bail application. However,' he inhaled a long breath before continuing: 'strictly speaking he made the correct decision.'

'Does that include the contemptuous manner with which he treated her?' Max retorted.

'Certainly not. Unhappily, certain of our magistrates are failed barristers who take a delight in insulting members of the private Bar. We shall not afford him a second opportunity. In principle, our best hope is to apply to a High Court judge. On the plus side, you have an excellent character, no convictions of any sort I believe.' Max nodded.

'Your defence has the singular merit of being capable of belief, a genuine mistake. But,' he grimaced, 'I have made some quiet inquiries and it seems that the PRC government are claiming that the money was stolen from the Autonomous Region of Tibet.'

'But that's ridiculous.' Max snapped. 'It was never theirs in the first place, it…'

'Forgive me Colonel,' Rougier interrupted him and put his forefinger across his lips before scribbling on a legal pad before turning it around for Max to read.

'These walls have ears.' Max rubbed his face in frustration. Rougier turned the pad back and wrote again before pushing it towards Max. 'Let's get you out of here first, then we'll talk.' He frowned as he spoke clearly. 'I must be brutally frank, Colonel, despite the factors in your favour, the odds are against us, even without anyone exercising political influence.' Max saw Miss Seto give the barrister a look of alarm, it added to his anxiety.

'What do you need from me?'

'Just that you keep your own counsel, if you'll pardon the unintentional pun. Miss Seto has been busy and it appears that someone of substance is willing to stand as a surety for you.' Max raised an eyebrow.

'Ours not to reason why Colonel, as Tennyson put it rather melodramatically.'

Max felt adrift in an alien world, nothing was what it seemed to be and he felt increasingly out of his depth. He had no serious alternative but to let the lawyers take over, even though it galled him not to be taking an active role, it went against the grain.

'I have studied Annie's notes of your account of the events. This will suffice for our present purposes.' This was said in a tone that did not invite comment. He signed some documents that they slid across the table for him, barely taking in what was written in them. Miss Seto gave him an encouraging smile.

'We'll be in touch shortly, don't despair, Colonel, Mr Rougier is the best silk in Hong Kong, you're in really good hands.' They all shook hands before leaving the little room. The same CSD officer collected him to take him back to his cell. As they walked across the barren yard towards his cell block, the warder broke his silence.

'He's a very good *dai lo see*, very expensive, you lucky man, ICAC hate him.' He grinned. Max thought that he'd never felt so abandoned by lady luck.

They were entering the Cross Harbour tunnel when Anita's mobile rang. She switched to hands free as she noted the caller's identity.

'Mr Chainrai.'

'Anita, hello.' The lightly accented voice sounded ingratiating. 'I imagine you have seen our friend, yes?'

'Yes, I'm with counsel now, we're on speaker phone.'

'Ah, good afternoon sir, I am so very pleased that you are taking this case.'

'Mr Chainrai.' Rougier was coldly formal. Chainrai continued.

'Miss Seto will have explained to you that there can be no mention of the Sikkim business?'

'I'm afraid I am not at liberty to discuss my client's case with you, Mr Chainrai.'

'But...' The Indian objected.

'Mr Chainrai, I appreciate that you are funding Colonel Devlin's representation. However that does not change the nature of my professional obligations to my client.' He softened his tone a fraction. 'I trust that you will understand.'

'Yes, yes.' There was a pause. 'Anita, we must talk.' The solicitor's eyes rolled up momentarily to Rougier.

'Of course, Mr Chainrai. Please call my secretary to fix an appointment.'

'Thank you.' The line went dead. The QC wore a slight smile as he spoke.

'What's all that about Anita?' She gave a throaty little laugh.

'I wanted to get you on board before I gave you the complete picture.' She gave him an apologetic grin. 'I guessed you would take the case after you met the client but I was apprehensive about your reaction if I filled you in first.' She gave a little wave towards Annie who was on the rear seat. 'She doesn't know either.'

'Is your car bugged?'

'I don't think so but you never know with the ICAC.'

'Fancy a cup of tea?' She nodded. 'Perhaps your driver can drop us off at the Mandarin?' A little later they sat in Café Causette, both barristers ordered cappuccinos and Anita a pot of Earl Grey. Rougier leaned forward across the table and smiled.

'You'd better come clean Anita.'

'Chainrai is just a front man for whoever's funding the defence. I don't know whether it's the Dalai Lama's people or the Indian government. At first I thought it was the Tibetans but when Chainrai told me that the funding was conditional on there being no mention of the PLA troops attacking the monks and stealing the gold and currencies I couldn't make sense of it, you know?' Rougier raised one eyebrow and the solicitor ploughed on.

'The fact that he's Indian makes it highly unlikely that the Chinese would use him and anyway, the DoJ have already indicated that they'll be claiming the money belongs to the PRC. The Dalai Lama's people have no reason to hide the fact that their people were attacked and robbed by the PLA. I did an internet search of the Indian newspapers for reports of the theft and murders but there was nothing, either in the national papers or the Sikkim ones. To my simple way of thinking, that indicates that the Indians don't want it broadcast.'

'But if Chinese soldiers did cross over into Sikkim and carry out this terrible attack, surely the Indians would be screaming blue murder?' Annie shook her head in disbelief.

'So, the Indians are keeping mum about it and…' Rougier raised his index finger, '…so are the Chinese. Neither of them want it publicised.' He leaned back in his chair. 'If you take the meat out of the sandwich, all you have left is the treasure being smuggled out of Tibet and ending up in our client's account in Hong Kong.' He blew air out through his nostrils. 'A perfect recipe for dealing in the proceeds of an indictable offence, which is what he's charged with.'

'And they don't need to prove that the money was stolen because the burden of proof will be on the colonel to prove that he didn't know or suspect it.' Anita banged her hand angrily on the table top. Annie spoke apologetically.

'He didn't talk to me about that, just that he rescued it from the PLA troops who had stolen it from the monks and had been instructed to return it to the Dalai Lama's people via their bank account in Hong Kong. He said that only his fee should have been credited to his account.'

'Not your fault, nor his, come to it. How were you to know that the prosecution would frame their case this way?' Rougier reassured her. 'In fact, we don't even know that for sure, we're just speculating on the basis of some informal guff that Anita has been given by her contact in our illustrious Department of Justice.'

'I'm pretty sure it's reliable.'

'Be that as it may, we're going to need a hefty surety to persuade anyone to give us bail.'

'How much do you think we should offer?'

'With almost 400 million Hong Kong dollars in issue, judging by past experience, we'll need sureties for at least 40 million.' Rougier sighed. 'Is Chainrai good for that amount?' Anita grimaced.

'He'll have to be.'

'Who's duty judge this week?'

'Horace Liu, I checked.' Annie's tone reflected what they all felt. 'Heaven forfend!' Rougier gestured to the air. 'He's not fit to sit on a chamber pot, let alone the High Court bench.'

'Do we have to get it in front of the duty judge?' Annie asked. 'The listing office clerks are inflexible.' Anita commented drily.

'Let's postpone it to next week, anyone's better than horrible Horace, with his level of xenophobia we won't stand a snowball's chance in hell. Meanwhile, you'd better get friend Chainrai organised.'

High Court

Admiralty, Hong Kong

'Court!' The stentorian tones of the CSD officer in the dock bellowed across the courtroom as Mr Justice Kenneth McIntyre entered, walked across and sat down.

'Good morning Mr Rougier, Mr Yang.' He smiled. 'I'm afraid that the CSD officers are unable to leave their parade ground manners outside. Yes, Mr Rougier.'

'Has Your Lordship had an opportunity to consider my skeleton submission?'

'Yes, thank you. As you say, it is rather a large amount that's involved.'

'Four hundred million reasons to abscond.' Yang rose and interrupted.

The judge motioned him to sit down.

'I appreciate your concerns, Mr Yang but I'm discussing this with Mr Rougier, you'll get your turn.'

'But the application is misconceived, my Lord.' Yang persisted.

'Mr Yang.' McIntyre's expression was angry. 'I have already said that you will get your turn, I expect counsel to conduct themselves with courtesy, both to the court and their opponents. I'm fully aware of the issues, now if you will condescend to allow Mr Rougier to complete his submission without further interruption?' The DoJ solicitor seated behind Yang leaned forward and plucked at his counsel's jacket, the anxious expression on his face enough to get the message across. Yang, disgruntled, sat down.

'Your client is an ex-Army officer with an impeccable record.'

'My Lord,' Rougier nodded. He sensed the direction in which the judge was going.

'And though 50 million US dollars is, as the prosecution put it so succinctly, a powerful incentive to abscond, not a cent of that money is presently available to your client.'

'Precisely, my Lord.'

'He is offering two sureties in a total of just over 10 percent of the sum involved?' Rougier confirmed this and McIntyre turned to prosecuting counsel.

'Are the sureties acceptable to the prosecution?' Yang turned to his instructing solicitor and there was a brief exchange. The judge's left eyebrow shot up momentarily.

'I would have thought you would have taken instructions on this, Mr Yang.'

'I'm sorry, my Lord.' Yang half turned back, flustered. 'I'm being given an update.' McIntyre looked at Rougier.

'When did the defence provide the prosecution with the information about the sureties, Mr Rougier?' Anita handed a copy of a letter to him.

'On the 17th, my Lord.'

'And today is the 23rd, so a full week, Mr Yang?'

'I am instructed that the sureties are acceptable as to their status but the commission is of the view that no less than 100 million Hong Kong dollars would be necessary.'

'Were the defence notified of this condition?'

'Oh yes.' Yang nodded emphatically.

Rougier rose to his feet shaking his head.

'Only just before we entered court this morning, my Lord.' McIntyre began writing. Max found the silence extraordinarily oppressive, the apprehension reminded him of sitting in an ambush, wondering whether they had been double bluffed and the enemy had them surrounded. Rougier was conferring silently with Annie. When Yang turned round to speak to his solicitor, he wore a satisfied smile. The judge's voice broke the spell.

'Bail will be granted until trial on the following terms: the two sureties accepted by the prosecution, each in the sum of 20 million, the defendant will report to a police station...' He looked up.

'Which would be the most convenient, Mr Rougier?'

'Aberdeen, my Lord.'

'…on Monday and Friday of each week between 10 am and 6 pm. He will surrender to the court his passport, not to leave Hong Kong, reside at the Ovolo Aberdeen Harbour and notify the ICAC of any change of address within 24 hours.'

The judge stood up saying 'Thank you, gentlemen', bowed and walked out of court.

Office of Commissioner for Ethnic Integration

Beijing

'He did what?' Bo's voice shot into a eunuch register as he exploded into his mobile. 'No, don't repeat it, you made me feel sick the first time.' He brought himself under control.

'You told me there was no chance of him being released from prison.' There was no hiding the bitter anger charging his words.

'It was a laowai judge.' There was a tremor of fear in the voice.

'So why did you allow it to get out of our control?'

'We cannot control everything in Hong Kong.'

'The other side obviously did.'

'No, sir, the listing clerks can't be bribed, they just follow the rules religiously.'

Bo was struggling to come to terms with a judicial system in what was, after all, a part of the People's Republic that was not controlled by the party, this demonstrated the fatal flaw in permitting such a system to operate. Now he would have to get instructions to the vulpine triad boss to get rid of Devlin somewhere in Hong Kong outside the closed community of the prison system. It would cost more, but the man had to be silenced, and soon.

Island Tang Restaurant

Central, Hong Kong
Same Night

'I thought you'd appreciate some rather more appetising food and a comfortable environment, Colonel.' Anita smiled at him across the table. 'I took the chance that we'd get a table, rather than give the ice-cream men a chance to bug the place before we arrived.'

'Ice-cream men?'

'Our nickname for the ICAC.' She laughed lightly.

'I see. But would the management here co-operate so readily?'

'It doesn't pay not to. They were originally set up to root out corruption in the Hong Kong police, but now they've spread their net so wide and they have draconian powers.'

'Yes, I think I've discovered that.' He smiled. It was pleasant to be able to joke about the past couple of weeks.

'Forgive this somewhat informal consultation but I was anxious to hear your full account without the risk of being overheard.' Rougier smiled apologetically. 'I'm afraid that your case is bristling with political "keep off the grass" signs.'

'Does that put you all at risk?' Max frowned.

'No.' All three answered rather too quickly for Max's peace of mind.

Rougier waved a dismissive hand.

'None of us know what the future holds, so when in doubt just follow the rules of the game. For we lawyers, that means adhering rigidly to our respective professional codes of conduct and chief amongst those is to represent our clients without fear or favour.' He gave a cynical laugh. 'I'm afraid that sounds very pompous but as a soldier you will doubtless be familiar with the way that the rules are there to protect everyone involved.' Max nodded slowly. The restaurant captain hovered and Anita beckoned him over.

'Shall I order for everyone? Is there anything you don't eat, Colonel?' He shook his head.

'Please go ahead.' The captain bent over her as she selected dishes, conversing in Cantonese.

'I believe you speak a number of Asian languages fluently, Colonel.' Rougier began. 'No-one can hide his light under a Google.' He laughed. Max smiled.

'I am fascinated by languages and the way they lift the veil on civilisations.'

'Done.' Anita announced, then turned a serious face towards Max. 'Would you please tell us the story of the Dalai Lama's treasure from your perspective?' She made an apologetic gesture with her hands. 'It is not idle curiosity, we need to know the full picture if we are to advise you properly.' Rougier signalled that he would take over.

'Colonel, my job is to represent you to the best of my ability as,' he said and waved towards Annie and Anita, 'are we all professionally obliged to do. Bitter experience has taught me that though I can cope with the limited edition that some of my professional clients sell me, someone of your character, unfamiliar with the arcane world of a criminal prosecution, can easily fall foul of the hidden hurdles just because you know that you are not a criminal and have nothing to hide. Indeed, your very intelligence can operate against your best interests. One golden rule that I observe is to ensure that, so far as practicably possible, my client gives me the full picture. All too often a defendant in the witness box will suddenly disclose something that he has not told me about and it is too late for me to reel him in. Put shortly, you have to leave it to me to decide what is important and what is not.' He paused as he looked hard into Max's eyes.

'It may sound arrogant but, believe me, I don't want to expose a chink in your armour simply due to a lack of total preparation.'

'Is there a chink in my armour?'

'That's what I need to know.'

'Fair enough.'

'It may strike you as rather cloak and daggerish to discuss your case in these surroundings.' He gestured towards the diners before continuing, 'But the ICAC has a bad record of bugging discussions between people they have charged and their lawyers, they even disregard judicial oversight. I cannot guarantee that my chambers have not been compromised. The background music and the ambient conversation level here provide a sufficient measure of protection.' He nodded towards his junior counsel.

'Annie gave me a concise account of what you told her in the magistrates' court but I would like to hear from you directly.' He indicated Anita. 'She will record our discussion.'

'I find it difficult to believe, my picture of Hong Kong was very different. Nonetheless, I must be guided by you, you're the professionals.'

'Thank you.' Rougier smiled.

Max was seriously troubled. The bail application had restored his faith in the system of criminal justice but what he was being told now put that faith on very unstable ground. All he had to go on was the mixed fortunes of his court appearances and his judgment of the lawyers whom he had not even chosen himself. It came down to personal assessment. He glanced at Annie who gave him a reassuring smile. He had adjudged her to be entirely honest and she, it seemed, had brought Rougier and Anita on board. The QC's complete mastery of the bail application demonstrated his ability, if any proof had been necessary and Max approved his candid exposition of the situation.

'There is one question that I need to ask though.' He looked from one to the other, settling on Anita. 'Who's funding all this?' The solicitor paused momentarily before speaking.

'As far as we know, a wealthy Indian businessman, Mr Chainrai has put my firm in substantial funds not only to cover our and counsel's fees but also for your hotel and living expenses pending trial. He explained that he is acting on behalf of an interested party but the truth is, we don't know who is actually footing the bill.' She bit her lower lip as though there was something else she wanted to say but added nothing. Max hated the feeling of being beholden to anyone but even more so when his benefactor was anonymous. On the other hand, without funds even now he would be sitting in Lai Chi Kok with no realistic plan to extricate himself from this mess.

'Well then, it seems that it would be foolish not to take advantage of my benefactor's generosity.'

Their first course of various *dim sum* delicacies arrived and Anita guided him through them. He decided to trust them with a potted version of his involvement with the treasure, starting from being tricked into rescuing the infant Dalai Lama from Tibet. He left out his involvement with Tashi and any mention of Fernandes. That limited the story to his retention by the Tibetan government-in-exile, mention of which brought a look of concern to Rougier's face. He was of two minds whether to come clean about ambushing the PLA special forces but realised that if he left them out of the account he would inevitably have to account for the murder of the monks. As he recounted the firefight, both Anita and Annie's eyes widened in disbelief. By the time he had completed his account he sensed that his credibility had been strained to breaking point. Rougier rested his chin on his cupped palms.

'So, there's been no outcry from the Indians about the PLA raiding into their territory nor outburst from the Chinese about the death of their troops?' Max's expression indicated that he found it as big a mystery as did the QC.

'But the Indian newspapers blame you for the death of the monks from Rumtek and robbing them of their money.' Anita's troubled expression was mirrored in Annie's face.

'I can understand the Indian government not wanting to admit that Chinese soldiers penetrated so deeply into their territory but ignoring the diplomatic leverage they could have gained from such an outrage?' Max left the conclusion hanging in the air.

'Equally, Beijing's silence about the fate of their troops is easy to follow.' Rougier sat back in his chair. 'The loss of face would be enormous, added to their failure to seize the treasure.' He frowned. 'But this was such an isolated incident that it smacks of a lone enterprise, perhaps even something that the central government was unaware of until after the event?'

'Some senior party cadre's head may roll?' Max interposed.

'Heads have rolled for far less than this.' Anita observed grimly. Rougier leaned forward.

'Beijing's lack of reaction is easier to follow than India's selective memory loss but,' he pointed his finger at Max, 'it leaves you as a convenient scapegoat and Beijing can get its hands on the money by way of a simple proprietorial claim.'

'Which can only be contested by the Dalai Lama's people, none of whom will be given a visa to enter Hong Kong.' Anita's voice was heavy with disgust. Max was about to inquire whether a statement from the Bhunnia that he had mixed up the two accounts would resolve the issue as far as he personally was concerned but he could see that it still linked him to what the Chinese regarded as stolen money.

'I think that we must also tell you that Mr Chainrai's instructions are that there must be no mention of the events in Sikkim.'

'So I'm just a sacrificial bundle, the court proceedings will just lend an artificial gloss of legitimacy.' He made no attempt to conceal his anger. Rougier held up his hand and smiled softly.

'Please understand, Colonel, you are our client, we take our instructions from you, not Mr Chainrai. We're guided only by what is in your best interests.'

'But he's the paymaster, doesn't he call the tune?'

'I'm tone deaf to some music.' Rougier smiled, then his expression shifted back into a more serious frame.

'But I'm not going to delude you, we have a major battle on our hands.'

'So what am I supposed to do?' Max's frustration infused his words.

'I'd like to say, leave it in our capable hands but that won't wash, I know. I need to think through everything that you have told us this evening and consider our options before we meet again.' He allowed a hint of a smile to edge his eyes. 'In the meantime, please review every step you've taken since you accepted the Tibetan government-in-exile's commission. There are aspects of the account that you have given us that don't quite knit together, perhaps you see what I mean?' Max said nothing. It was plain that Rougier believed that there was more to the story that had not been disclosed to him. It put him in a quandary, despite wanting to come clean to the barrister, Max held onto the notion that the account he'd given was sufficient for the purposes of devising a defence to the money laundering charge. The rest of the evening seemed a little stilted and he was glad to pray in aid the onset of fatigue after a somewhat dramatic day.

He asked the taxi driver to drop him off at the fish market so that he could walk along the harbourside and digest what he had been told. In his own mind he was convinced that it had been no mistake, Dariwallah had transferred the Dalai Lama's money into his personal account as his way of getting his own back. Doubtless the bastard thought it would cause confusion but whether his aim had been to get Max arrested for money laundering he really couldn't be sure. A simple confusion over account numbers could easily be explained away to the Tibetans. It was tempting to call Deepraj and get him to teach the Bhunnia a lesson he wouldn't forget but he dismissed it immediately, it would do nothing to resolve his problems.

He stood and looked across the harbour at the lights on Ap Lei Chau, he wondered if Miles Strachan was propping up the bar in the Aberdeen Boat Club, it would be good to get out on the water, sailing was such incredible therapy. His mind ran on to the possibility of borrowing a blue water cruiser and jumping bail to Thailand. But even if he could escape from Hong Kong he'd be a fugitive with few places to go and no discernible future. The ICAC had seized his mobile phone and though he had bought a cheap Huawei and a SIM card he had lost all his contact data and could not call either Geljen or Fernandes. Anita had promised to press the ICAC to return his mobile but he guessed they would have doctored it so as to monitor his calls. A cruel gust of wind reminded him of Rougier's brutally frank opinion of his chances of an acquittal. He berated himself silently, he probably had done himself no favours with his leading counsel by omitting parts of the story. A drop of rain fell on his face and as he turned to take the aerial walkway back to his hotel the heavens opened and he was soon drenched. He looked up into the sky and shouted at it.

'Shit!'

Garden Lounge

The Hong Kong Club
Central

'Can you arrange all your future consultations here, Peter?' Anita grinned at Rougier.

'Provided they are paperless, you know we can't be seen to consult any documents here.'

'Oh well, it was worth a try.' They had each chosen their dishes and were ensconced at a corner table that Danny, the head captain, had placed so that it was strategically removed from other diners. Rougier looked at both of them as he spoke.

'I think he's keeping something back.'

'But you don't think it's anything sinister, do you?' Annie asked anxiously.

'Well, it can't get much more sinister than bumping off a bunch of the PLA's special forces.' He acknowledged.

'So does it matter?'

'We don't know, do we? That's my problem.' There was a silence for several seconds before Anita posed the question that was in all their minds.

'Do you think it's true…about the PLA?' Annie wanted to voice her belief in their client but out of deference to her leader she waited for his reaction.

'I admit that I did an internet search of the Indian newspapers for the period and came up with zilch, which, in the circumstances is decidedly odd. Why publicise Devlin's attack on the monks when the Chinese would be so much more attractive a culprit?' No-one offered an explanation and they busied themselves with their food, the ramifications were uncomfortable. Anita put her knife and fork down firmly.

'It sounds a bit sneaky but I'm going to do some snooping of my own.' They looked at her expectantly.

'There was a girl from at LSE at the same time as me, Kim Namgyal. She was two years behind me but we were both badminton players and we became quite friendly. I'm going to see if I can get in touch with her, assuming she's back in Sikkim and try to find out if there's some local scuttlebutt that hasn't reached the papers.'

'Bit of a longshot.' Rougier observed doubtfully.

'Worth a try, surely?' Annie said enthusiastically.

'Well, it can't do any harm, can it? I think I've got her email somewhere.'

'Alright, let's just hope that we're not opening another can of worms.' Rougier had the sense that both his junior and instructing solicitor were a bit less objective in their attitude towards the client. Not altogether surprising, he thought ruefully, they would doubtless think him attractive in the way that women found adventurers more exotic than yeoman barristers. Devlin's account of becoming involuntarily involved in Tibetan politics stretched credibility to the full but his antics on the Nepal-Tibet border paled into insignificance beside the story of events in Sikkim. If, contrary to his account, he had ambushed the monks from the Rumtek Monastery, unquestionably the money in his account was the proceeds of an indictable offence in respect to which he could not possibly believe other than that he was guilty. Unless the Indian government issued a request to the Hong Kong Special Administrative Region for his extradition the Department of Justice would have no evidential basis on which to prefer a charge based on theft from the monastery, which, he pondered, was probably why they were ignoring that sequence of events and resting the case on robbery from the Potala Palace. His gaze wandered across the heads of the diners, assuming that the Indians were funding the defence, if they had stipulated that there be no mention of events in Sikkim they were also trying to tie his hands, all of which struck him as wholly contradictory. He broke out of his thought process.

'Have you tried to contact the Tibetan government-in-exile, Anita?'

'Mm.' She nodded, her mouth full of food. 'They were very uncommunicative, said that I'd be hearing from them. That was four days ago.'

Rougier leaned back in his chair, toying with a chopstick. If anyone had asked him whether he believed his client he would have given them the stock answer that he was not paid to believe his client, just to represent him to the best of his abilities. To himself he admitted that despite the extraordinary circumstances, he did.

Office of Secretary for Justice
Hong Kong

'The head of the Liaison Office has been pressing me for news of the Devlin case.' He looked to the Director of Public Prosecutions for information. The DPP smiled courteously at the government's senior law officer, a man he despised. Sergei Sze was a political appointee of the very worst kind; a man of dubious legal expertise and even less judgment who owed his appointment to his servile propensity to parrot whatever Beijing laughingly called the Basic Law. Short, fat and balding he was the personification of malevolence.

'It's a work in progress.'

'Tchh!' Sze hissed. 'The central government won't be fobbed off with such prevarication, Brian. The case has to be prosecuted swiftly so that the *gweilo* is imprisoned for many years and the money returned to the motherland.' Brian Kong checked an intemperate response. He spoke slowly and quietly, disguising his anger.

'Sergei, you know as well as I do that once charges are preferred, unless fresh evidence comes to light that bears directly on the validity of the prosecution the criminal justice system must take its course, regardless of the wishes or interests of you, me or the central government. We've briefed Allan Chu, he's expensive but against my better judgment I've authorised his outrageous fees because you told me to instruct him.'

'He's politically sound, a member of the Guangdong CPPCC, so any of the judges will know which side their bread is buttered.' Kong rubbed his chin slowly. He fully appreciated that this was precisely the message that the Secretary for Justice wanted to send but how many of the District Court judges would disregard their judicial oath to return a verdict that would advance their judicial career? Selecting trial by a District Court judge rather than a High Court jury already weighed the case heavily against the defendant. Not for the first time, he reflected on the wisdom of his decision to leave the private Bar and accept the appointment. He had genuinely believed that he could be serving the public interest but he had not factored in the extent to which the Department of Justice was not only deeply committed to the Hong Kong government but dancing to the discordant tune of Beijing. He was rapidly developing a siege mentality, keeping as low a profile as possible in the hope that he could keep the prosecution division as free from political influence as possible. The Devlin case was testing his objectivity to the limits. Sze tapped his file with his Montblanc pen.

'Make sure the listing officer in the District Court assigns the case to a safe pair of hands.' Kong was on the point of saying that he'd do no such thing but satisfied himself with a grunt of acknowledgment. Even if the case finished up in an 'unsafe' pair of hands, there could be no comeback because no-one would go on record for such tampering with the criminal justice system. As a sop to his own conscience and a temporising response he said as he closed the file, 'Without anyone to back up his account of being commissioned by the Dalai Lama's office, his defence will be as futile as it sounds. It's inconceivable that he could be acquitted.' The Secretary for Justice treated him to what he probably thought was a smile but which Kong read as a constipated grimace.

'You'd better be right.'

Residence of His Holiness the 15th Dalai Lama

Dharmasala

Tashi was still struggling with the English language as her eyes followed her finger as it traced the lines of the brief summary on her tablet. She chided herself gently as she registered that though she took the tablet for granted, reading the English script was still a problem whereas Dondhup was fluent in the use of both. They had found a clever app for her that translated, more or less accurately, the English into Tibetan but she tried not to resort to it unless there were new words or phrases. But the words she had read needed no further expansion. Max-la was in very serious trouble, trouble that he would never have encountered if she had not allowed her name to be used to persuade him to recover the treasure. The shadow of a headache reminded her that she had slept very badly as she tried to think of a solution. Her concentration was broken by the tapping at her door.

'Come in.' She turned as the elderly Abbot of Shadung bowed his wrinkled old head before greeting her.

'Come, sit by me.' She indicated the low armchair next to hers. 'We have serious matters to discuss.' He eased himself slowly down and she thought she saw a brief grimace of pain twist his already distressed features. She poured him a cup of *pu-erh* and offered it to him in both hands. Though his face was endlessly sad his eyes conveyed both strength and kindness.

'Devlin-la.' It was a statement, not a question. She nodded and indicated the screen on her tablet. He shook his head and the ghost of a smile haunted his face for a moment.

'The talking book is not for these eyes…my *chela* tell me all that I need to know and all that I would not wish to hear.'

'He is in trouble and it is my fault.'

'No.' He shook his head. 'The men in Beijing, they must destroy those who make them lose face, it has always been so.'

'But it was a mistake by the Indian money broker, he must go and tell them.'

'These merchants will not put their own lives at risk.' She frowned and her words had a lining of steel.

'I have seen the message from the Indian confirming that the money was sent to two different accounts in Hong Kong with the correct account numbers. That message proves that the mistake is not Devlin-la's.' The Abbot nodded gently, his eyes closed and she wondered if he had fallen asleep. She raised her voice.

'Doesn't it?' He opened one eye and regarded her silently.

'What it proves is that there is a direct connection between His Holiness and a very large sum of money sent from India to Devlin-la's account in Hong Kong, which is what the men in Beijing are also saying. That the two account numbers were mixed up does not break the link between him and money which the Chinese authorities in Lhasa claim was stolen.' The force of his logic only added to her sense of frustration.

'So, are we just going to do nothing, lose the funds and allow him to be sent to prison?'

'Peace.' He raised both hands, palm out. 'We made inquiries with the Chinese embassies in Delhi and Kathmandu, it seems that anyone with a Tibetan or Bhutanese name will not be given a visa for Hong Kong until the trial is over, so even if we wanted to, none of us can give evidence.' He raised one hand to signal her that he had not finished.

'I have an idea, I think it will work but it will depend on whether the judge who controls the trial is himself controlled by Beijing.' Her face flushed a little.

'And you're not going to tell me what the plan is?' He smiled and put one hand on her forearm.

'Consider it the foible of an old man, I just wanted to tease you a little.' Then he told her.

Gangtok

Sikkim

As she ended the call and returned her mobile to her pocket Kim was still recovering from the double surprise of hearing from Anita Seto and then being asked about the Rumtek murders. Her old badminton companion had been up front about her interest, telling her that she was making inquiries on behalf of a client in Hong Kong but she had clammed up when Kim asked her who the client was. But she knew in her bones that it had to be Max. The Indian newspapers had reported that he had fled to Hong Kong but the uncanny coincidence that his solicitor was an ex-LSE alumnus stunned her. She had been doing her best to consign Max to the lowest levels of her subconscious mind but like recurrent trauma he kept re-entering her life. Despite all the evidence that pointed to him having masterminded the attack on the monks and the theft of their treasure, against her better judgment she still clung to the idea that the man she thought she was in love with could not possibly have been responsible.

Anita's inquiries seemed to be directed to determining first whether there had been such an attack and secondly who was believed to have been involved. Kim had been very frugal with her information, trying to draw Anita into disclosing her interest. It was the direct question, 'Were there any foreigners involved in the attack as far as you know?', that had confirmed her suspicions about the Hong Konger's client.

'According to the Indian newspapers.' Then she suddenly blurted out, 'But you know how unreliable newspapers can be.' She was tempted to mention the rumour that had been circulating in the bazaar recently that Chinese soldiers had been involved somehow but she felt she was clutching at straws. Promising to email Anita if she heard anything more they had ended their conversation agreeing to keep in touch.

She caught sight of herself in the full-length mirror in her bedroom and stood staring at her reflection.

'He walked out on you without a word of explanation. For all you know he's a murderer and a robber, so why can't you forget him and get on with your life?' Talking to herself, the first sign of madness, so the saying goes. She could hear her mother's voice: 'Never chase after a man, it's his job to pursue you.' But was she chasing him? In her heart of hearts she knew that she wanted him, wanted him to be the kind, clever, inspirational man she had fallen in love with, wanted to believe against the known facts that he was not the vicious assassin who had killed the monks and stolen their treasure. In her head she heard Barbra Streisand singing 'I am a woman in love…' She turned away from the mirror and picked up her tablet. The only question was whether she took a flight from Paro or Calcutta.

Chung King Mansions

Tsim Sha Tsui

Max checked his watch, 11.15. The directions were for him to be on the steps of Chung King Mansions at this time, nothing more. When Anita gave him the message she sounded as puzzled as he was but she assured him that the request had come from the same source as the funds for his defence. If it was a representative from Geljen, it still occurred to him that there were better places to meet.

'Saheb.' The familiar voice came from behind him. He turned and smiled automatically when he saw Deepraj's grin.

'What the hell are you doing here?'

'*Colonel sahib ko pahli ayo.*' Deepraj did not have to sing the song for him to get the message.

'Who says I need a bodyguard?' The Gurkha's eyebrows rose a fraction.

'I haven't a clue, Wangdi Saheb gave me an envelope with cash, a return ticket to Hong Kong and told me to wait until I got here for instructions. These are my instructions.' He opened his arms to embrace the street.

'Where are you staying?'

'Here.' Deepraj jerked his thumb back towards Chung King Mansions. 'Right. Check out and move into my hotel in Aberdeen. If you're here, I don't want you on the wrong side when I need you.' Max called reception at the Ovolo and told them to reserve another single room in his name.

That evening they were both in the bar of the Aberdeen Boat Club listening to Miles entertaining a group of sailors with an account of taking his cruiser to Thailand and persuading a fantastic girl to join him on board only to discover that 'she' was a ladyboy. As the laughter subsided, Miles ordered another round of drinks for them. Max put a restraining hand on his arm.

'Thanks Miles, it's generous of you. Please let me square up with you, I know it's a club but I can't accept your open-handed hospitality.'

'OK. We'll work it out.' He frowned a little. 'Time must be a bit heavy at the moment, why don't you take my cruiser out?' He looked at Deepraj. 'Can you crew?' The Gurkha looked puzzled.

'Crew?' Max explained and he shook his head.

'I can show him what to do, I'd love to get out on the water.'

'You can use the speedboat too, there's a couple of mono-skis on board.'

'Great.' Max smiled his thanks.

'Any time, just top up the petrol tank, that'll be payment enough and give me a call beforehand in case I plan to take the cruiser out.'

That night, Max left the club with mixed emotions: wondering how he would feel with the deck under his feet, running with a strong breeze, knowing all the time that the probability was that such freedom would be short-lived.

Office of Director of Public Prosecutions

Justice Place

Hong Kong

'Criminal damage?' Brian Kong demanded incredulously. 'He's a 14-year-old schoolboy who wrote a few words on a wall in chalk that will wash off in the next shower of rain!'

'Yes, but it's what he wrote that's important.' Archibald Ho's unwavering appetite for prosecuting anyone for anything was what had driven him so rapidly up the ladder of promotion. He flourished a photograph of the offending graffiti.

'Hong Kong and PRC separated by a heart shape which has been crossed out, the message is very clear, it's incitement for an independent Hong Kong.'

'In that case it's not criminal damage and until Article 23 is turned into an offence of sedition, there's nothing we can charge him with and even then he could argue that it simply means that they've fallen out of love.' He laughed lightly.

'But Sergei says we must make an example of him.' Ho persisted. If the DPP had been irritated before, all he needed was this reminder of the Secretary for Justice muscling in on his territory yet again to break through his carefully constructed patience.

'Fine. Charge him with criminal damage, behaviour likely to cause a breach of the peace and charge both his parents for failing to exercise proper control over the son.' He watched the satisfaction spread over Archibald's features. 'And,' he lifted an admonitory finger, 'make sure that the chalk is confiscated and seek an order for its destruction.'

'Yes, of course, Brian.' Kong shook his head in disgusted disbelief. 'Archie…'

'Yes Brian?'

'Forget the rubbish I just told you. Offer no evidence against the boy but tell the court prosecutor to try to get him to agree to being bound over to keep the peace for 12 months.'

'But Sergei…'

'But Sergei nothing! Just do what I say.' The senior prosecutor's face was a mixture of disbelief and shock that segued into the venomous.

'Whatever you say, Brian.' Kong pushed the file back across his desk signalling that the matter was closed. Ho almost collided with a slim middle-aged woman with her hair tied back into a tight bun and wearing an equally tight expression burning through her large designer glasses. They exchanged expressions which conveyed a mutual distrust of their boss. Kong noted that she had not troubled to give even a perfunctory knock on his door, not that it surprised him, Phoebe Lam was very firmly in the Secretary for Justice's camp.

'What can I do for you, Phoebe?' He inquired courteously.

'I just came to let you know that the PTR in the Devlin case is fixed for this Friday.' Kong did a quick mental calculation.

'That suggests that it has been expedited.'

'Oh yes. We want to get it done and dusted as soon as possible.'

'Do we know what the defence stance is on this?'

'It's bound to be the usual time wasting that all defendants try on.'

'Well, just keep me informed.' The case was largely out of his hands now but he was uncomfortable with the political dimensions that it had assumed.

District Court

Wan Chai

'How many witnesses will you call, Mr Rougier?'

'As presently advised, two, Your Honour.' District Court Judge Jonathan Tang Ching-yee continued to write as he asked the next question without looking up.

'Including the defendant?' Rougier smiled.

'That's a decision that we don't have to make until the prosecution case is closed.' He did not add 'as Your Honour bloody well knows' but it was not a good sign that a judge who was very experienced in criminal law would even think of trying to get a commitment from the defence at this stage. Still, he would have to be humoured, they could not afford to antagonise the man.

'And you're asking for a subpoena to HSBC to produce the bank records of the Dalai Lama?'

'Our position is very simple, Your Honour. The funds that ended up in Major Devlin's HSBC account should have been credited to the account of the Dalai Lama and on the same day a credit of US$1.2 million which ought to have been remitted to Major Devlin was incorrectly credited to His Holiness's account. Once the court has sight of both accounts the mistake will be apparent.' The judge looked at Allan Chu.

'Well, of course, Your Honour, the court cannot possibly countenance such a blatant breach of the Personal Data (Privacy) Ordinance,' Chu said, his lip curled as he glanced sideways at Rougier, 'let alone granting access into a total stranger's bank account, it would be ridiculous.' The judge stared at Rougier for a few heavily silent moments.

'What evidence do you have to support your theory that there is such a deposit in the lama's account?' Rougier knew before he made the application that this was capable of boomeranging back into his face but he could see no way of obtaining the evidence that would avoid his client admitting that he had knowledge of the source of the massive sum. What made it so incriminating was that because both remittances were made on the same day, there was a powerful inference that Devlin's fees were linked to the funds. As far as the Chinese and the prosecution were concerned, that squared the circle.

'My instructions are simply that both remittances were made by the same money exchange business and that is where the mix-up occurred.' He picked his words carefully, avoiding an outright denial of any connection between the two.

'My solicitors are endeavouring to obtain evidence from the remitting agency.'

'Until which time you only have your client's instructions.'

'Correct, Your Honour.' He wanted to say: 'Inevitably, as you must well know.'

'I'm against you, Mr Rougier.' The judge reached for his file. 'So the time estimate still holds good at five days?'

'Yes, Your Honour.'

'Mr Chu, you're asking for an early date for trial.'

'If Your Honour please.' Rougier eyed his opponent sideways on, the swept back hair with the touches of grey that he suspected were the result of a hair stylist rather than natural ageing, the John Lennon glasses that ill-suited the predatory style. The judge turned to the defence counsel.

'Is there any objection from the defence?' Rougier had no intention of disclosing the problems they were facing in trying to secure a witness to confirm Devlin's engagement on behalf of the Dalai Lama but they needed time.

'I can put it no more succinctly, Your Honour, the defence is not yet ready to go to trial. We need two months and after that I am committed to a six-week trial.'

'Your Honour.' Chu was on his feet, all concern and false anguish. 'I'm sure that my learned friend has a full diary but the prosecution is anxious to have this matter resolved swiftly. The Autonomous Region of Tibet wants to recover their funds as soon as reasonably practicable and we are ready to proceed.' Rougier stood up and leaned on his lectern.

'The Dalai Lama,' he emphasised the words, 'would also like to get his money back soon but, as Your Honour will be aware, title to the funds in the account is the subject of competing claims which touch directly on the serious allegations against my client. I don't need to remind the court that the liberty of the individual has to be given priority.' Chu was back on his feet, impatiently tapping his papers with his fingertips.

'Your Honour, this is a straight forward case. The unemployed defendant has to satisfy the court that he neither knew nor believed that nearly US$50 million in his bank account was the proceeds of an indictable offence.' He gave a dismissive laugh.

'We're not talking about Li Ka Shing here.' He sat down and Rougier rose slowly to his feet before picking his words slowly and carefully.

'Now is not the time to rehearse the opposing arguments nor for me to remind my learned friend where the burden of proof lies in a criminal trial. We are telling the court, as we are obliged to do, that the defence is not ready to proceed and asking that the trial take its place as in the normal course of events.' Max sat in the dock wondering where all this was going, the judge did not appear to criticise the way in which Chu had twisted the facts which did not augur well for his prospects.

'Gentlemen, let me look at my diary.' The clerk of the court stood up holding a large book which he placed in front of the judge. Max could not hear the conversation between the judge and the clerk but whatever he was being told seemed to surprise the judge.

'It seems that a lengthy trial that I was due to hear the week after next has been re-assigned to another judge so that I am now free to take this case in ten days' time. I am always disposed to extend an indulgence to the defence for good reason but other than a vague assertion that the defence is not ready, Mr Rougier has not referred me to any specific matters that are preventing the defence from proceeding to trial. I must therefore, in the interests of all parties, accede to the prosecution's application. The trial will commence on the 15th of this month. Bail will be continued on the same terms, the surety need not be taken afresh. Thank you, gentlemen.' He rose, bowed and walked out of the court.

'Is it always as bad as this?' Observing Anita's strictures against discussing the case anywhere that could be overheard by the ICAC, Max had contained his anger until they were all sitting in the Grand Hyatt's coffee bar. Rougier nodded.

'Invariably. The District Court is seen as a step on the judicial ladder and the higher the conviction rate the better the prospects for promotion to the High Court. Only the prosecution has the right to elect whether the trial will be before a District Court judge sitting alone or in the High Court with a jury, so the cards are stacked against a defendant from the start.'

'So I really don't stand a snowball's chance in hell?'

'The odds are not quite that bad but they're not brilliant either.' Rougier rubbed his chin reflectively.

'Judge Jonathan Tang is a curious judicial bird. Unlike so many others, he gave up a very good practice at the Bar to take this appointment. It's rumoured that his daughter is not well and he wanted to have a more settled life. What makes it rather intriguing is that his wife, Bonnie Wu, also a barrister, is a very outspoken libertarian, defends people whom others would run a mile from and does a fair amount of *pro bono* work too. I thought she might temper his zeal for convictions but apparently not.'

'I can't see why there's room for any optimism whatsoever.' Max shook his head. Anita looked up from reading her smartphone and turned the screen so that Max could read it.

'This is the confirmation note from the money exchanger to the Dalai Lama's office.' Max peered at the small print which recorded the two remittances having been made to the correct accounts.

'Well, at least now you'll believe me though I'm damn sure that the bastard deliberately switched account numbers.' Rougier shook his head.

'Forgive me if I sound uncommitted: it's not a question of whether we believe you or not. Our job is to test the prosecution's case to see if it holds water. To do that, we start from the premise that you, our client, are giving us a truthful account.' He breathed in heavily through his nose.

'If you ask me as your counsel whether or not I believe you I will tell you that it is no part of my professional duty to do so.' He held his hand up to stop Max from interrupting.

'In my personal capacity however, I have no reason to doubt that you believe that the funds are the property of the Dalai Lama.' Max relaxed back into his chair, his eyebrows flicking up momentarily. He reached across the table and touched the screen of Anita's smartphone.

'Assuming that you download this note, I think I understand enough to know that you still need someone to produce it to court and the Chinese have effectively blocked anyone able to do so getting into Hong Kong.' Anita closed the screen.

'I'm working on it.'

'In the meantime,' Rougier rested his chin on his hands, 'do you have any paperwork anywhere to support your claim to these fees?' He gave Max a lopsided grin and said, 'Something that did not involve snatching them from either the monks of Rumtek or the PLA.'

'I suppose I could stretch my original brief to cover it without departing too far from the truth, delivering the funds was part of what the project turned out to be and the expedition to catalogue the Buddhist iconongraphy of Nepal was a massive task, even if I was duped into a fundamental change of plan.'

'I'm not asking you to lie.' Rougier's expression was grim. 'Once you're caught out in a lie our defence vanishes. Everything turns on the judge accepting that you genuinely had no reason to believe that the money was illegally come by.'

'I'm as sure as I can be that the gold and the currencies were the legitimate property of the Dalai Lama, but you're asking me to omit all the killing and mayhem caused by the PLA's attempts to capture it.' He threw his hands up in disgust.

'I know, I know.' Rougier slid himself forward to the edge of his chair and stared hard at Max.

'Look, you know just as well as I do that this is a political trial and the other side is bending every damn rule in the book. All I'm advising you to do is to come up with a credible basis to account for these fees. I don't know what the terms of your retainer were, only you know that. I'm playing this by the rules, acutely aware that you probably think I'm allowing my integrity to get in the way of your defence and that Chu is counting on it. But if this case goes to the Court of Final Appeal that same integrity will weigh the scales in our favour.' He sat back in his chair, exasperation puffing through the pores of his features. They all sat in uncomfortable silence for a little while, Max's fingertips slowly tapping the tabletop.

'Actually, it's not unlike soldiering: we're governed by the Geneva Convention, the rules of engagement and an individual sense of what's right, but our enemies have no such compunction. When you lose one of your own, the urge to ignore the rules can be overwhelming…so hard to justify clinging to civilised norms.' Max stared into an unfocused middle distance.

'The ultimate irony, civilised warfare.' He blinked and his eyes swept across them.

'I'm in uncharted territory, in your capable hands and since there's little if anything that I can do to progress my case I think I'll get out on the water and enjoy my freedom whilst I still have it.' He rose and walked away, threading a path between the tables.

The frustration was still churning away at him as Deepraj steered the motor boat out of the Aberdeen typhoon shelter heading out towards the Middle Island. Max registered that it was an almost perfect day: being a weekday there were no other pleasure craft out, the sun shone, the breeze was gentle, the sea incredibly calm; yet the fates had turned their backs on him. He pointed to an area just below the Ocean Park.

'Stop over there and then we'll ski parallel to the shoreline.' He balanced his mono-ski on the broad transom, stepped up, put his feet into the cups and checked that the tow rope would run free, then nodded to Deepraj to cut the engine before he jumped into the water. Once the boat had drifted away, the Gurkha watched as he drove forward to take up the slack. Max pulled himself upright and signalled for acceleration. The weight of the water travelled up through his legs and as he cut figures out of the grey-green mass his sense of his own power began to return. On both the previous days there had been a swell that had forced him to keep the speed down but today conditions were perfect and he threw his head back and revelled in it.

The distinctive high-pitched scream of a jetski intruded into his peace. He made a conscious effort to disregard it but the noise grew louder. Someone else had seized the opportunity to enjoy the calm waters, a pity that it should be the noisome jetski fraternity. The scream of its engine grew uncomfortably loud and he glanced back over his shoulder. There were two black-clad figures riding it, both wearing helmets which made him wonder whether they were Marine police sent out to make sure he did not make a run for it. Now the noise became uncomfortably close and he glanced back again, noting that it was directly in his wake and still gaining on him. He swung out to his left towards the cliff face below Ocean Park, bringing them into his peripheral vision only to lose sight of them as they tracked his course, confirming his suspicion that they were targeting him.

The scream of the engine filled his ears and he twisted round to his right just in time to see the pillion passenger standing up and leaning towards him wielding what looked like a large butcher's knife which he had swung back preparatory to taking a swing at head height. Max twisted himself into a violent stem turn, hunched down over his ski and shot out of reach. For all its power, the jetski could not match his manoeuvrability. Swinging himself to his far right extremity without losing traction he yelled to attract Deepraj's attention. Whether it was his shout or the proximity of the jetski, the Gurkha looked back, the expression on his face comprehending the immediate threat. With his eye still on Max, Deepraj reached for the throttle and Max held on grimly as he was wrenched forward. The jetski now altered course and aimed for him and it was obvious that it had the legs of the speedboat so that if he tried to swing back to his left he would cross their path and afford them an easy target. He considered dumping his ski and diving under the water to evade them but abandoned it as narrowing his options too far. An idea began to form in his mind but it was hedged around with uncertainties: nonetheless he had to seize the initiative. He pointed away to his right and Deepraj nodded and headed out towards the shipping lanes. Now the jetski had to follow him and then come up alongside to get within striking distance. It took no time for them to get parallel to him but he managed to maintain a 50-metre gap of open water to his left. The speedboat was at maximum and the jetski was bouncing across the broken surface of the boat's wake. Deepraj was steering with one hand and watching for his signal: Max swept his hand across his throat and though there was a momentary pause as the Gurkha registered both the meaning and the effect, he cut the engine. As Max lost speed so the jetski shot ahead of him. Then he signaled full speed and the towline jerked taut. Slewing to his left, Max crouched over his ski and sped in an arc using himself as the pendulum with the jetski at the mid-point between himself and the boat. The men on the jetski suddenly saw the danger they were in and began to turn to their left but Max's momentum was even greater than theirs and he braced himself for the impact, aiming the line to cut them just below head height. The pillion passenger made a futile slash at the towline a fraction of a second before it struck him under the armpit and across the neck then both men were in the water. The force of the impact swung Max in towards the jetski and he struggled to keep his balance. The jetski was locked in a turning circle from which Max concluded that the idiot driver had not attached the dead-man's control to his wrist.

One of the figures was floating lifelessly on the water, kept afloat by his buoyancy jacket; the other was floundering, making gurgling noises. Tempting though it was to ski straight at his head, Max judged discretion the best course and signaled Deepraj to pull him in the direction of Middle Island. As he sped towards the isthmus of water between Middle Island and Repulse Bay he chided himself for allowing his guard to drop. The only possible inference was that the Chinese wanted him dead. Hong Kong may well be a special administrative region but it was well within Beijing's reach. What was the death of one more foreigner in the overall scheme of things? He signaled Deepraj to pick him up and hauled himself into the speedboat. The Gurkha was grinning.

'That was a bit close, Saheb.'

'Thanks.' Max grunted as he toweled himself dry. 'Drop me off over there.' He pointed to where the road curved beside the sea on the opposite side to the Yacht Club. Pulling on a pair of shorts and a T-shirt he told him to take a circuitous route back to Aberdeen.

'If the jetski's still turning circles, report it to the Marine police. You didn't see anything else and I'm in enough shit without having the cops taking an undue interest in me. If they ask what you were doing, tell them I instructed you to meet me here but as I didn't turn up you gave up on me.'

'Huzoor.' There was nothing to be gained by behaving like a good citizen, his attackers would be anxious not to draw attention to themselves, even if they survived.

'You'll have to watch my back from now on.' The Gurkha gave a peremptory nod that also conveyed that this was an entirely superfluous order.

Bauhinia Chambers

Duddell Street

'*Sifu*, have you seen this?' Annie walked into Peter Rougier's room holding a scanned document in her hand. The blank look on his face was sufficient answer.

'It's the prosecution's witness statement claiming title to the money in our client's account. It's in Chinese but I've done a rough translation for you.' He reached out for it and started to read.

'Looks as though they've found a turncoat Tibetan to provide a legal basis for their claim.'

'Mm.' She pointed to the first paragraph. 'He calls himself the financial controller for the Potala Palace.'

'What a curious coincidence.' Rougier tapped the page. 'The amount he claims was stolen matches the sum credited to Devlin's account.' He gave a disgusted snort.

'It's very vague, just refers to "assets". That's the nearest translation I can come up with. You know how imprecise the Chinese language can be.' She smiled. 'But that'll give you plenty of room for cross-examination.' He shook his head.

'Even if we can show that the amounts can't possibly correspond, it won't make much difference, the charge is framed as knowing or believing that it *or any part thereof* were the proceeds of an indictable offence. In other words, Devlin has to establish, on balance, that no part of the funds in his account could have come from the Potala Palace. His explanation is that his instructions came from the Tibetan government-in-exile.' He looked at her in frustration. 'It's virtually proving their case for them.'

'But surely, sifu, it's not the only inference? Why couldn't it be funds to which the Dalai Lama was legitimately entitled?'

'The gold and the US dollars perhaps but the Chinese yuan?' He shook his head. 'Don't forget that the receipt we were hoping to rely on, even though we have no-one to prove it, specifically refers to an amount in yuan.'

Annie wanted to press her argument, emphasising that the lamas who had fled from Tibet would have brought *renminbi* with them but she could tell that Rougier was firm.

'The point is, Annie, our instructions are that these are the very funds that were brought over the Himalayas at the time of the Dalai Lama's escape and handed over to Devlin and his Sherpas. So, we can't mount a positive case that they're someone else's funds because we *know* that they're not! We're trapped by our own professional ethics.' Annie sat down and Rougier felt sorry for the glum expression on her face.

'Look,' he swung himself round in his chair so that he faced her, 'Devlin's dilemma is that he genuinely believes that these *assets*,' his tone was contemptuous, 'belong to the Dalai Lama and it's Devlin's state of mind that's on trial. You and I probably believe that he's right but frankly, the prospects of a District Court judge accepting his belief against sworn testimony on behalf of the government of the PRC are less than a snowball's chance in hell.' He threw his pencil down on the desk top.

'So, it's a political trial.'

'What else would you call it?' They sat staring at each other in a darkly coated silence which was broken by his telephone ringing.

'Yes, put her on.' He mouthed to Annie, 'It's Anita.'

'You what?' His eyebrows rose and fell. 'In your office now?' He picked up his pencil and started to doodle on a scratch pad. 'Don't tell me any more, Anita. Take the statement, have it sworn as an affidavit, lock the original in a safe and then bring us a copy. Oh, and advise him to keep a very low profile.' He replaced the handset and turned his face towards Annie, an enigmatic half-smile illuminating his features.

'It seems we do have a witness after all.'

Park Walk Residence

Kowloon Tong

'*Jo-jiu*, can you take April to the doctor tomorrow morning? I have a trial in Fanling.' Bonnie frowned, anticipating the response.

'You know I start the Devlin case tomorrow, how can I justify a late start, especially when we both know that my handling of it will determine whether I get onto the High Court bench.' Jonathan screwed his face in frustration. How could Bonnie begin to compare some trifling magistracy case with the trial that he had been told, albeit unofficially, would decide his promotion.

'Why can't Grace take her?'

'Because Grace is our domestic helper, not her mother or father and one of us needs to hear what Dr Lai has to tell us about the results of the biopsy.' Bonnie stood up and put her hands on her hips, a sign that Jonathan recognised from old.

'You said you gave up your career at the Bar so that you could devote more time to our daughter.' She had been containing her increasing anger as Jonathan had avoided his share of their responsibilities for April, always excusing himself on the grounds of his judicial duties.

'I really think you care more about your bloody career than your daughter's needs.' She had the bit between her teeth now and she cut him off as he started to speak.

'No! You've changed. When you started sitting you set out to be a model of fairness but your ambition has blinded you to everything that used to matter, just so long as you get to wear the red dressing gown. I was willing to make compromises in my own practice to help you but now that your fucking career takes precedence over April's health. You're not the man I married.'

Jonathan felt the fear in his stomach: everything had been going so well it had never occurred to him that Bonnie saw him in this light. But the panic he was experiencing now was the dilemma of losing his family or his elevation to the High Court bench.

'But don't you see the massive benefits for all of us once I get promoted? Luxury flat, chauffeur-driven car, bigger salary and pension?' Even as he spoke he knew this was the wrong way to win the argument. Bonnie shook her head in disgusted dismay.

'At what price? How many innocent people do you have to convict to get all these,' her hand sliced the air contemptuously, 'benefits!' She picked her mobile up off the kitchen table and waved it at him dismissively.

'Go! Go! I'll ask Marcus to brief someone else.'

'I,' he began but she stormed out of the room. He felt sick. Just when the fruit was in reach, he could feel his fingers around it…now this. His own anger filled up the space. She wasn't being fair, spouting off about innocent people. Hong Kong was a better place with all those triads and fraudsters locked up. She always defended the indefensible. He snatched up his cigarettes and lighter and walked out of the flat, slamming the door behind him. One thing was for certain, Devlin was going down.

District Court

Wan Chai

As the prosecuting counsel opened his case, Max watched the judge's face, trying to interpret any expression and felt his spirits sinking as he noted the nods of acquiescence to the points being made against him. The judge's purple robe sent his mind off at a tangent, if a scarlet woman was one without shame, what did that make a purple judge? From where he sat in the dock he only had a side-on view of Chu's face but he quickly developed a distaste for the way the man's lips seemed to burble the words. Rougier's body language signaled an anger that he contained and once or twice he got the distinct impression that the QC was restraining Annie's disagreement with Chu's submissions. One time she turned around to look at him and let him see the contempt on her face.

'And so, Your Honour can see that there really is no defence to this charge. Indeed, with all due respect to my learned friends, the not-guilty plea is a gross waste of the court's time and simply delays the inevitability of a guilty verdict.'

'I believe that decision rests with me, Mr Chu.' To Max's surprise, this was delivered in icy tones. Was Chu guilty of some sort of judicial *lèse majesté*?

'I take it that concludes your opening, let's hear some evidence.'

'If Your Honour please.' Max noted Chu's sudden reversion to the sycophantic tone. 'The prosecution calls Mr Chin Yee-man. He is the HSBC employee who reported the extraordinary credit into the defendant's account.' The judge looked at Rougier.

'Are you challenging the veracity of the HSBC account statement?' Rougier stood up.

'Not the veracity, no.'

'What then? It seems pointless to call a witness to swear to something you don't challenge.' The tetchy comment was not lost on Max.

'If the court will permit me?' Rougier left his question hanging in the air.

'Oh, very well but I hope you are not wasting time.' Rougier inclined his head in acknowledgment and sat down. Chu took the man through the formalities and asked him to produce the bank's record, then sat down. Rougier looked briefly at Max who nodded.

'My client, Mr Devlin, produced his HSBC premier account card and asked you to show him his bank statement, didn't he?'

'Yes, sir.' Chin's pale face matched his nervous manner.

'And when you showed him his account statement, he told you that there had been a mistake, didn't he?' Chin looked towards Chu.

'Please do me the courtesy of looking at me when I am addressing you, Mr Chin. I want your answer, not Mr Chu's.' Chu shot to his feet.

'I have not said a word, I object to the inference.'

'I'm not suggesting that Mr Chu has said anything, Your Honour, but the witness plainly looked at Mr Chu rather than answering my question.'

'Answer the question, Mr Chin.' The judge spoke sharply and motioned for Chu to sit down.

'I expect counsel to treat each other with courtesy, Mr Rougier.'

Chin's face was drawn and he answered hesitantly.

'Ye…s.'

'In fact, Mr Devlin told you that the credit of US$50,120,800 was not his money and ought to have been credited to another account.'

'I…don't remember clearly.'

'But that was the gist of what he told you, wasn't it?' Again, Chin's eyes flicked towards Chu before he replied.

'You may say so.'

'You mean you agree with me?'

'Mmm.'

The judge tapped on his desk.

'Mr Chin, I need a Yes or a No, not an "Mmm".' The witness looked as though he would crumple. Very softly, he responded, 'Yes.'

'And Mr Devlin asked you to check another HSBC account, the number of which he gave you, to see if there had been a credit of US$1,200,000.'

'I told him that I could not disclose the status of someone else's account.' Chin had suddenly discovered some courage.

'Correct, but he gave you a specific account number and mentioned that amount.'

'I don't remember.'

'But you made a note of your conversation with my client, didn't you?' Chin shook his head. Rougier tapped the file open in front of him.

'In your witness statement made to the ICAC on the same day, you said and I quote, "*I made a note of what Mr Devlin told me, the bank requires us to make a record of what is said when we suspect money laundering.*" So, where is your "note", Mr Chin?'

The witness's complexion turned grey as he looked at the ICAC officer seated behind Chu.

'I gave it to him.'

Rougier turned towards the ICAC senior investigator.

'Do you mean Mr Alexander Yuen?' Chin nodded his agreement and Rougier raised one eyebrow in Yuen's direction. The ICAC officer conferred with Chu who rose to his feet, his scowl matching the bad grace with which he responded.

'Mr Yuen will try and find the note, Your Honour.' The judge nodded. Rougier whispered to Annie, 'Let's break the rules.' He then turned to the witness.

'But you did check on that other account, didn't you, Mr Chin and saw that there had been a credit in precisely the amount mentioned by Mr Devlin?' Rougier held his breath. Chin nodded slowly, saying: 'Yes.' Rougier motioned to the court usher to hand a document to the witness.

'Please don't read it out, but the number of the account you checked is the same number written on this note confirming that a credit of US$1,200,000 had been remitted to it.' Chu was on his feet.

'We have been given no notice of any such document, I object to its production.' The judge looked at Rougier.

'Can you prove this document, Mr Rougier?'

'Yes, Your Honour.' Rougier watched as only the judge's eyes moved in his face, switching between Chu and himself.

'Let the witness answer the question.'

'Can you ask me the quesiton again?' Rougier repeated it for Chin.

'I think so, yes.' Annie underlined the answer in her notebook. Rougier sat down and waited to see if Chu would try to undermine the evidence. Chu leaned over his lectern as though he could cower the witness by his proximity.

'How can you possibly remember such detail at this remove in time?'

'Mr Chu is cross-examining his own witness, Your Honour.'

Both leading counsel were on their feet. This time the judge's perturbation was more obvious.

'Perhaps you could phrase your question differently, Mr Chu.'

'Are you able to remember the exact amount that the defendant mentioned to you?'

'Well…' The witness squirmed with discomfort. 'No, not the exact amount.' Chu gave Rougier a sneering glance.

'But I remember being surprised that the sum he mentioned was identical to that in the account.' Rougier bent his head towards Annie. 'Bulls eye.' Chu looked at the clock on the wall of the court.

'Would that be a convenient moment, Your Honour?'

'Yes. Court is adjourned until Monday.'

Café Causette

Mandarin Oriental
Sunday

'You can confide in me you know.' Anita reassured him.

'I know, but you don't need to know the details, just that an attempt was made to silence me. It failed and I want to change my accommodation.' Max's smile was firmly persuasive. Anita felt that she really ought to have been told everything but she also recognised that he could be very stubborn when he wanted to, especially if there was anything that could compromise her. His expression became more serious.

'How secure is the information given to the police? What I mean is can third parties get hold of it?' She grimaced.

'The police hate the ICAC, they're traditional enemies and they'd be disinclined to do anything to help them. On the other hand, the police leak information like a paper bucket.' She gave him an inquiring look which made him want to confide a little more in her.

'I don't know who is in league with whom but as I'm plainly seen as China's number one enemy, I assume that everyone regards it as their patriotic duty to shaft Devlin.'

'It's really not that bad.' Anita had a musically throaty voice which lent her words a credibility she did not feel.

'I don't blame them.' His tone was apologetic. 'Everything I read tells me that Beijing is breathing down Hong Kong's neck, so self-preservation is instinctive.' He paused. 'But mine is on high alert.' She brushed her hair away from across her face to compose what she wanted to say.

'The station commander at Aberdeen is a pretty straight guy. If I ask him to guard your address closely, I think he'll do it.'

'Thanks.' She leaned forward speaking softly.

'You don't want to tell me what happened?' He shook his head. She sighed.

'OK.' She tapped her mobile's screen and spoke briefly in Cantonese but he heard 'Shama Apartments'.

'I've booked it in my name, here's the address.' She wrote on a small note pad, tore off the sheet and handed it to him. He read it and handed it back, then stared at her and she noted that mocking humour in his eyes.

'Tell me truthfully, how are we doing?'

'You can see for yourself, the judge is being fairly even-handed. Apart from refusing our application to postpone the trial he hasn't given us cause to suspect that he's any more biased than usual.' Max gave a snorting laugh.

'Is that supposed to comfort me?' She detected the bitterness and found herself responding defensively but he gave a dimissive wave of his hand.

'You're right, I'm over critical.' He felt no such thing but she did not deserve to be the butt of his anger.

'Peter says we'll start our case tomorrow.'

'Didn't he say something about a submission of no case to answer?'

'Yes, but he says it's just to make the judge think more carefully.'

'So I'm likely to be in the witness box by tomorrow afternoon?'

'Mmm.' She nodded.

'And I'm not to say a word about the events in Sikkim.'

'It would be fatal, you know that.' Little worry lines divided her brow. He stared at her in silence for half a minute.

'What I *know* is that I've been set up by a conspiracy between the Indian and Chinese governments and that I am now being put through this charade which will result in my imprisonment.' His sense of betrayal surged through the earlier intention not to lay responsibility at her door. 'Forgive me Anita if I go and enjoy what remains of my freedom for a few more hours.' He gave a peremptory wave of his hand as she opened her mouth to speak, pushed back his chair and walked away from the table. It was the sense of having no control over events that was crippling him, it was surreal and ran counter to the way he had managed his life to date. He could taste the contempt he had for the justice system but he was damned if he'd just be a leaf in a Kafkaesque storm. Time for an exit strategy.

An hour later he stood in the bar of the Aberdeen Boat Club nursing a San Miguel and only half listening to Miles' description of his last race in the San Fernando competition. A deeply tanned man with a strong Australian accent clapped Miles on the back.

'How're you doing mate?' Miles made the introductions. 'Eamon Durning, this is Max Devlin.'

'Devlin? You must be the poor bastard the papers are talking about.' He grinned. 'Maybe not such a poor bastard with all that loot slopping around in your account.'

'That's in bloody poor taste, Eamon.' Miles face darkened. He turned to Max. 'This godforsaken Aussie reject has the manners we associate with convict stock. Max, I apologise on his behalf.' The concern lines corrugated the Australian's face like a prune.

'No offence intended, just a bad joke. What are you drinking?' Max indicated that his glass was almost full and made a dismissive gesture.

'None taken.' Durning looked around to see who was near them, then dropped his voice.

'If ever you feel like a long sail, you know, Vietnam, Thailand, I'm your man fella.' He dug into his jeans pocket and tugged out a wallet from which he extracted a business card which he handed to Max.

'I've got bugger all to do with my time and any excuse to take off works fine for me.' Max managed a half-smile and a flick of an eyebrow.

'I can't say it wouldn't be tempting but I'm trusting to Hong Kong's justice system, for now.'

'Rather you than me mate, from what I hear it ain't what it used to be.' The Australian's clear blue eyes focused on Max and his expression hardened.

'Joking aside, my offer's genuine. Give me two hours' notice and we can slip our mooring and be gone. Don't much care for what's happening to old Hong Kong.'

'Let's change the subject, shall we?' Miles said firmly. The conversation drifted on aimlessly allowing Max to let the notion roll around in his head.

He would go online and find out how many countries had extradition treaties with Hong Kong. That could not hurt. It went against the grain to even contemplate going on the run but he was being forced to accept that he was on the rim of a vortex of political forces with increasingly fewer options to avoid being sucked in. The mental picture dissolved into one word: sucker.

District Court

Wan Chai

Monday

'Please state your name, ordinary address and occupation.' Chu's question was translated into Tibetan. Max stared at the witness, the creases on his face looked as though they had been engraved. Balding and slightly stooped, he guessed his age at late 60s, maybe mid-70s, it was hard to tell, the years had not been worn lightly. His voice was a thin rasp.

'Thukchuk Lachungpa, Potala monastery, Lhasa, Tibetan Autonomous Region of China.' He answered hesitantly but Max noted his sunken black eyes were searching the courtroom and came to rest on him.

'Your occupation.' Chu prompted. There was a quiet discussion between the witness and the interpreter before the interpreter turned to the judge.

'He's using a word I don't understand. I think it must be Tibetan. I think the gist of it is some sort of financial controller.' The judge looked at both counsel.

'Are you content with that, gentlemen?' Max attracted Annie's attention and she got up and walked over to the dock.

'He's the government's appointed treasurer of the Potala Palace.' Annie conveyed this to Rougier. 'My client, who is fluent in the Tibetan language, says that the witness is the Autonomous Region's treasurer for the Potala Palace.' The judge looked inquiringly at the interpreter who nodded acquiescence.

'So be it. Carry on, Mr Chu.' The prosecutor passed a piece of paper to the usher and indicated the witness.

'Do you recognise this document, Mr Lachungpa?' The Tibetan extracted a wire-rimmed pair of spectacles from his jacket pocket, put them on and studied the paper.

'Yes. My writing.'

'The date?' There was further discussion between the witness and the interpreter.

'It's the Tibetan calender, Your Honour, approximately two years ago.'

'What does it refer to?' Rougier rose to his feet.

'Pardon my interruption Your Honour but we admit that the document appears to record various currencies and gold bullion totalling US$51,320,800.' The judge nodded. Chu shrugged his shoulders inside his gown and tapped his lectern with his pen.

'What can you tell us about this document?'

'It records what went missing from the Potala.'

'Two years ago?'

Rougier looked at his opponent and said quietly, 'Please don't lead.'

Chu spun round angrily. 'My friend admits the contents of the document and as a Tibetan linguist his client must know that the date *is* some two years ago, so I am only restating the obvious.'

Rougier rose wearily to his feet. 'None of which entitles my learned friend to feed the answers to his witness.'

'Yes, well, let's get on.' The judge's tetchy reply avoided making a ruling.

'Does the date on that document have any particular significance, Mr Lachungpa?' The Tibetan looked slowly around the courtroom as though he was searching for someone, then bowed his head a little.

'They say it was then that His Holiness was kidnapped and taken to India.' Chu smiled and sat down. Max shook his head in disbelief, when had this story been concocted? Rougier smiled towards Max as he got to his feet.

'*Tsashi Delek!*'

'*Tsashi Delek.*' The Tibetan's face cracked into a broad grin. 'Tibetan greeting, Your Honour.' Rougier explained to the judge.

'You have identified the writing on the document as yours, is it correct that you wrote it on the date that we see written there?' Max watched the Tibetan's face as the question was translated. He detected a nervous flicker of the eyes before Lachungpa answered more like a question than a statement. 'Yes?'

'And the currencies listed on that document, Mr Lachungpa, where did you get the exchange rates for them to convert into US$?'

'The Bank of China in Lhasa.'

'Of course, the exchange rates two years ago were very different from those of today?'

'Mmm…yes.' The man's face seemed to shrink in on itself as he sucked in his cheeks. His head seemed to twist a little to the side as though his clothing was uncomfortable and he added, 'I don't know.' Rougier handed him a copy of that day's *China Daily* opened at the exchange rates page and a computer printout of the renminbi rate 24 months previous.

'Please look at those two documents, then you will know.' The witness's eyes shifted from one to the other, then he looked up.

'Yes, different.'

'Very different, you agree?' The witness nodded. 'Please say yes or no.'

'Yes.'

'Now calculate the value of the renminbi listed in your document at the rate that it was two years ago; would you like a calculator?' He turned round and Anita handed him a large desk calculator. The witness's eyes did not stray from the paper.

'Don't need.' He was calculating on his fingers. He looked at Rougier.

'Not the same.'

'Approximately 20% higher than the rate two years ago.' Rougier picked up another document and tapped it with his forefinger.

'I have here a printout of the exchange rates published in *China Daily* for three months either side of the 12-month period you referred to. None of them vary more than 1.5% over that period.' Rougier handed a copy of the printout to Chu.

'Mmm.' Lachungpa nodded slowly.

'How could that be, Mr Lachungpa? Or is it that this document in your writing was only created very recently, not two years ago?' The Tibetan stared at Rougier, his mouth working silently, then he switched his gaze to Chu.

'Can you help us, Mr Lachungpa?' The judge inquired irritably. The man looked up at this new inquisitor, his head moving very slowly from side to side.

'No.'

'Do you mean that you did not create this document recently?' Rougier pressed him.

'Yes, that's what I mean.' Rougier continued to look directly at him, then sat down.

'Thank you.'

'Do you have any re-examination, Mr Chu?' The judge inquired. Chu was in earnest conversation with his junior and Yuen, the ICAC officer and ignored the judge.

'Mr Chu?' The judge's tone was peremptory. Chu turned a coldly angry face towards the bench. 'No, Your Honour.'

'Is that your case?' Chu bent down and whispered to Phoebe Lam before straightening up.

'It is.'

'Now you can tell me whether your client is going to give evidence, Mr Rougier.'

'May we have a short adjournment, Your Honour, 20 minutes?'

'Very well.' Judge Tang stood, bowed and swept out of the court. Rougier pointed to the rear of the court and Max was allowed out of the dock. Annie escorted him into a conference room.

From her seat in the furthermost left-hand corner of the courtroom Kim had been observing Max. Even though she could only see part of his right-hand profile, she could not take her eyes off him, straining to catch each facial reaction to the exchange between counsel and the witness. She had sneaked into the court the previous Friday determined to find out the truth about the attack on the Rumtek monks and the robbery of their money. The revelation that it had found its way into Max's bank account in Hong Kong was devastating confirmation that he had indeed been behind the murder and robbery. She had crept out of the courtroom lest he catch sight of her. She had been so shaken that she had wandered aimlessly along the streets, condemning her stupidity for blind faith in a man she now felt she really did not know. The weekend had been spent mainly in her hotel room with the

TV on but her mind going back again and again over the time in Delhi. Cold reason told her to pack her bag and take the first flight back to India but emotionally she needed the closure of witnessing this trial to its conclusion. Something just didn't add up. What they were all talking about had nothing to do with what had occurred in Sikkim, why were they focusing on events in Tibet two years ago when surely the answer was so much closer in time? But her fiercest dilemma was her inability to divorce her inner, irrational feelings for him from the hard evidence of him as monk killer and robber. Unable to sleep on the Sunday night she had finally dropped off with mental exhaustion having decided to return to the court on Monday morning in the belief that he would have to explain himself in the witness box.

'That was impressive, you caught him out there.' Max congratulated Rougier.

'Regrettably it was only of limited forensic value. Chu knows we can't challenge them on the central fact that a quantity of mixed currencies and gold have been removed from the Potala Palace and that the money in your account is the proceeds of such a mixed bag of currencies and bullion. On top of that, it is our case that you were paid for work done for the Dalai Lama. It all ties together too conveniently, regardless of the amount or the relevant date.' Rougier removed his wig and ran his fingers through his grey streaked hair. Max saw the tension in the barrister's body language. He had spent too long pondering the incriminating circumstances to miss the objective of this summary.

'So, I won't be giving evidence?'

Rougier rested his forehead on his hand and gave him that curious half-smile of a secret shared. 'You're too intelligent a man to fob off with anodyne words. Our only chance, and it's a thin one at that, is to plump for the fact that it's not your money, you've never laid claim to it and if our witness is believed, it should never have found its way into your account. That's a solid defence,' he broke off with a short deprecatory laugh, 'or it would be if this wasn't a political trial.'

'But the judge appears to have been fairly even-handed.' Max objected.

'Of course he has to be, just in case people conclude that he was biased against you from the start.'

'So you're telling me that I haven't a chance?' Max allowed his anger to leech into his words.

'No.' Rougier put his hands on the table palm down. 'I'm giving you my best opinion of our prospects but I'll continue to fight your corner tooth and nail.' He paused, picked up his wig and let it hang from his fingers. 'I'm afraid I misread this judge, not that there would have been anything we could do about it but he was a pupil of one of our great criminal barristers and I hoped that his influence had not worn off.' He put his wig back on. 'My advice is, don't give evidence, you'll be a hostage to further misfortune. I'd like to gamble on a valid defence that will survive on appeal if worst comes to worst.' The empathetic smile was back in place as he looked Max in the eye.

'It's your decision.'

'Forgive the inappropriate analogy but having bought the dog why would I bark myself?'

'Fair enough.' Rougier grinned, then turned to Anita.

'Is our surprise witness here?'

'I've got him secreted in one of the conference rooms. I'll go and get him to stand by.'

After all the counsel had returned to court, Kim left the ladies' lavatory where she had been hiding and slipped back to her corner seat on which she had left a shopping bag to reserve it. As she sat down she heard the judge addressing Max's counsel.

'As you are not calling your client now, do you have any other witnesses, Mr Rougier?'

'I call doctor the Venerable Michel Girard.' All eyes in the courtroom turned towards the entrance door which Anita held open to admit a shaven-headed, middle-aged Caucasian dressed in the robes of a senior Tibetan lama. Kim was immediately struck by the air of contentment that he seemed to carry with him. Once in the witness box he bowed gravely to the judge before making the affirmation.

'Please tell the court your name, residential address, occupation and qualifications.' The monk turned to face the judge.

'My name is Michel Girard, my preferred place of residence is partly at Budhanilkantha Monastery in Kathmandu and partly at Dharmasala. However, my responsibilities to His Holiness the Dalai Lama require me to travel extensively. I trained as a biochemist in which discipline I hold a PhD but my work is as principal trustee of the funds of the Gelugpa school of Buddhism.' His voice was clear and embracing, with the very slightest of French accents. Rougier handed him the confirmation email.

'Do you recognise this document?'

'Yes, it was handed to me on the same day that it was received in Dharmasala.'

'To what do these two remittances of funds relate?'

'As you can see, the larger sum was destined for His Holiness's account with HSBC in Hong Kong. The smaller amount was payment due to Colonel Devlin for work that he had carried out at the behest of His Holiness's representatives in India.' Rougier handed up Max's HSBC bank statement.

'Can you explain why the sum you say was destined for the Dalai Lama's account ended up in my client's account instead?' The monk's eyebrows rose momentarily.

'As my instructions to the hundi merchant, the money exchanger, were unequivocal, I can only assume that either they confused it or there was a mix-up at HSBC.'

'You say *your* instructions?'

'Yes, I instructed the hundi firm to make these remittances.' Max was watching the judge's face and noted a quick furrowing of his eyebrows.

'By what authority did you give those instructions?' Girard smiled as he turned to face the judge. 'As a trustee of His Holiness's funds.' Rougier thanked him and sat down. During this evidence the prosecution team had been in quiet but intense whispered discussion. Chu stood up and stared at the witness.

'What proof do you have that the funds that were remitted into the defendant's account were not stolen from the Potala monastery?' Girard steepled his fingers and rested his chin on the fingertips.

'Can one steal from oneself?'

'Don't ask me questions.' Chu shot back at him. 'I'm here to ask them and your job is to answer them.' Girard simply smiled gently and lifted his head a little.

'Everything in the Potala Palace is the property of the Gelugpa school of *Buddhisme*.' He pronounced the word as in French. 'The Dalai Lama is the head of our school and the principal trustee of its property.' He separated his hands as if to signal that nothing could be more apparent.

'But Tibet is part of the People's Republic of China and all property belongs to the state, so you cannot be correct.'

'Surely this is where the doctrinaire parts company with the pragmatic?'

'Don't bandy words with me!' Chu allowed his frustration at not getting the answer he wanted to boil into his tone.

'Any property removed from Tibet without specific authorisation from the government of the Autonomous Region is, by definition, dishonestly come by and the proceeds of a serious offence, isn't it?' Girard cocked his head slightly as he looked at Chu, then turned to face the judge.

'Your Honour, no such allegation has ever been made before regarding property brought out of Tibet by its citizens.' He looked briefly towards Chu. 'This is the first time I have ever heard such a proposition. It is true that much of our *Buddhiste* iconography was destroyed in 1951 when the then Chinese government invaded Tibet but the Han Chinese did not claim that the monasteries belonged to them. Indeed, I believe it would be contrary to Communist doctrine.' The judge leaned down towards Girard, his manner impatient.

'Dr Girard, surely you understand that Hong Kong is part of the People's Republic of China and we must recognise its proprietary claims?'

'Your Honour, ownership of material things, money, gold, is of no consequence to our philosophy.' He raised his right arm in an open gesture. 'But we need funding for our schools, retreats, pilgrim hostels and to sustain our teaching, these make enormous demands on His Holiness's funds. That has always been recognised by the authorities in the Autonomous Region.' Max watched the effect that the lama's words had on the judge's expression and he knew, instinctively, that he rejected the reasoning. The judge switched his head questioningly towards Chu.

'If you are not prepared to answer with a simple yes or no, we can take it that you are not in a position to challenge the proposition I put to you.' The lama looked at Chu with what Max felt was a pitying expression.

'I think I have answered your question M'sieu.' Chu threw his left hand into the air in dismissal and sat down.

'Re-examination, Mr Rougier?'

'When you gave instructions for the money to be remitted to Hong Kong,' as though in an aside he added, 'regardless of which accounts the two sums were destined for, did you have any reason to believe that they were dishonestly come by?'

'None.' The lama shook his head slowly.

'That is all I wish to ask you, Dr Girard.' He looked towards the judge. 'Does Your Honour have any questions for the witness?' Tang looked hard at the lama, as though he was forming a question for him, then gave a quick shake of his head.

'No. You are free to leave. Is that your evidence, Mr Rougier?'

'If I may have a moment, Your Honour.' Rougier bent down and conferred with Annie and Anita, then looked at Max, one eyebrow raised. Max could not free himself of the niggling thought that as it was his state of belief that was on trial, he ought to give evidence. But they had argued this back and forth between them and he could see Rougier's worries: once in the witness box the prosecution would ask him questions the honest answers to which would sink him without a trace. He shook his head grimly.

'That is our case, Your Honour.' The judge was writing as he spoke.

'Your closing speech will be completed by lunchtime tomorrow, Mr Chu?' The prosecutor agreed.

'We'll sit until your speech is finished, Mr Rougier.'

'Your Honour.'

The judge looked up. 'Bail is withdrawn. The defendant will remain in custody until further notice.' Max felt as though he'd been punched in the stomach. Rougier looked angry as he rose to his feet.

'There has been no change of circumstance, Your Honour. My client has honoured every provision of his bail punctiliously. The court has his passport and his bank account has been frozen, he is not an absconder. With the greatest respect, there are no valid grounds for withdrawing bail. I would urge you to reconsider this direction.' Chu started to rise only to be signalled to sit back down by the judge.

'I have considered the points you make so cogently, Mr Rougier but on the basis of the evidence at this stage of the trial I consider it a prudent step in the overall interests of justice. You are welcome to apply to a High Court judge, that is the defendant's right.' He closed his note book, stood, bowed briefly and walked out of the court.

Back in his chambers, Jonathan put his wig on the wooden head that Bonnie had given him when he was appointed. A ripple of guilt broke the surface of his sense of achievement. He had a judicial studies seminar to attend tonight, that would mean him getting home late and he could avoid discussing the trial with her. As he sank back into his desk chair he saw the envelope propped up against the photograph of his family. He tore it open, anticipation making him dispense with a letter opener. He had recognised the vice-president of the Court of Appeal's handwriting on the envelope. The note was brief but everything he could hope for.

'*The powers that be are very impressed with your handling of the case, I hope to see you in a full bottom wig very soon.*'

He returned the letter to the torn envelope, unlocked a desk drawer and deposited it on top of his collection of letters congratulating him on his District Court appointment, then locked the drawer again. Withdrawing bail had not been his own idea, but the anonymous telephone call had left him in no doubt that it was in his very own best interests to do so. After the seminar, he would come back to his chambers and start writing his verdict, nothing said in the speeches would make any difference.

Kim was stunned by the sudden decision to withdraw Max's bail. She had been trying to fathom out the significance of the lama's evidence; if Max had been on some sort of engagement for the Dalai Lama it simply did not make sense that he would have attacked the Rumtek monks. It was as plain as could be that a mix-up had occurred resulting in His Holiness's money being wrongly credited to Max's account and vice versa and she could not understand why they were prosecuting him. Once the lama had explained that the money belonged to His Holiness, not Max and that he had not been responsible for the mistake, it followed logically that he had not committed any crime. It was in that frame of mind that the judge's decision about bail shocked her. She shrank back into her seat in the corner of the courtroom as Max's barristers hurried over to talk to him through the bars in the dock. It was a curious cameo, their gowns flowed from their shoulders to the floor as they bent over to speak to him, the greyish wigs making them look like some mythical creatures, they sent a shudder through her body. She registered that there were several reporters leaving the court in haste and the other spectators were talking animatedly amongst themselves. It dawned on her slowly that she was isolated, solitary and emotionally in turmoil. She became aware that her hand was across her mouth, whether in shock or self-defence she could not divine, she allowed it to drop. From the movement in the dock it was apparent that Max was being led away through the door in the wall behind him. His barristers stood talking quietly to each other and Anita where they were joined by a short well-built man who was obviously Nepalese. It was at that moment she decided she had to abandon her anonymity. The barristers picked up their files and walked out of the courtroom talking to each other, leaving Anita talking to the Nepalese. Getting up from her chair she noted that her legs felt weak and she had to pause a moment to get her balance. As she approached the row of seats in which Anita had sat, the solicitor looked up, surprise stretching her features.

'Kim?'

'Anita.' The solicitor turned her head from side to side, staring at her.

'What…what are you doing here?' Kim glanced towards the Nepalese and Anita gestured at him. 'This gentleman is a friend of our client.' She smiled at him and he backed diplomatically away.

'Can we talk?' Kim thought that it sounded as though she was begging. 'I know him, Max…your client.' Realisation found a seat in Anita's eyes and she put her hand on Kim's arm.

'I have to go and see him in the cells, I won't be long. Can you wait for me on the ground floor, near the front entrance to the building?'

Kim felt her throat go dry as she nodded. Anita turned to Deepraj.

'I'll try and get them to let you see him for a few minutes. Come down with me.' She picked up her capacious bag into which she had been stuffing papers as she talked and motioned him to follow her, looking back over her shoulder she called out to Kim.

'Downstairs, see you in a bit.'

Park Walk Residence

Kowloon Tong

It was past midnight by the time Jonathan reached home. He closed the door as quietly as possible, the light was still on in the kitchen and he shucked his shoes off and walked there in his stockinged feet. He was relieved to find it empty. A note pinned to the kettle told him to make himself some pot noodles if he was hungry. Pot noodles, that said it all, she was still angry with him. He sighed as he switched the kettle on, better that they did not meet and quarrel. The sound of shuffling made him look up but it was only Grace rubbing the sleep out of her eyes.

'Is there anything you'd like, sir?' He waved her away.

'No Grace, go back to bed.' The kettle boiled but all of a sudden he had no appetite. Why couldn't Bonnie understand that it was for all their benefits that he was doing whatever was necessary to get that High Court appointment? Once there, who knew how far up the judicial ladder he could climb with the sort of influential backing that he now had?

At the same time that His Honour Judge Jonathan Tang was deciding against the pot noodles, Max was stretched out on the thin mattress in his cell in the Lai Chi Kok Reception Centre, his head resting on his hands placed behind him on what passed for a pillow and his mind refusing to let go of the inescapable realisation that he was facing a lengthy period, what… two…three years or more of this mind-numbing institutionalisation, not even in a culture with which he had any affinity whatsoever. Rougier's assurance that if it came to the crunch, the Court of Final Appeal would almost certainly quash his conviction was as much comfort as a bikini in the Arctic Circle, the estimate being that it would take two years to get there. He knew that all his training in resistance to interrogation was worthless in this situation and escape was virtually impossible. As the dread weight of prison folded its clammy wings over him it struck him that he was in a breeding ground of triad gangsters, the same people, he reasoned who had been instructed to get rid of him at sea. He looked at his cellmate, a large Nigerian charged with drug running. Not, he decided, a likely candidate for executioner. But once he was sentenced, every 24 hours would be at maximum risk. Loath to leave anything to chance, he tore two strips off the mattress cover and used them to secure top and bottom of the barred cell door, then jammed an old newspaper that he folded tightly as a wedge under the bottom edge. It was far from perfect but would give him time. He permitted himself an ironic laugh, the door was meant to prevent him getting out, not stop others getting in.

Anita was sufficiently intrigued by Kim's presence – she guessed that there had been some sort of relationship with Max – to suggest that they meet for dinner and a girls' chat. She arranged to pick her up from her hotel on Hollywood Road and directed the taxi to drop them off at the Kee Club. Sitting at an unobtrusive table in a corner of the room, it had not taken much to wheedle Kim's story out of her. As she listened to how Max had abruptly disappeared from her life, she empathised with the Sikkimese girl's predicament.

'D'you think he wanted to protect you, knowing that what he was doing was dangerous?' Kim inclined her head, acknowledging the possibility. Anita did not want to make excuses for the man but as far as she could judge, he was not so callous. When Kim recounted the story of the attack on the Rumtek monks Anita had to stop herself from interrupting. She thought carefully before posing the next question.

'Do you know anything about a Chinese army unit ambushing the monks?' The way Kim's eyes stared widely at her indicated that this was not an unwelcome prospect.

'Chinese army? I don't…' Kim's eyes looked away, unfocused. What was it that Lyangsong had said, something about the man that forced him to stop the truck.

'There was a survivor from the attack, I talked to him…he told me that the soldier who made him stop the truck told him to get out, he said something a bit funny, that the soldier had Chinese eyes.' Anita nodded thoughtfully.

'But the Indian government has said nothing about this?'

'No.' Kim shook her head. Why would Anita mention this unless there was some truth in it? Lyangsong had also said that, what was his name, Tenzing, had been looking for someone called Devlin and his interest was plainly hostile. What had Max got himself into? She looked hard at Anita.

'Tell me, is Max in over his head?' Anita smiled to buy herself time. For all she knew Kim had been sent to work as much information about Max out of her as possible. Then she remembered that she was the one who had contacted Kim. Her intuition told her that this was a woman whose interest in her client was seriously emotional. She decided to go with her gut feeling.

'Just between you and me,' she held up an admonitory finger, 'if you tell anyone that I told you, I'll deny it flatly.' Kim shook her head and leaned forward.

'Please.'

'There's too much mainland Chinese political weight behind this prosecution. We understand that it was the PLA that killed the monks and stole their treasure; Max recovered it.' She watched the young woman's facial reaction to this news, it was as though life surged back into every feature.

'Our defence is good in law but liable to be submerged under facts that tell against him, especially if the judge thinks his career prospects will be helped by a guilty verdict.'

'But that's so unfair, where's the justice?' Kim blurted out.

'It's human behaviour, any system of justice is only as good as the people who administer it, and even judges have human frailties, some good some bad.'

'But what can we do?' Kim pleaded with her whole body.

'We do our job as best we can, Peter Rougier is the best criminal defence counsel in Hong Kong. We have to hope that the system works the way it should.' Kim shook her head in frustration.

'But *you* don't trust it.' Anita was torn between telling the truth and giving Kim hope, however false.

'It's all we have.' Kim closed her eyes and held her face in her hands. 'Can I see him?'

'Is that wise?' Anita frowned. Since when had she become a mother hen? 'I'll see what I can do.'

Office of Commissioner for Ethnic Integration

Beijing

'How could they fail?' Flecks of angry spittle spattered the mouthpiece of the phone.

'Why should I care if they're dead? It's the laowai who should be dead. What are you doing about it now?' He listened with impatience billowing in his chest.

'You must have people inside who can do a professional job.' The voice was one of abject subservience.

'Promise them anything you like, just get it done.' He slammed the handset back down onto its rest as he turned to face his PA. 'Clean up afterwards, we don't want anyone leading back to me.' His PA knew that this involved yet more people to be disposed of despite the fact that there would always be a lead back. It would be very risky, he had to protect himself too so he needed an untraceable cut-out. At least with the laowai in prison the operatives in Hong Kong had a variety of people available to get the job done. He would have to engineer a transfer to a different department, this entire operation had backfired disastrously.

District Court

Wan Chai

'This court must accept the PRC evidence.' Chu was in didactic form but whereas Max would have expected the judge to resent being hectored, he was nodding in apparent agreement. Prosecuting counsel had been addressing the court for an hour and a half already and it was obvious that Judge Tang was hanging on his every word. He saw Rougier write something on a pad and pass it to Chu who glanced down at it and nodded.

'Would that be a convenient moment for the morning break, Your Honour?' Tang snatched a look at the wall clock.

'Twenty minutes.' He made a note, rose, bowed and left the court room. The defence team huddled together at the dock before the CSD officers took Max inside. Rougier tapped on the wooden balustrade.

'Chu's shot his bolt: he's said everything he can say, from now on it'll be repetition.'

'What he's saying is logical, though I don't like the way he says it.' Max gave a grim quarter smile. 'But he can't marry up the amount they claim was stolen with the sums paid into the two HSBC accounts.'

'He doesn't have to. There's sufficient similarity between the composition of the stolen property and the breakdown on our own confirmation of remittance.' Rougier shook his head. 'No, our defence lies in a proper construction of the law.' The CSD officer interrupted.

'Have to take him inside, sir, if you want to continue, you can talk in the corridor.' He nodded towards the door at the back of the dock.

'No, don't let me interrupt your chain of thought.' Max stood up to leave. 'You've explained it all to me.'

'Thanks.' Rougier smiled his appreciation, composing the shape of his closing speech demanded his full attention and this was no ordinary case. Conducting a criminal defence always involved taking on the government in one form or another, that was his bread and butter, but Beijing's presence in this case was almost palpable and for the first time he wondered whether the time was approaching when troublesome *gweilo* counsel would find themselves increasingly frozen out. Well, that was for the future, right now he had to find a route into Jonathan Tang's mind. He assumed that Tang would find that the money in Devlin's account was derived from assets removed from the Potala Palace and that the evidence of the treasurer, Lachungpa, would be accepted. That established that in fact the money was the proceeds of an indictable offence. All that remained was whether Devlin either knew or believed that it was dishonestly come by. The big gamble had been to call no evidence so that Devlin's state of mind now had to be inferred from the surrounding circumstances. He was still fashioning an even more basic submission, one which he hoped would cause His Honour Jonathan Tang to think long and hard. If he made a fundamental error of law, that would hardly commend him to the disinterested chief justice, but would Tang pin his hopes on the strength of his backers?

When he returned to court, Rougier noticed a highly attractive young woman talking to Devlin through the bars of the dock. He raised an interrogative eyebrow to Anita and glanced in their direction. Anita waited until he had resumed his seat before she leant forward and whispered in his ear.

'It seems my old LSE alumnus friend is an even closer friend of our client. Poor girl, she seems to have found him only to lose him again, this time for much longer.'

'Oh ye of little faith.' Rougier gave her one of his quizzical looks, half-serious, half-joking. She had a really soft spot for him. 'Have you no confidence in the counsel of your choice?' She managed a guilty grin.

'Worst case scenario.' They were interrupted by the knock on the door that announced the judge's imminent entrance.

Rougier studied Tang's face for any clue as to his state of mind but he was not giving anything away. Max was momentarily disoriented. Kim's sudden presence had shocked his system so that for a few seconds he forgot to breathe. He sensed that his mouth was moving like a fish in a bowl as she put her finger to her lips to silence him.

'You left me because you feared all this.' The arm that swept in a wide arc that embraced the courtroom was as definitive as her words. He opened his mouth to deny it but her face just lit up and with a toss of her hair she challenged him.

'Don't deny it.' The noise of the judge's entry closed off further communication. She kissed her fingertips and turned them towards him before walking to the back of the court. A CSD officer tugged his shirt to make him sit down. Everything was totally unreal. He, the defendant, should have been the centre of the court's attention but he was relegated to the role of interested spectator, all eyes were on Rougier and the judge. Some part of his cognitive faculties heard his counsel's words but they fell like autumn leaves, indistinguishable from their bronze and red fellows that furzed the ground. He ought to listen but he kept looking at her, wondering what had prompted the dramatic change of heart. There could not have been a less auspicious time for them to come together, the legal and physical impediments rendered everything utterly hopeless.

'Let me assume, for the sake of argument, that Your Honour is against my client on the question of his belief. He has not spoken but, as Lord Devlin stated so succinctly, the failure of a defendant to give evidence is itself not evidence. On which basis there is no sworn testimony. Doubtless, Your Honour will heed my learned friend's submission that Mr Devlin's denial to the ICAC interviewing officers is no more than a self-serving statement and carries no weight. Yet if it is consistent with the rest of the collateral evidence it cannot be weightless. And,' Rougier tapped his lectern to emphasise his qualification, '...and if he had no knowledge of the money being in his account until Mr Chin, the HSBC officer, told him and,' he paused for effect. 'His immediate response was that there had been a mistake. Then to put the matter beyond doubt, Mr Chin's evidence is clear even though the ICAC appears to have lost his original note,' Rougier turned a grim face to Alexander Yuen sitting behind Chu, 'because it was Your Honour who insisted on a positive yes or no answer when I put to him that Mr Devlin said that the funds in his account were not his and he agreed. Consequently, he never dealt with the money the subject matter of the charge. The court can only begin to consider his state of mind if he actually *dealt* with the money. If I mistakenly transfer funds into my learned friend's bank account and he tried to use them in whole or in part, he'd be guilty of an offence because the funds would not be his. Ironically, if he thought they were dishonestly come by and he returned them to me, he would be guilty of the offence.'

Max found the logic impeccable but the look of dissatisfaction on the judge's face indicated that he was not impressed. Rougier thrust his hands behind his back under his gown and leaned forward.

'There is no evidence before this court that my client knew or even had grounds to suspect let alone believe that the money erroneously paid into his account without his knowledge and to which he had no proprietorial claim were the proceeds of an indictable offence. Title to the money is now being contested between His Holiness the Dalai Lama and the treasurer of the Autonomous Region of Tibet. Ignoring if Your Honour will, the fierce animosity towards the Dalai Lama by the central government in Beijing, prima facie, His Holiness has a claim of right made in good faith. That alone must mean that the prosecution cannot invite the court to draw the only possible inference, namely that it was stolen.' There was an anguished expression on Tang's face.

'But are you not forgetting, Mr Rougier, that Hong Kong is a part of China, two systems maybe but one country. So the central government's stance as regards the Dalai Lama must be binding on me.' Rougier tried to disguise his impatience.

'But that does not automatically invalidate a claim by a private citizen, simply because the other party is the state. Think, if you will, of all the claims brought by Hong Kong citizens against various organs of the Hong Kong government, these are always entertained by our courts.'

'But the Hong Kong citizens are not advocating independence for Hong Kong.' Tang gave Chu a quick reassuring smile.

'Political differences of opinion don't have the effect in law of disqualifying the protester from asserting his or her title to property, Your Honour.'

'I don't think that can be right Mr Rougier.' Max's mind had been engaged as the argument was developed so that the wisp of hope that had trailed enticingly across his head evaporated with the judge's dismissive comment. Rougier's physical stance seemed to transform from persuasive to pugnacious and Max became apprehensive. The judge continued addressing Rougier.

'These are wholly different circumstances.' Tang made a note in his notebook. 'But irrespective of the conflicting claims to the money, the central fact remains that the defendant not only makes no claim to it, he positively asserts that it is not his.' Rougier stabbed the bench with his finger as he spoke the final words. The judge appeared to glower at him for several seconds before he wrote something down.

'That is the ultimate thrust of our submissions on behalf of Mr Devlin: the money is not his, he makes no claim to it and has never dealt with it. Its presence in his account is a processing mistake by a third party for which he cannot be held responsible.' Rougier paused. 'By reason of which we submit that he is not, nor could he be found guilty by a jury properly directed as to the law.' He remained standing, waiting for the judge to stop writing.

'Is there any other matter upon which we can assist the court?' Tang stared at him silently, then gave a curt shake of his head.

'No, thank you Mr Rougier, you have said everyting possible that could be urged on behalf of your client.' Rougier gave a little bow and sat down, then whispered to Annie.

'That's the kiss of death.' He put a restraining hand on her arm. 'Don't turn round and look at our client, your face will give it away. He has enough to worry about.'

Just before the CSD officers led him out of the dock, Kim found the few nervous minutes of exchanges with Max excruciatingly artificial, neither of them could say what they really felt and everything was circumscribed by the situation. She put her hand between the bars just so that she could touch him fleetingly, expressing more than any words could at that moment. He managed a grin.

'It'll work out, don't fret.' Then he turned away as he was ushered out of the dock and through the door into the secure zone. She was no lawyer but her instincts were telling her that even Max did not believe in a positive outcome. Suddenly she became aware that Anita was talking to her.

'Sorry…I didn't catch what you were saying.' Anita gave a nervous little cough of a laugh.

'Like me to keep you company this evening?' Kim was on the verge of refusing when the prospect of nursing her fears alone hit home.

'Yes, please.'

Jonathan Tang remained in his chambers in the court building writing his verdict. Conscious of the fact that it would be studied by those responsible for appointment to higher judicial office, he focused on crafting it in a way that would make it impossible to appeal on the facts and set out the law in a succinctly accurate restatement. He found his concentration slipping from time to time as his line of sight caught the photo frame of the three of them leaving the hospital after April's birth. They had been so deliriously happy until they learned of her rare condition. Not enough to blight the pretty girl's life completely but something she would have to take precautions about for all her days. Bonnie with her usual positive approach had researched the condition and established a routine that gave April as normal a life as possible, but there were still these regular checkups that either parent would normally take her to. He found his mind wandering away from his analysis of the evidence, the picture of Bonnie's almost contemptuous expression yesterday as she had undone her hair and let it fall angrily onto her shoulders, the clear signal that she would not be going to court. He had struggled with his righteous indignation that she failed to appreciate the momentous step up in his career that he was so close to making and his inner recognition that he was putting his career before their child and, if her words had really conveyed her feelings, their marriage too. Why did it have to be one or the other? Though he tried to ignore it, her remarks about him abandoning his sense of fair play in order to build a reputation as a conviction-minded judge had hit a chink in his armour of judicial probity. She had told him when they first dated that she had fallen for what she called his Atticus Finch character. That had given him a sense of the self-worth that he secretly yearned for but thought he could only aspire to. He re-read the last sentence he had typed: '*I am satisfied so that I am sure that the Defendant either knew or must have believed that the money in his account, the mere presence of which constituted a "dealing", could not have been honestly come by, the very amount argued against its legitimacy.*'

He saved it to its file and shut down his device. Time to go home and mend the domestic fence.

He walked into the bedroom and closed the door behind him. 'Hello love.' Bonnie looked up and put down the book she was reading. He felt his muscles stiffen when he saw the look on her face.

'Why did you withdraw your defendant's bail? Did the ICAC spin you some tale about him being about to fly?' He tried a smile of least resistance, his hands opening in front of him in an explanatory gesture.

'Don't give me a load of bullshit.' Her eyes were hard. It was a look he had seen when she was cross-examining a prosecution witness she had cornered in a lie. He dropped the smile and went on the attack.

'I didn't need to be told anything, it was the proper exercise of my judicial discretion. The case against him had hardened to a certainty of guilt, I couldn't risk him doing a runner.' Her expression changed to the triumph of closing the trap on him.

'Precisely. You had no evidence on which to base your decision.' The glare from the reading light hid her face for a moment as she continued. 'And you have no evidence of him dealing with the money that was mistakenly credited to his account either but you'll still convict him.' She brushed her hair back from her face in a gesture that conveyed disgust. 'My pupil has been in your court giving me a blow by blow account. You're sucking up to that thin-lipped bloodless government stooge Allan Chu, just to secure your place on the High Court bench.' There was no way he was going to admit to the truth of this, even as he knew she was right.

'You've been spying on me!'

'Since when were criminal court proceedings not open to the public?'

This sparring had to stop, it was time to have it out with her. 'Why? Tell me why?'

Her voice was ice cold as she picked her words. 'Why? I'll tell you why, because I didn't want to believe that the man I fell in love with and married and fathered my child had become a gutless, self-seeking bastard who had abandoned all the high principles he once professed so proudly.' She swung her legs out of the bed on her side and stood there, the lace cups of the black silk chemise he had bought on her last birthday moulding against the perfect roundness of her breasts which swelled and fell as her anger flowed through them.

'You know why I found you so irresistible?' She did not wait for an answer. 'You were my ideal of a defence barrister, polite but never submissive to judges and you never allowed a prosecution witness to go off on sidetracks, you dragged them back, remorselessly even when the judges tried to intervene to salvage a failing prosecution. Without fear or favour, you gave that phrase meaning. But now…?' It was as though she crumpled, suddenly the fight went out of her. She flapped her hand in a dismissive wave, her words carrying the weight of their disgust. 'You can sleep on the couch, I'm not sharing a bed with you…any more.'

She sat back on the bed, swivelled herself around pulling the sheet over her, switched off the light and left him standing there in darkness save for the thin frame of light around the door. His stomach felt as though he had been empty retching. Why did women say the things they knew would be most hurtful when they were angry?

He felt for the door handle and let himself out, closing the door behind him as quietly as possible. Urgently in need of an emotional salve, he crept quietly into April's bedroom and looked down on her little face softly illumined by the nightlight. Where had things gone wrong? He argued his own defence even as he registered that it was indefensible. Sinking down onto the floor in a corner of the room he could pick out the cartoon characters that they had pasted onto the wall around April's cot and his mind went straight back to the time that he and Bonnie had decorated the room together. He felt a tear well in the corner of his eye. Why didn't she understand?

Lai Chi Kok Reception Centre

Hong Kong

Max's mind was like spaghetti junction: different issues running towards unknown destinations, overlaid and criss-crossing each other in a series of loops none of which had resolution. The usual night noises of the prison struck him with greater intensity and he wondered whether to give up trying to sleep altogether.

Suddenly, he could not breathe, the earth pressed down on him and in that instant he awoke to the realisation that it was not the earth but some sort of cloth being held over his face whilst great force was exerted on it. In the fraction of a second that he registered he was about to lose consciousness, he knew instinctively that he was awake and would only have one chance. With his mind slipping away he drew on every atom of his body and exploded up from the bed. Whatever it was that was smothering him moved very slightly, enough for him to suck in air and he punched up and out towards the open side of his bed and contacted with someone but it was not sufficient to dislodge what he now realised must be a pillow. His right hand grabbed at his assailant's clothing which was loose, using his grip on it for traction he yanked himself to his right and felt the pillow move again as he turned to roll off the edge. Just as he did so, he felt a hand pressing the back of his head into the pillow and sensed that he was losing consciousness again, there was a weight pressing down on him but then pressure released and he clawed away the fabric over his face.

'You okay, man?' His eyes were open but in the darkened cell it was hard to make anything out clearly. He felt a hand clutch his shoulder.

'You hear me, man?' It dawned on him that it was the Nigerian. He stared into where he thought the man's face was.

'Sorry, man, ah'm real sorry.' As his mind cleared he saw that his cellmate was holding someone in a neck lock. He began to piece it together, his fuddled mind told him that the Nigerian must have pulled his assailant off him, only just in time. Why the hell was he apologising?

'They told me ah'd be next if I did'n let'm open the door.' The Nigerian's eyes seemed to widen. 'I just one black guy...'n all these Chinese.' He shook his head and Max began to register the fear in the man's face. 'Then I see him smotherin' you...I did'n sign up for no killin'...so I hit 'im.' Max shrugged himself free and checked on his assailant who was not moving.

'Hold his arms behind his back.' The Nigerian followed the instruction. Max felt for a pulse in the man's carotid artery, it was there but very faint. He checked the cell door which was unlocked: that meant that at least one or more CSD officers were in on the operation and would have to come back to lock it, presumably leaving one dead Devlin inside and the Nigerian to take the blame. He spoke softly to his rescuer.

'Hold him for a minute or two while I check out the landing.' Without waiting for an answer he opened the door gently and did a quick assessment of the geography. It was as he remembered, about 15 metres to the left was the head of a staircase that descended some six metres to the next level. It would have to do. Easing himself back into the cell he ordered the Nigerian to let the Chinese prisoner drop to the floor, then he stooped over the inert body and gathered the head in one arm from behind whilst holding the shoulder still with the other hand, then with a practised violent twist he broke the man's neck.

'Pick up his feet, we're going to get rid of the evidence.' The Nigerian was now sweating with fear, standing stock-still.

'Listen, their plan was to kill me, lock the door and then blame you, so if you don't want to help me, more fool you.' Perspiration was running down the Nigerian's face in rivulets. His mouth opened and shut but no words came out. He managed a nod and grabbed the dead man's feet. Max opened the door and peered out along the landing which was deserted. Holding the cell door open with his foot, he bent down and heaved the body unceremoniously towards him, took a grip under the armpits and then edged out onto the landing. The Nigerian's head was moving frantically from side to side looking for anyone who might see them.

'Come on!' Max whispered the order and between them they carried and dragged the body to the head of the staircase.

'Now we throw him down the stairs, on three...' The Nigerian's eyes looked as though they would pop out of their cavities but with one more terrified glance behind him, he nodded.

'One, two, three.' The body hit the stairs about three metres lower down, bounced, rolled over and tumbled inertly to the bottom.

'Quick, inside.' He shooed the man back into their cell.

'The screw who unlocked the door will have to come back and lock it so that you get the blame.' He pointed to the man's bunk.

'You get back in your bed. I'll lie on the floor as if I'm dead.' The Nigerian wiped the sweat across his face, he was trembling with fear. Max whispered harshly.

'Bed. Now.' The big man's eyes never left Max as he lay down and pulled the sheet up tight against his chin. Checking that the cell door was fully closed, Max lay on the floor with the pillow resting against his face and the sheet half on half off the bed. He estimated that it would not be too long before the complicit CSD officer returned. Fortune smiled on him: for no more than 10 minutes had passed when he heard the sound of boots on the fretted iron web of the landing floor. The one thing he had gambled on was that the officer would not enter the cell to ensure that he was dead. He held his breath as the footsteps stopped on the other side of the door. He had to picture the man checking through the inspection glass. A susurring of fabric against fabric felt as though it deafened his ear, the proximity meant that it was the Nigerian moving. What the...? Then it stopped and his heart responded to the sound of the key in the lock. As the footsteps receded he kept a grip on his nerve ends, trying to discern in which direction the officer was walking. Unless he returned the way he had come he was bound to see the body, the sound diminished and when it ceased without an explosion of noise, he let out a long controlled breath. So far, so good.

District Court

Wan Chai

The courtroom was packed with journalists and a variety of spectators who had an interest in the outcome. Rougier spotted several of the mucky-mucks from the Department of Justice as well as the ICAC's director of operations and one or two faces he recognised as belonging to the Beijing favour-currying legislators and their acolytes. Their smiling faces told him what he did not want to know: it was Christmas Day, the Dalai Lama would get his come-uppance, the Tibetan government-in-exile would be embarrassed and the PRC would collect over US$50 million. He nodded grimly at Monica Yau, his favourite court reporter who sat quite close to counsel's row. Annie touched his elbow and he turned towards her.

'The dock officer let our client in a bit early so that he could have a few words with Kim.' Rougier glanced back and saw them talking, their faces strained. He flicked his head towards the back of the court.

'Too much like the Roman circus for my taste.' He looked towards the rear right-hand side of the court where all those favouring the prosecution were seated. 'They're here for blood.' Annie passed him a few sheets of typewritten paper.

'I worked on this last night. I think we have arguable grounds for an appeal, so I've drafted some provisional grounds in case you feel like asking for bail pending appeal, at least it would anticipate the prosecution a bit.'

'Thanks Annie.' He turned his grave eyes on her and spoke softly.

'We'd never get bail, not from a District Court judge anyway – but we're not convicted yet.' He saw the impatience in her face.

'I know, sifu, but it's all a foregone conclusion.' She pointed her thumb towards Chu behind her, he was enjoying a joke with his junior, Phoebe Lam.

'It's as though they know something we don't.' Her voice was accusing.

'I'm afraid they probably do.' He picked up his fountain pen and endorsed the date on his brief. He had been reasonably content when they found out who their trial judge was to be. He remembered him at the Bar, a quietly effective advocate who never made pointless submissions. He had welcomed Tang's appointment to the bench even though he was surprised that he had given up his practice. But all that was in the past: the writing was on the wall for all who could read to see, Jonathan Tang Ching-yee was destined for a red dressing gown.

Kim had rehearsed what she was going to say and she blurted it out the moment he stood in front of her behind the bars of the dock.

'I love you Max Devlin, don't you ever decide what's good for me in the future. I'll make my own decisions and right now I'll do whatever it takes to get you acquitted.' He gave her a wry smile.

'A hacksaw and a lock-picking kit?'

'Oh,' she frowned impatiently. 'Don't joke, this is serious.'

'My love, from where I'm standing, I can assure you it is serious.'

'But…' His smile was forced through eyes that were hooded and the strain was etched into the creases that she had thought of as laugh lines. There was an incongruous greyness to his skin that underlay his tan.

'No buts.' He gave a slight shake of his head. 'I've been set up but I was stupid, I walked into it and now I'll have to pay the price.' He could see her face squeezing back tears and put as much warmth into his voice as he could muster.

'Let's not give up hope. My lawyers say there are grounds for an appeal.' As he spoke the words he felt guilty, knowing that there was no realistic hope and he was only feeding his own need to cling on to her.

'I don't have an answer to it now but we have to think positively.' He touched her hand softly as the knock on the judge's door announced his imminent entrance and the dock officer told him to stand up. He looked towards the bench, trying to read the judge from his expression, only to see that it was impenetrable. Everyone sat down and he quartered the courtroom. Those he had labelled the pan-prosecutors were displaying their appetite for blood. His thoughts returned to the dead assassin in Lai Chi Kok, no-one had fingered him for that, yet. But that made three triad members who had been sacrificed in the course of trying to kill him. Once convicted he would be a marked prisoner. Hacksaws and lock-picks might very well become a reality…if he was to survive he would have to escape. Breaking out of one of Hong Kong's prisons was a pipe dream, he already stuck out like a sore thumb amongst the Chinese prisoners; it would have to be either from the courtroom or whilst in transit. Transit would have been a distinct prospect if he had a team in place, but on his own, Deepraj couldn't do it. He examined the courtroom again, this time with a different agenda. Surprise would only get him so far, then he'd be in the court building and blind to its structure. Rougier had told him that sentence would be adjourned to a later date, so there was time to brief Deepraj and get the necessary intelligence on the layout of the building which, he recalled, housed more government departments, not just the District Court. He began to compile a plan in his head.

Rougier groaned inwardly as the familiar pattern of a guilty verdict judgment took shape. All the signals were already there.

'Mr Rougier, with his customary skill and persuasiveness has advanced all the arguments that could possibly be raised.' How he hated the hypocrisy of these judicial blandishments, all the more vacuous because they came out of the judicial textbook on essential courtesies. Since counsel knew how utterly insincere they were it could only be to lend an artificial air of even-handedness when the Court of Appeal came to consider allegations of judicial bias.

'Mr Chu SC's cogent submissions on the issue of the provenance of the money in the defendant's bank account are, I am satisfied so that I am sure, incontestable. The defence are unable to contest the evidence of Mr Lachungpa, the government of the Autonomous Region of Tibet's appointed treasurer of the Potala Palace. The precise value of the assets stolen from the Potala is necessarily subject to exchange rate variations so that the fact that the value of the amount stolen two years ago is virtually identical to that in the defendant's bank has no evidential value.'

'Bollocks.' Rougier muttered under his breath. Either he missed the impossibility of such precision or he was deliberately fudging the point. Annie nudged him and put her finger to her lips. He'd have to keep his stage whispers down to a less audible level.

'An essential element of the offence is knowledge or belief that the property in question is the proceeds of an indictable offence.' The judge looked across at Devlin.

'The authorities establish that this is a subjective state of mind and not what the court finds a reasonable man would believe if faced with such a set of circumstances. However, we have not heard from the defendant as to what his state of mind was, therefore the court is compelled to draw the necessary inference that in these circumstances it is impossible for the defendant to have believed other than that these assets were indeed stolen.'

The judge looked at the clock and then addressed counsel.

'We'll take a short break before I complete my judgment.' He rose and the people in the courtroom got to their feet and returned his bow. Anita pulled gently on Rougier's gown.

'He's sewing us up.' Rougier nodded.

'Better go and prepare the client for the inevitable.' She frowned.

'I'll go too.' Annie pushed past him and together the two young women lawyers bent over Devlin's seated form.

'Well, you went through the motions, Peter.' Rougier's head whipped round to face his opponent who had come up beside him in counsel's row.

'Don't you ever say that to me again…I've half a mind to take you outside and make you pass some bloody motions out of your arse.' Chu's face lost its superior smile.

'You can't say that to another member of the Bar.'

'Well, I just did, now fuck off.' Rougier pushed his way out of court and marched along the corridor as he fought to control his temper. He was furious with himself for allowing Chu to get under his skin and though he justified it to himself he knew he ought to have treated the remark with utter disdain. He had a sneaking feeling that his client might very well have reacted in much the same way he had, which made him feel better.

Max had wanted to have a few quiet words with Deepraj but the two lawyers were intent on explaining the possibilities of a successful appeal and by the time that he managed to interrupt them, the court was reassembling in anticipation of the judge's entrance. Max felt physically sick. All the legal niceties were nothing more than a charade to clothe his conviction and imprisonment with the appearance of legitimacy. He knew only too well that Beijing could not possibly permit him to be acquitted. He almost felt some sympathy for the judge, knowing that he was a cog in a machine that ticked to the central committee of the Communist party's time, he'd probably be consigned to the equivalent of a judicial re-education camp if he departed from the party line. He was almost as much a captive as Max himself, compelled to carry out Fernandes's instructions. He wanted to look at Kim, see her in an almost natural surrounding rather than have her visit him in prison. She caught his eye and her smile put a lump in his throat. He turned to stare at the judge who was reading from his prepared script. He lost all sense of fellow feeling and cursed him under his breath.

'The final element to constitute the offence is dealing in the proceeds. I have already found that I am satisfied so that I am sure that the proceeds were indeed the product of an indictable offence, and that the defendant believed that they were stolen.' Jonathan looked up from his papers and stared at Rougier. He was exhausted. He had sat looking at April all night, occasionally getting up to stroke her head when she became restless. She inherited her hair from her mother, it was so soft, so atypical of Chinese hair. His imagination had already distanced him from Bonnie; he was living in a well furnished but empty apartment and the full bottom wig of a High Court judge stood on a stand beside his desk next to a colour photograph of him on the day of his investment, standing alone.

'Once the money was in the defendant's HSBC account he had control over it. That, Mr Chu SC contends, is to all intents and purposes a dealing. Not so, says Mr Rougier QC, for he disavowed any title to it the moment he became aware of its presence in his account.' Bonnie's words wormed their way into his head. Had he really abandoned all the high principles he had once professed so proudly?

'I find myself curiously impressed by Mr Rougier's argument. In my opinion, a dealing requires a positive assertion of ownership over the property in question. The defendant positively rejected ownership. In these circumstances, I cannot be satisfied so that I am sure that there was a dealing.' He paused, acutely aware of the weight of apprehension in the room.

'Consequently, I find the defendant, not guilty.'

For at least two pregnant seconds there was pin-drop silence in the courtroom, then uproar smashed into the vacuum. Audible exclamations of denial erupted from the right-hand side of the court and the judge's expression moved from a bland quietude to one of anger.

'Silence! I will have silence in my court.' Rougier got to his feet not quite believing what he had just heard.

'May the defendant be discharged, Your Honour.'

'Yes.' Tang stood up, bowed and walked out of the court. No-one noticed the almost imperceptible smile of relief on his face. Rougier turned towards the dock and gestured to the dock officers to release Max. One of them opened the half door and he stepped out, strode over to Rougier and shook his hand.

'Can't thank you enough.' They smiled at each other. Rougier gave a little nod of his head in the direction of the prosecution team.

'This is not legal advice, just a friendly idea that popped into my head: first plane out?' Max grinned.

'Sound idea.' Kim was beside him, tears streaming down her face. He put a comforting arm around her and looked for Deepraj. The Gurkha's grin was occupying half his face.

'Three tickets on the first flight out of here by the time we get to the airport, book them online.' Max shouted it over the heads of the reporters who were surrounding him and throwing questions. Deepraj nodded and borrowed Kim's tablet. With the reporters crowding around him, Max walked forcefully out of the courtroom and along the corridor to the lift. Deepraj had to push people aside to make room for Kim. On the ground floor the three of them made their way out of the building with the reporters clinging to them like bees around a queen. Deepraj hailed a taxi and Max pushed Kim into the backseat, then followed. As Deepraj climbed into the seat next to the driver he told him to take them to the Airport Express.

Office of Director of Public Prosecutions

Justice Place

Hong Kong

Sergei Sze stormed into Brian Kong's room.

'How could this happen? No, don't explain. I want him arrested immediately.'

'What for?' The Director of Public Prosecutions looked askance.

'How do I know what for? You're the DPP, get him for conspiracy to defraud the central government of funds or breach of his visa conditions, it doesn't matter, just arrest him and refuse bail.' The DPP stared at his superior's rat-like face.

'Sergei, we can't just fabricate criminal charges. This is a civilised common law legal jurisdiction. If you have proper grounds to arrest him, tell me and I'll set the wheels in motion.'

Sergei Sze's eyes bulged out of his face. He turned abruptly and signalled Phoebe Lam to follow him. When they were in the corridor he stopped and faced her.

'Tell the police commissioner to arrest Devlin. It doesn't matter what the charge is, just arrest him and have him thrown back into gaol, and tell immigration to put him on the stop list.'

Phoebe's eyes shone, this was her opportunity and she would not lose it.

'Certainly, Sergei.'

South China Sea

The sun shone with laserlike intensity out of a cloudless blue sky as a Force 5 wind filled the sails and the cruiser cut through the blue water at an effortless ten knotts.

'Here, take the helm.' Eamon beckoned Kim towards the stern and she moved cautiously across the deck, holding on to the superstructure as the boat heeled over at 30°. He pointed to the wind direction indicator.

'Keep the needle at about 40 to 45 degrees.' She took a firm grip on the wheel and shook her hair out of her eyes.

'I'll try.' Eamon grinned and walked over to the open door to below decks and called down into the cabin.

'You can come on deck now, Max. We're in international waters, have been for about half an hour but I wasn't taking any risks, the Chinese have a plastic approach to territorial waters.' Max climbed up the stairs and stepped out onto the deck sucking in the ozone-laden air.

'God but that feels good. Your accommodation is marvellous but I was beginning to feel a bit queasy down there.'

'You'll get used to it.' Eamon grabbed him by the shoulder. 'Time for a quick beer.' He turned towards Kim. 'You up for a beer love?' She shook her head.

'Just water, thanks.' Eamon nodded.

'Great idea of yours to have Kim with me on deck when we motored out of Aberdeen, the Marine police only had eyes for her.' He ducked down and went below. Max sat down and looked at her, the wrap around sunglasses hid her eyes but nothing could hide the happiness in her mouth.

'I've been trying to work out a plan for us but…' She took one hand off the wheel and held it up to stop him.

'You're always trying to plan things. Right now we don't need any plans: I'm on this beautiful boat with you, the sun is shining and you're free. Isn't that enough for today?' She gave him an admonitory grin. He leaned back and let the sun play on his face. The movement of the boat through the sea, the rush of the water past the hull, her presence, all combined to leech the stress out of his system.

'Sufficient unto the day is the evil thereof.'

'What?' He began to formulate the phrase in Nepali, then abandoned it.

What the hell, she did not need lessons in philosophy.

The Great Hall of the People

Beijing

The prime minister of India and the Chinese premier were ushered into an ante-room with their interpreters. The Chinese premier suddenly broke into English.

'Perhaps we can dispense with the interpreters for a little while?' The Indian smiled his agreement and the two language experts looked at each other, gave a little bow and then left the room. The Chinese indicated the comfortable chairs positioned side by side and they both sat down. Leaning slightly across to the Indian, he spoke softly.

'The secret protocol to aid each other in the fight against Islamic terrorists binds our two countries together in a way that is not open to conflict like economic or political disagreements. Our feet are clad in identical fabric as we tread the silken path together.'

The Indian smiled. He had become accustomed to the Chinese affinity for metaphors. 'The fundamentalist Islamic winds have blown us onto the same course.'

It was the Chinese premier's turn to smile. The Indian continued, 'I regret the loss of your people in the Sikkim incident. It was not attributable to our military personnel.'

'Quite so.' The Chinese premier nodded. 'Your aircraft could have destroyed our rescue team. It was that that convinced me we had a basis for an understanding on greater issues.'

'So, we can say that the death of your people was a very small weight in the scales of mutual understanding between our two great countries.' The Indian premier scratched his beard for a moment as he waited for the Chinese to respond.

'There must always be sacrifices for the benign winds of the world to blow evenly across the people.' He extended his hand and the two men shook firmly.

'Shall we?' The Chinese premier indicated the door.

Acknowledgments

I am indebted to His Holiness the late 14th Shamarpa Rinpoche for his exposition of the conflict within the Karma Kagyu school of Buddhism over the reincarnation of the 17th Karmapa and the right to occupy the Rumtek Monastery, a struggle which underlies this story.

The inspiration to turn *The Dharma Expedient* into the Max Devlin series emerged from the many readers who asked, 'What happened next?' or 'Will there be a sequel?' I had not appreciated how fulfilling it would be to get such detailed commentary and feedback.

Devlin is a complex character whose academic and linguistic skills sit comfortably with an almost clinical detachment from the savage survival skills that are second nature to him. His ability to command fierce loyalty is a redeeming feature in one so ready to resort to violence whenever the need arises.

The unflagging encouragement of my ex-Gurkha chum Christopher Lavender is a tremendous boost. The major editing of this book, no easy task given my propensity for excess capitalising, and for which no thanks are too great has been undertaken by Angel W Lau. The wondrous cover illustration was designed by my brilliant friend Giulio Acconci. His cover design inspired the sculpted image of the Dharma chakra by Psyche Chong, for which much thanks.

My publisher Bidur Dangol's appetite for these adventures is, happily, undimmed.

The process of writing, whilst seemingly a solitary occupation, is soon peopled by characters who assume their own inimitable identities. Some of them, companions who travel with one stride for stride whilst the dark characters conspire and collude in counterpoint.

The next book, *The Chakrata Incident*, covers an earlier period in Devlin's life when he is seconded from the Royal Gurkha Rifles to the British Secret Intelligence Service.